Investing in Stocks
How To Win Big!
Strategizing, Positioning, and Leveraging
for Success

&

Your Personal Guide to

- ❖   Money and Economics
- ❖   Investing in Stocks
- ❖   Bonds, Mutual Funds, and ETF
- ❖   Options, Futures, and Forex
- ❖   Personal Finance
- ❖   Tax and Retirement Planning
- ❖   Insurance
- ❖   Will and Estate Planning
- ❖   College Prep Process
- ❖   Social Security Benefits
- ❖   Great Investors and their Strategies

Kishore Mishra

Copyright© Materials

Proprietary Notice

Disclaimer

Appreciation

I want to thank my family (wife Suprava, son Aniket, and daughter Tamanna) for their relentless support and unwavering encouragement for writing this book. I am thankful to my motherland, India where I grew up and got most of my education. Lastly, I am grateful to the land of opportunity that is the United States of America where things are possible, and dreams are not just dreams.

To all the individual warriors who fight every day to bring better opportunities to their families and take control of their own financial lives.

Contents

Contents

Contents

Contents

Contents

Contents   13

Preface

> An investment in knowledge pays the best interest.
> -Benjamin Franklin

An informed investor is an intelligent investor, and an informed decision is an intelligent decision. As human beings, we are reluctant to make a decision, or we make wrong decisions mainly because we do not have all the information or simply are not knowledgeable about something. Many people are fearful about the stock market and are unwilling to invest in stocks because they have been burnt in the past or know someone who has lost money in the past. They are not wrong, and they are not alone.

We are not taught about finance, investing, and stocks in school or college. We learn it by trial and error, and along the way, many of us are left with a bad taste that makes us fearful or overly conservative in our investments. The recent scars of 2000 and 2008 have been so deep that many individual investors just left the field forever. In addition, the perception is that one has to be an expert in economics, company details, and has to spend a lot of time to be successful in investing – that only the big guys in Wall Street can make it. It is not true. These things are not difficult, and we can build basic understandings of how things work slowly and steadily. In the beginning, it will need some effort, but slowly, it will become second nature.

This book will go a long way toward that and will make the process easier. There are no recipes for overnight success or cut-and-dry method to be successful in the stock market. It is the proverbial slow-but-patient tortoise that beat the fast-but-inconsistent fox to the finish line. There are many ways to make money and plenty of ways to lose money. Investing in stocks is a learning process, and you will walk sure-footed as you gain more experience along the way. This book will be your companion with many useful tips, insights into how things work, and proven strategies that have been successful. It will be your strongest and closest ally to help make money in stock market and be financially successful in life!

The book is divided into four main sections. **Section I** builds the foundation for a long-lasting investing journey – it introduces and refreshes basic economics, accounting, math, government systems, and legal implications. It serves as the foundation on which you are going to build an investment structure that is solid and will stay solid for years to come.

Section II brings the investment choices available in the market place with their pros and cons. However, the main focus and coverage is on investing in stocks. It provides an in-depth analysis on how the stock market works and offers strategies to make money consistently while minimizing risk. **Section III**

Preface

discusses about other investment choices, such as Mutual funds, ETFs, Options, Futures, Forex, and real estate.

Section IV discusses about personal finances, how to make more money at work, how to reduce expenses without sacrificing benefits, how to be savvy about taxes and tax planning, and importantly, how to enjoy money and explore possibilities that would be available. I strongly believe that this book will be your true friend and a source of knowledge that you could always count on.

I was born in a middle-class family in India and migrated to the USA twenty-five years back. Both of my parents were schoolteachers, and I am very grateful to them for giving a simple upbringing, teaching the value of hard work, teaching how to manage finance, and most importantly, encouraging to aim big and high. I learnt, firsthand, from my parents, many lessons that are applicable today. Rice is the staple food in many parts of India. We would buy rice for the whole year during the rice-harvest season when the price is low. The same applies today – buy the things you need in bulk when they go on sale. I was exposed to critical life finance lessons that have become my lifelong companions.

Though I had a good foundation on managing money well and savings money for future, I had little exposure or experience in investing in stocks. When I look back, my initial investment days were hit and miss. I had very little understanding of how and why the stock price changes – I would consider a stock cheap and buy when it drops by 50 percent and keep putting more money as the stock went down further, only to see that the company went out of business in a few years and lost most of my money. I did not give up. I studied books and did a lot of research. I analyzed each investment in details and tried to understand why it happened the way it happened.

As I gained more experience, something was getting clearer to me – *Though the stock market is highly unpredictable, there are a few things in stock market that work or repeat in clockwork precision.* The stock market goes through cycles. Both the positivity and the negativity get amplified in much bigger way than the reality. The market and stock price would go up very high or go down very low diverging far away from the real intrinsic value. These are the points where you can lose a lot or make a lot. Speculation can make you some quick money, but on a continual basis, you would lose what you gained.

On the contrary, if you can choose stocks that are fundamentally strong and pick them up when they are out of favor, it increases the probability of good returns while reducing the risk of losing money. It is the experience, the patience, the discipline, and the desire to be successful that will make you a good investor.

Preface

Stock investment is part science, part art, but mostly it is the mind and the psychology.

I am an engineer by profession with my first love toward computer architecture and chip design. I am also an entrepreneur and have founded successful companies. However, my secret love has been stock investment and economics! I have made investment mistakes in the beginning and still do. I value the experience I gained from investments where I lost money as much as the ones I made money. I have learnt from my mistakes and try to be a better investor today than I was yesterday.

People, who know me, say that my strengths are in getting to the point quickly and in a simple objective way. I have authored one of the best-selling books on computer design, "Advanced Chip Design." I have taken the same approach to bring useful, insightful, and actionable information in this book. I have immensely enjoyed writing the book; hope you do the same reading this book and make a lot of money!

Kishore Mishra
Silicon Valley, USA

Introduction

Chapter

1

1 The Individual Warriors

We are all individual warriors working hard to take care of our families; and, do well in our professions as well as in our financial endeavors. Though we are well prepared to navigate through our professional careers, we are not that sure when it comes to navigating the financial world – what the good investments are, how to invest and grow wealth, and how to figure out the good advices in the midst of information deluge. Is the individual investor at a disadvantage compared to the professional money managers? Yes and No. There are pluses and minuses. Yes, to manage money on your own, specially investing in stocks, an individual investor has to learn the basics and gain experience to be good at it. However, these are not insurmountable obstacles and are completely within the realm of possible achievements. Once you have it, the benefits are huge.

Professional money managers have some advantages that they have dedicated staff to do research and make the best decision. However, the reality is that information is also available to individual investors quickly and easily from many sources. An individual investor just needs to have the basic understandings to sift through the diverse information and come up with his or her own assessment. Many pundits will say many things, but nobody has the crystal ball to tell how the stock market is going to behave the next day, the next month, or the next year. As long as you understand that stock market can move in any direction, and you strategize and position yourself accordingly, you are very likely to come out a winner.

The big money managers and the mutual funds have their limitations as well. They generally have large positions in a stock and cannot buy or sell positions easily without affecting the price. Though stocks are highly liquid assets, they are not that liquid without influencing price. Individual investors do not have this constraint. They can get in or get out of a stock easily without affecting price. Big funds are answerable to their clients and may not have complete flexibility in their decision-making. The individual investors do not have such constraints.

You can take more risk or less risk depending on the current conditions. Not everything is stacked against the little guy or the individual investor. There are more pluses than minuses, and the minuses can be overcome. The goal of this book is to help the little guy to achieve these goals.

1.1 Building Wealth

Building wealth has many components to it, and one needs to be smart about each of the components. For example, many high-earners have ended up broke due to mismanagement of personal finance and lack of basic financial knowledge. People get stuck in low-paying jobs as they cannot afford to be out of work long enough to look for better opportunities. People do not invest in stocks due to lack of interest and fear of the unknown. The obstacles in each of these areas are not huge. Having a good understanding in each of these areas and desire to do something about them will be surer ways toward building wealth steadily. Let us look at the four areas of wealth creation:

Earnings (E)

Have a predictable and steady source of income from a job or a business. Having a steady source of income is critical that it provides stability not only in personal life but in financial life as well. How do we maximize this? Refer to chapter 25 that talks about personality development, how to be successful in workplace, and how to negotiate for better salary and compensation.

Spending (S)

Spend wisely so that there is money left for investments; so that you can build a cushion to be able absorb shocks from unforeseen events in life. It needs money to grow money. It matters how much you are earning, but what matters even more is how much you are saving. You need the steady savings to plough it back to investing. How do we minimize expense without being miserly or compromising basic needs? Last part of the book covers personal finance, tax planning, and strategy for retirement savings.

Leveraging (L)

Leveraging simply means borrowing to grow. Debt, in general, is shunned and advised to be avoided. There are two types of debts – bad debts and good debts. Debt, incurred to live beyond the means, is bad, and debt, undertaken for investment, is good debt. Having a reasonable amount of good debt, that you can digest, is a smart way of building wealth, given the low interest rates on loans. The debt should always be a reasonable percentage of your net worth, and you can undertake larger amount of good debt as your net worth grows.

Investing (I)

Invest wisely so that it grows and becomes a major part of building wealth. With a little bit of investment in time to understand the basics of investing, you will have a very rewarding outcome. Chapters 11 to 21 focus on understanding the stock market and offer strategies to maximize gain while reducing risk.

Formula for building wealth = (E − S + L) * I

- Maximize E (Earnings)
- Minimize S (Spending)
- Reasonable Leverage (L) that you can digest
- Maximize I (Investment growth), must be greater than 1

Note: I have seen many financially smart and financially conservative people who are very good at taking care of the first two (E and S). However, they don't take advantage of L, and they use I very conservatively. They are doing the right things by taking care of the first two but missing out on L and I.

Enjoying

When you are firing all the cylinders (the previous four going well), you will be on your way to building serious wealth. Wealth not only enables to have the security and basic comforts in life but also gives many choices, such as donating to charity, volunteering in charity, or anything you want to do in your life. It will give you the freedom to choose options that would not have been possible otherwise.

1.2 Why Invest?

If you understand something well, it becomes easy to execute it, including taking calculated and informed risks. If you start investing early and understand the trade well, it has the possibility to augment your active income or even surpass it at some point in your life. Once you are financially independent, you could do many things that would not be possible otherwise.

Do not work for money, let money work for you – Robert Kiyosaki. There are two parts to this. The first part is about your career choice, and the second part is about investing. Do not choose a dead-end career or something you do not enjoy. If you love what you do, you will be highly successful, and you will earn a lot of money in the process. Equally important is the second part – let the money work for you. If you smartly invest money, it will generate a lot more money for you.

Most of us are regular people working hard to lead a better life, take care of our families, and provide the best education and opportunities to our children. In the first 20-25 years of our lives, we focus on studies, sports, and learnings with a goal to get into a good stable job. Some, who are entrepreneurial, risk-takers, and are willing to go beyond the confines of safety, will go on to build companies, business, and many other wonderful things that not only make them rich but also provide opportunities and jobs to many. For majority of the people, however, having a steady good-paying job is a critical foundation for financial success in life. That is the first pillar. However, we should not stop there! We can use the power of investing to make the money work for us. We are deterred by the possibility of losing money and stay away from investing.

When not investing, we are losing a big opportunity of money working for us. One hundred dollars today will be worth only a fraction of it in thirty years. Money is constantly losing value due to inflation. By not investing, you are losing money slowly but steadily. If nothing else, the attrition of money due to inflation should prod you to take some risk. With a good understanding of investment vehicles (stocks, bonds, mutual funds, and real estate), taking interest in personal finance, and having determination to succeed, you will feel comfortable in taking calculated and informed risks. Investing will be the other pillar of financial success.

1.3 A Slow and Steady Approach

> A journey of a thousand miles must begin with a single step.
>
> – Lao Tzu

You get better and better in your job as years go by, and at some point, things become natural. You are more confident in your work. The same is true in investing. Investing is not a random thing, winning a lottery, or making some quick money. It needs passion, love, and determination to understand the trade. Most of all, it needs patience. It needs a slow but steady approach. There are many great books in investing that are very helpful, and I highly encourage you to read and understand the ideas. You do not have to invent the wheel every time. However, there are somethings that you can learn only on the job.

Investing involves risk and the possibility of losing money. When your hard-earned money is at stake, it is very difficult to stay rational and not commit costly mistakes. One has to live through one's own investment decisions during the difficult times. After a couple of times, you will be able to stay calm and accept that investment is a risky business. But, most importantly, you would learn how to play it to your advantage. It is very hard to buy stocks when the stock market has crashed and everything in future looks bleak. However, these are the times to invest and make big money when market recovers later.

Take a slow and steady approach. When you are starting out, start with small; may be $10,000, $20,000, or $50,000. Use a strategy and stick to it. Stay the course and execute your strategy. Always look at the percentage of returns, not the absolute amount of money you are making. Fifteen percent of gain on $10,000 investment is $1,500, which may not look like a big deal or a life-changing gain. But, the percentage is important. If you could make 15% gain consistently with a strategy (not by random pick or luck), you can scale it up as you gain more experience. It has to be a well-understood strategy that is repeatable and is expected to behave similarly under similar conditions. When you scale that strategy to $100,000, you could be making a $15,000 gain. Bring it to a million dollars, it is serious money. You could be making $150,000 gain. There is no limit.

Once, I was with a group of friends talking different things. One thing that came up was investing in stocks. What is the best investment strategy? Everyone was giving opinion based on his or her knowledge and experience – pretty regular stuffs. But, one friend told something that caught my attention. He said,

"Whatever Works." I am not sure if he himself was serious about it or just said in a casual fun way.

Whatever works, and I will add the word "consistently" to it. We all need to find out, what is that "whatever" that will work for us. Once we find it, we should use it to our benefits. I have discussed many different successful strategies later in this book, and I strongly encourage you to go through them and find one, or may be invent your new way - find your **"Whatever Works Consistently."**

1.4 Good Debt versus Bad Debt

Debt is a very personal issue, and debt has the connotation of something to avoid at any cost. While this may be true for most situations, you need to understand the vice and virtue of debts. Done properly, it can be used for significant financial gains. Incurring debt to live beyond means and sacrificing the future for the present gratification are examples of bad debts. Debts for investments in assets (stocks, real estate, and education) are examples of good debts. When you invest in fundamentally solid stocks at low price, there is a very good chance that the stock price will recover in a year or so. In some cases, it may happen even before that. Real estate goes up in the long run. You need to give time for investment to bear fruit. A good education now is going to pay dividends in terms of higher salary and other compensation down the roads.

Low-interest longer-term debts are better than high-interest short-term debts. When a loan is for a longer duration, you know the worst-case scenario as to how much you have to pay in interest. Many companies take out longer-term loans to give time for the business to succeed and not run into cash-flow crunches. Same is true for individuals. As long as you are not in a long-term negative cash flow situation, you would be able to tackle short-term negative cash-flow problems. Important thing in using debt is to know how much you can handle. If you have invested in real estate, make sure that the house can be rented even during down markets. If you have used margin money to buy stocks, make sure that you chose stocks that are fundamentally strong and have a good history of paying dividends. The dividends will absorb some of the margin interest costs. Also, make sure that the debt you incur for investment is not too big to service. If needed, you should be willing to temporarily cut expenses and work extra to get over the tough times.

The cost of debt is also very important. If the cost is too high, it becomes risky as the gain may not be that good, and the debt servicing may be too burdensome. On the same note, it may be an opportunity to use debt judiciously when interest rate is low. Let us look at the current Fed interest rate. It has been very low for almost a decade. Given the amount of US debt and its trajectory, it will be practically improbable for the Fed to raise rates by several percentage points, as interest payment alone would be significantly high. At 5% interest rate on $20 trillion debt, the interest burden would be a trillion dollar every year, roughly one-third of the current yearly budget. Another important thing is that major world economies have rates close to zero. Given the present contexts, it will be reasonable to expect that lower interest rate is going to stay for the foreseeable future. It may go up one or two percentage points, but we are unlikely to see a large jump (if there is high inflation, the Fed probably will raise rate to fight inflation but only temporarily). Why is the Fed interest rate important, and why are we discussing this? Because, the interest rates we get from risk-free investments are tied to the Federal interest rate.

It will be reasonable to believe that the interest that we can expect from safe investment vehicles, such as savings account, CDs, and government bonds will not be lucrative for the foreseeable future. We cannot use these vehicles for building wealth other than for meeting short-term liquidity needs. This means, we need to look into other areas, such as stocks and real estate for long-term gain. The low interest rate is not good for people who are on fixed income and do not have the time horizon to take risk, specially people who are retired, or anyone who cannot afford to take any risk. However, for other people, the low interest rate also provides opportunity to get loans at very low rates. It makes easy to buy a house, buy investment properties, start a business, and use margin for investing in stocks. Remember, being too conservative in using debt, you are missing out opportunities. Being overly aggressive can wipe you out. Using it, judiciously and at manageable levels, is a smart way of building wealth over the long run.

2 The Investment Landscape

There are many investment choices and investment vehicles available, and it is not an easy task to choose the right one. The investment choices range from no-risk, low-return to high-risk, high-return investments. In the no-risk or very low-risk end of the spectrum, are the savings account, CDs, and federal bonds. These are also called fixed income investments as the rate of returns is fixed during signup. In the middle of the range, are the mutual funds and ETF that provide better returns than the fixed income but involve higher risk. In the high-risk end of the spectrum, are stocks, options, and futures. These involve the highest risk, but they can generate the highest returns as well.

With so many choices, how does one select the right one? It depends. The choice would have been easy if an investment vehicle were available that provided the highest returns without any risk. Unfortunately, such a thing does not exist! If someone offers one, be aware, and just stay away from it. What to choose depends on one's risk tolerance, knowledge of how an investment scheme works, and experience in it. Though, getting the highest rate of return at zero risk is the ideal situation, we could target to get the highest returns while minimizing the risk. The other thing is that much of the risks of the high-risk investment choices such as stocks originate from lack of knowledge and lack of a good understanding of how these things work. The goal of this book is to present more details on these various investment choices with a significant focus and emphasis on how to be successful in stocks while minimizing risks.

CHAPTER 2   The Investment Landscape

2.1 Fixed Income (Savings A/C, CDs, Bonds)

Fixed-income investments have very low risk but provide very low return as well. The money in savings account and CDs in banks are insured by FDIC up to $250,000. What it means is that even if the bank fails, the US government is going to pay the money to the account holder. However, in this low-interest rate era, the returns are nonexistent - close to zero. The inflation will erode the value of your money faster than the returns you would get by putting money in savings account and CDs as investment vehicles.

Federal bonds provide better returns (10-yr yield is around 2%) compared to savings account. Federal bonds can also be considered no-risk investments as they have never defaulted. Fed bonds also provide tax advantage as the interest earned is tax exempt at the state and local levels. However, the returns are much lower now than historical returns from stocks (around 10%). It may be OK to have some percentage of your investment assets in Fed securities, but it would be too conservative to put a large percentage. Municipal bonds (Munis) come under the same category as Fed securities from a yield and risk perspective. They have a little higher return than Fed bonds but also have a little higher risk. There is no federal tax on the interest earned from Municipal bonds.

Corporate bonds from good, established companies provide a little better return (3-5 %), with higher risk than municipal bonds. On the far end of bonds spectrum, are the junk bonds where the returns and risk are high. They provide higher returns (6to 9%) but have high risk of losing the principal.

2.2 Stocks

Stocks have historically provided very good returns. Stocks have the risk of losing money, but with a good understanding of how to choose the best stocks and keeping the horizon long, stocks are the best investment vehicles to generate sizable returns. We will be devoting a substantial part of the book on investing and winning in stocks.

The graph below captures the returns from DOW for last 20 years (1996-2015). DOW Jones has provided an annualized return of 11.2%. If you include the dividends, it would be a couple of percentage points more, bringing the total returns to13.2 percent.

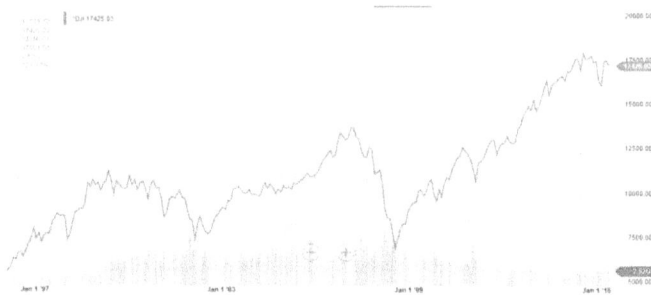

Fig. 2.1   Dow Jones (1996-2015): Yahoo Finance

Dialing back by five years, the graph below captures the returns from DOW for a twenty-year period from 1991-2010. The annualized return was 16.2%. If you include the dividends, it would be 18.2%. As we can see, investing in stocks has historically provided the best returns in the long run.

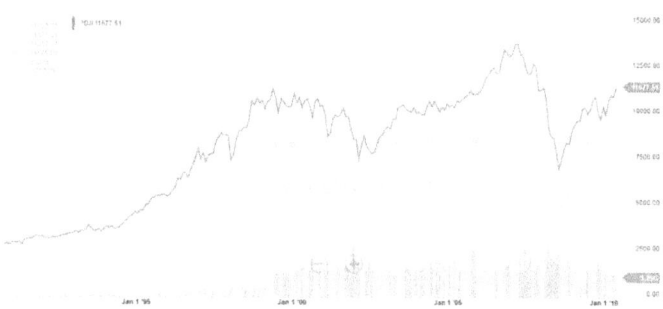

Fig. 2.2   Dow Jones (1991-2010): Yahoo Finance

2.3 Mutual Funds and ETF

Mutual funds are investment vehicles managed by professionals where a fund represents a group of stocks, bonds, or cash. In general, mutual funds provide better returns than CDs and bonds. Many mutual funds hold regular stocks. The major benefit of mutual funds is that these are managed by professionals. If you do not have time to invest in stocks on your own, investing in mutual funds is a good choice to get good returns. Some of the safe mutual funds are index funds where the fund mimics the popular indices, such as DOW30 and S&P 500.

ETFs are the efficient cousin of mutual funds. ETFs are similar to mutual funds in many ways. ETFs can be specific to sectors, such as financials, commodities, semiconductors, or real estates. ETFs are cost-efficient compared to mutual funds. One of the drawbacks of mutual funds is the fees associated with mutual funds that the manager of the funds charges for managing the funds. ETFs are structured differently than mutual funds and do not require much managing. The other benefit of ETTs is the flexibility in trading. ETFs can be traded during normal trading hours in the open market like stocks. Mutual funds, on the other hand, can only be purchased or sold at the end of the day from the fund company. Because of these many benefits, ETFs are gaining popularity among many investors.

Mutual funds and ETFs definitely have a place in the investment portfolio. Many people have their 401K invested in mutual funds. As you gain more experience and get more confidence in investing in stocks as an individual investor, you can gradually shift more money into stocks from other investment choices. The main idea is that you can produce better returns by investing in individual stocks rather than investing in mutual funds and ETFs that are diversified more than individual stocks.

2.4 Options, Futures, and Forex

These are at the farthest end of the investment choices – these provide very high returns and involve very high risks. These are typically of short duration. These investment vehicles use high leverage where you can make a large profit for a small investment. If you understand these instruments well and want to take additional risk, you can play in these areas to make good profit.

In options, you bet that a company stock will go up or go down, and you make money if your analysis was correct and if the stock price moved the way predicted. In Futures, you bet that a commodity price (gold, oil, corm, even stock index) would go up or down, and you make money if your prediction comes true. Forex works on the same principle but provides even higher leverage compared to options and futures. You are betting certain currency will appreciate or depreciate against another currency. There are stories of people making a lot of money in short times, but there are probably more number of cases people losing money that go unreported. If you want to explore these options seriously, go slow and small in the beginning.

2.5 Real Estate

Real estate, done right, can be a very lucrative investment vehicle. In the long run, home prices have always gone up outpacing the rate of inflation. At least, you should buy one house that you call home. It has many benefits. You would have the privacy and memories associated with your home. Keeping aside the intangible aspects, it provides many compelling benefits from an investment angle. Part of the mortgage payment will go toward building your equity. You also get the benefit of itemized tax deduction. The best part is that the home value appreciation is tax free up to $500,000 for married couples if you were to sell your home at some point. Even if you do not sell, you could use the equity in your house to fund children's 529 plans and other investments.

Beyond buying your home, one can buy more houses/condos as rental properties. It has its plus and minus. It depends on the market and the areas where you want to invest in real estate. Home values typically move in cycles. It would go up for a few years and then stagnate or even go down for some years, before going up again. In addition, it requires time and effort to take care of the rental properties. One also needs to think about liabilities and other considerations. All these things can be addressed, and may people do invest in real estates and make great money. It varies from person to person.

Section I

The Foundation

Chapter

3

3 A Little Bit of Math

The good news is that you do not need to know complex math to be successful in investing. The basic concepts of percentage, simple interest, compound interest, rounding, probability, and statistics are all you will need. We will brush up the basics without going into esoteric details. We will leave the complex algorithms and complex math behind high frequency trading for someone else.

3.1 Millions, Billions, Trillions - A Perspective

- On thousand thousands is a million   (1,000,000)
- One thousand millions is a billion   (1,000,000,000)
- One thousand billions is a trillion   (1,000,000,000,000)

Millions

- US population was 323.6 million as of April of 2016.
- By end of 2014, there were around 10M households in the US with $1M or more investible assets excluding the primary residence – data from Spectrum Group
- Largest lottery ever in the world is the US "Mega Millions" on January 13 2016, worth $1.586B that surpassed the long-standing largest lottery, "Spanish Christmas Lottery" in 2012, worth $942M.
- Second largest ever lottery in the US is "Mega Millions" on March 30 2012, worth $656M
- You have two offers – first one, you get $1M dollar every day for five weeks (35 days). The second offer, you get 1cent on the 1st day, 2 cents on the 2nd day, and 4 cents on the 3rd day, doubling every day from the previous day. Which one would you take? Answer at the end of this section.

CHAPTER 3   A Little Bit of Math

Billions

- The world population, in 2015, was 7.2 billion, with the top five countries as:
    - China – 1.36 billion
    - India – 1.25 billion
    - USA – 0.321 billion or 321 million
    - Indonesia – 0.256 billion or 256 million
    - Brazil – 0.204 billion or 204 million
- The top ten corporations by market cap on May 5, 2016
    - Apple $509B
    - Alphabet Inc. (Google) $479B
    - Microsoft $392B
    - Exxon Mobile $364B
    - Berkshire Hathaway $354B
    - Johnson & Johnson $310B
    - General Electric $278b
    - Wells Fargo $247B
    - China Mobile $231B
    - JPMorgan Chase $224B

Trillions

- US GDP in 2015 was: $17.5T
- US Debt as of April 2016: $19.2T
- Market cap of all US companies: $18T
- US personal wealth in 2016: $88T

Answer to which option is better

First option: **$35 million**

Second option:

Total money in 35 days: $1c + 2c + 4c + 8c + \ldots 2^{34}c = 2^{35} - 1 =$ 34,359,738,368 cents or $343,597,383 **($344 million)**

3.2 Rounding

> The farmer took 28 cows to the field for grazing. When he rounded them up at the end of the day, he had 30 cows.

Rounding is useful to get a quick and rough estimate of something. It also acts as a check that you have not made any gross error. Rules for Rounding:
- Go to the digit you are rounding to (hundred, thousand etc.)
- If the next digit is 5 or larger, round upwards, else (smaller than 5), keep the digit same.

Let us work through some examples.

Example1: Round 35,200 to the nearest thousands
- The digit representing thousand is 5, and the next digit is 2, which is smaller than 5
- The answer is thirty five thousand (35,000)

Example2: Round 3,285 to the nearest hundreds
- The digit representing hundred is 2, and the next digit is 8, which is greater than 5
- The answer is three thousand and three hundred (3,300)

Example3: Round 10,585,000 to the nearest millions
- The digit representing million is 0, and the next digit is 5, which is equal to 5
- The answer is eleven million (11,000,000)

CHAPTER 3   A Little Bit of Math

3.3 Percentage

Genius is one percent inspiration and ninety-nine percent perspiration.
-Thomas A. Edison

Percentage means the value per hundred. Suppose you scored 22 out of 25. It is 88 out of 100 or 88%.

Finding Percentage of a Number

Finding out percentage of some number is straightforward. You multiply the number with the decimal value of the percentage. Let us work through some examples.

Ex1	20% of 500:	500x0.2 = 100
Ex2	15% of 350:	350x0.15 = 52.5
Ex3	50% of 750:	750x0.5 = 375

Finding what Percentage a Score or Gain Represents

This is slightly more involved than finding the percentage of a number. You scored 22 out of 25. What is it in terms of percentage? I use a method called **Unit Method.** First, find out the score out of unit (one). Then find out how much it would be, out of 100 by multiplying the result by 100. Let us do this systematically.

Step1.   Out of 25, score is 22

Step2.   Out of 1,   score is $\frac{22}{25}$

Step3.   Out of 100,   score is $\frac{22 \times 100}{25}$ = 88 or 88%

Most of the time, you can skip step2 and go to step3 directly when you are figuring out in your mind. In this case, 100 is four times of 25, and so would be the result - 4 times of 22 or 88. Percentage is always calculated on the base value. You bought certain number of stocks for $800 and sold for $900 excluding commission. What is percentage of profit you made?

Base value is $800, on which you made a profit of $100. You can arrange it in paper or do it mentally as follows.

For $800,   profit is $100

For $1,   profit is $\frac{100}{800} = \frac{1}{8}$ (may skip this step and move to next directly)

For $100,   profit is $\frac{1 \times 100}{8} = 12.5\%$

You bought stocks for $800 and sold for $720. What is the percentage of your loss? For $800 investment, the loss is $80 or 10%.

Percentage is used in many aspects of our lives - bond yield, dividend yield, or percentage gain in our stock holdings. Let us look at another example that we come across frequently. There is a dress on sale that has a price tag of $50 before any discount is applied. You have two coupons, one gives 30% off and the other one gives flat $20 off. Which one should you use?

30% of $50 = 50x0.3 = $15

Now you know which coupon to use. If the original cost of the dress were $100, would your choice be the same? Let us look that as well. In this case, the discount with the 30% coupon will be $30; so using the 30% coupon makes sense.

When the stock goes down by 50%, it has to gain back 100% to breakeven. Portfolio of $10,000 declined by 50%, meaning it is now at $5,000. To get back to $10,000 from $5,000, it has to go up by 100%.

Lesson: It is very critical that you are not over-leveraged (used up all cash and may have used some margin as well) during the peak phase of a bull market. If your portfolio lost 30% (quite possible), it needs to gain 43% to breakeven, and it may take a while to be there.

Percentage wise…

- One percent is equal to 100 basis points. When we hear 75 basis point, it means 0.75%.
- A Jellyfish is 95 percent water.
- Gold types:
  - 14-carat gold: 58.33% gold. Rest copper and silver
  - White Gold: 75% - 85% gold. Rest nickel and zinc
  - 22-carat gold: 91.6% gold. Rest silver, copper, and zinc
- 70% of our body is made up of water.
- 47% of dogs in the United States sleep in a family member's bed. - The Week Magazine, 8/10/07
- Baseball is ninety percent mental and the other half is physical - Yogi Berra
- Don't tell your problems to people: eighty percent don't care; and the other twenty percent are glad you have them - Lou Holtz

3.4 Simple Interest

Simple interest is based on the interest rate, the principal, and the time period. It does not provide further interest on the interest you earn. You have a CD that pays 3% per annum. What this means is that if you deposited $100 for one year, you would get $3 interest at the end of the year plus your principal of $100.

Example1: You opened a CD for $500 that matures in 2 years and offers 3% interest per annum. What would be the interest earned after 2 years?

The formula for Interest earned, **I = P x R x T**, where P is the principal, R is the interest rate, and T is the time period.

$$I = \$500 \text{ x } 0.03 \text{ x } 2 = \$30$$

Example2: You bought US 10yr bond for $5000 with current yield at 2.4% and held it to maturity. What is the total interest you would get?

$$I = \$5,000 \text{ x } 0.024 \text{ x } 10 = \$1,200$$

3.5 Power of Compounding

No one got rich overnight. May be it is possible with someone who inherited a fortune. However, many of the rich people have built their wealth over time. Warren Buffett's net worth of $67 billion (2016) started with 10 thousand dollars. Rome was not built in a day.

The idea of compounding is that the base or the principal keeps on growing whereas in simple growth, the base or the principal is fixed at what you started with. Let us compare two investments, one paying simple interest and the other one paying compound interest. In the first scheme, it pays simple annual interest of 10%. In the other scheme, every year the interest is added to the principal on which is interest is calculated.

	Start Yr1	Start Yr2	Start Yr3	Start Yr4	Start Yr5
Simple	$100	$110	$120	$130	$140
Compound	$100	$110	$121	$133	$146

	Start Yr6	Start Yr7	Start Yr8	Start Yr9	Start Yr10	End Yr10
Simple	$150	$160	$170	$180	$190	$200
Compound	$161	$177	$195	$214	$236	$259

In simple or linear growth, the rate of return is fixed at 10%, and the money doubled in 10years. With compounding, it took only seven years to double the money, and at the end of 10 years, the principal had grown by 160%. If we extrapolate the growth for another 10 years, difference in results between simple growth and compound growth would be stark. On simple growth, $100 will be $300, whereas in compounding growth, it will be worth $673. In compounding, the growth is higher because, each year, the interest is added to the principal; you are earning interest on interest. There is a formula to find compounded value at the end of certain period.

$$\text{Amount} = P \left(1 + R/100\right)^{n}$$

Where P is starting principal, R is the rate of yearly interest, 'n' is the number of years, and Amount is the amount accumulated at the end of 'n' years. Let us plug the numbers for our $100 compounding at 10% for 20 years example.

$$\text{Amount} = 100 \left(1 + 10/100\right)^{20}$$

$$\text{Amount} = 100 \left(1.1\right)^{20}$$

$$\text{Amount} = \$673$$

We can use the power of compounding in stock where you can reinvest the dividend resulting in compounded growth. Compounding can be used in 401K account where you do not have to pay tax until you withdraw after retirement. All the gains and dividends would grow compounded.

3.6 Rule of 72

Rule of 72 is an easy and approximate way to find out how many years it would take to double the money with compounded growth. Divide 72 by the rate of returns, and that would give the number of years. For example, if the rate of returns is 6% and the gain is invested back, it would take $72 \div 6 = 12$ years. For rate of return at 9%, it would take 8 years and so forth.

Rate of Returns	Number of years to double your money
1%	72 years
4%	18 years
5%	14.4 years
6%	12 years
7%	10.2 years
10%	7.2 years
12%	6 years
15%	4.8 years

One thing is clear that investing very conservatively (savings account for example) is not going to double the money anytime soon. Stocks provide the best chance to generate higher growth and the chance to double the money much quicker. The other assumption is that there is no tax payment. The perfect example would be tax-deferred retirement accounts such as 401K where the money grows tax deferred.

3.7 What is APR?

APR stands for Annualized Percentage Rate, which is different from the ordinary interest rate. Interest rate reflects the borrowing rate for the principal amount of loan whereas APR includes other charges, such as loan fees, points, and other costs that the borrower has to pay along with the interest payment. The total money to be paid for the duration of loan is divided by the number of years. From this one-yr. amount, APR is calculated by determining the amount one has to pay for each $100 loan. APR is higher than interest rate as it includes other charges as well. APR makes it easier to compare different loans, as just the interest rate may not give the true picture. For example, one loan with lower interest rate but loaded with other fees could be more expensive than another loan with higher interest rate but lower fees.

Note: While comparing loans, consider the APR as well, not just the interest rate. Sometimes, not all fees are included in APR calculation; so check out what is not included in APR calculation.

3.8 Probability

Probability is also known as chance in common parlance. Another form of probability is called odds, which also expresses chance but a little differently as we will see later. If an event is certain to happen, the probability is 100%. If an event is never going to happen, the probability is zero. If an event may or may not happen, the probability lies between 0% and 100%. If the probability of something happening is more than 50%, it is **likely** to happen, and if the probability is less than 50%, it is **unlikely** to happen.

Example1

There are five balls in a bag, and all are red in color. If you close your eyes and pick a random one, the probability of picking a red ball is 100%, and the probability of picking a blue ball is 0%.

Odds and probability are two different ways to describe the chance of an event occurring. Odds describes the chance as a ratio of success to failure - the number of desired outcomes to the number of undesired outcomes. Probability expresses chance as a ratio of the number of desired outcomes to the total number of possible outcomes.

How to calculate probability of an event

Find out all the possible outcomes and find out the outcomes that are favorable to the event. The probability is calculated by dividing number of favorable outcomes by all the possible outcomes. When you multiply it by 100, you get the probability in terms of percentage.

Example2

There are three red balls and three blue balls in a bag, and you picked a random one form the bag. What is the probability of it being red?

The ball you picked could have been any one of the six balls, and favoring being a red ball is three. The probability is $(3/6) = 0.5$ or 50%. The odds of getting a red ball are 3:3 (desired to undesired outcomes).

Example3

There are two red balls, two blue balls, and one green ball in a bag; you picked a random one form the bag. What is the probability of it being green?

The ball you picked could have been any one of the five balls; the number of all possible outcomes is 5. Total number of favorable outcomes (being a green ball) is one. The probability is $(1/5) = 0.2$ or 20%.

How to calculate probability of sequence of events

Find the probability of the first event, and then find the probability of the second event. Then multiply probability of both events happening. If you want to find probability of three things happening, find the probability of the third event, and multiply all three - so on and so forth.

Example4

There are two red balls, two blue balls, and one green ball in a bag. You picked a random one form the bag and noted its color, and then put it back in the bag. Then you picked another ball from the bag. What is the probability of the first pick being green and the second one red?

The probability of the first one being green is one out of five or $1/5$ (20%). Since you put the ball back into the bag, the probability of the second pick being red is 2 out of 5 or $2/5$ (40%). The probability of the first pick being green and the second pick being red is $(1/5)*(2/5) = 2/25 = 0.08$ or 8 %.

Let us say you put the second ball back into the bag and picked for the third time. What is probability of first pick green, the second pick red, and third one being blue?

The probability is: $(1/5)*(2/5)*(2/5) = 4/125$ or approximately 3%.

One thing we notice is that the probability of occurrence of multiple things happening goes down quickly than any one of the events happening. Let us see how we can use probability to make financial decisions or other decisions in life. Should one play Mega Millions lottery; and, for how much and how often?

Probability of Winning Mega Millions Jackpot

Players may choose six numbers from two separate pools of numbers - five different numbers from 1 to 75 and one number from 1 to 15 – or, select Easy Pick where the computer will pick the numbers for you. You win the jackpot by matching all six winning numbers in a drawing. The jackpots start at $15 million.

What is the probability of winning the jackpot by buying one ticket for a dollar? In the winning number, the first five numbers are unique, but the last one could be any number between 1 and 15.

- The probability of any one of your five numbers matching the first winning number is: 5 out of 75 or 5/75.
- The probability of any one of your remaining four numbers matching the second winning number is: 4/74.
- The probability of any one of your remaining three numbers matching the third winning number is: 3/73.
- The probability of any one of your remaining two numbers matching the fourth winning number is: 2/72.
- The probability of your remaining one number matching the fifth winning number is: 1/71.
- The probability of your sixth number matching the 6th winning number is :1/15

Your probability of winning the jackpot is:

$(5/75)*(4/74)*(3/73)*(2/72)*(1/71)*(1/15)$ = 1 in 258,890,850, roughly one in 259 million.

If I spend $5 per week and play it for next 40 years, will I increase my chance of hitting the jackpot and make it big? Five dollars per week is not much, and I can afford to do it. It seems innocuous, or is it? Over 40 years at $5 per week, you would have spent $5 x 52 weeks x 40 years = $10,400. Wow, that is a lot of money! If you invested and got 8% compound growth per year, it would have grown to $80,000. **It is not a trivial amount of money for most people.** Moreover, what is the chance of winning jackpot in these 40 years? It is 10,400/259 million or one in 25,000. Still the probability is close to zero for all practical purposes. To put it in another way; if 25,000 people spent $5 every week for 40 years, only one person would hit the jackpot! **It is Hail Mary Pass!**

Lesson Learned

In financial decisions, do not make Hail Mary Pass decisions when the amount is non-trivial. If you really want to play just for excitement, may be spend $10 per year. Your probability would still be close to zero, but if you win, you could make it big; and, you are not going to lose non-trivial amount of money.

3.9　Graphs and Charts

Line Graph

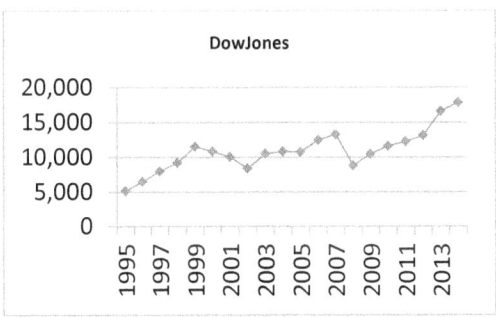

Fig. 3.1　　　　　Line Graph Example

Bar Graph

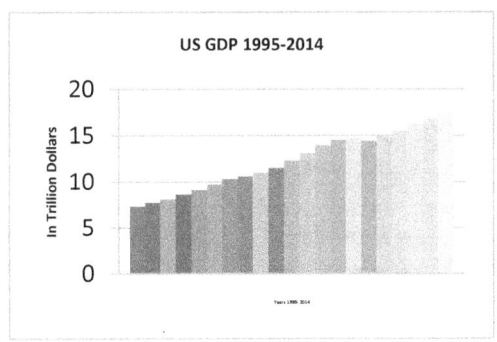

Fig. 3.2　　　　　Bar Graph Example

Pie Chart

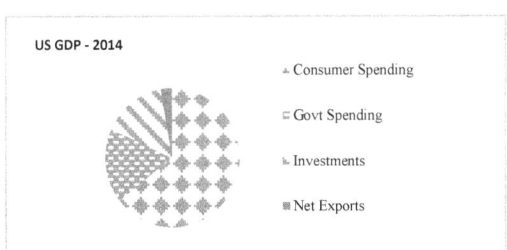

Fig. 3.3　　　　　Pie Chart Example

3.10 Statistics – Mean, Mode, Median

Some of the most commonly used statistical measures are mean, mode, median, variance, and standard deviation. We will explain these concepts with a data set – gain of DOW index in last 20 years (from 1995 to 2014).

Courtesy: Yahoo Finance

Year	Year-end Dow Value	Year-over year % gain	10yr Treasury Yield - Jan. 1st
1994	3,835		
1995	5,117	33.4%	7.78%
1996	6,448	26%	5.65%
1997	7,908	22.6%	6.58%
1998	9,181	16%	5.54%
1999	11,497	25%	4.72%
2000	10,788	-6%	6.66%
2001	10,022	-7%	5.16%
2002	8,342	-16.8%	5.04%
2003	10,454	25.3%	4.05%
2004	10,783	3%	4.15%
2005	10,718	-0.6%	4.22%
2006	12,463	16.3%	4.42%
2007	13,265	6.4%	4.76%
2008	8,776	-34%	3.74%
2009	10,428	19%	2.52%
2010	11,578	11%	3.73%
2011	12,218	5.5%	3.39%
2012	13,104	7%	1.97%
2013	16,577	26.5%	1.91%
2014	17,823	7.5%	2.86%

3.10.1   Mean

Mean, also known as average, is found by adding all the values in a data set and then dividing the sum by the number of members in the dataset. Let us calculate mean of 20 years of Dow yearly gain from 1995 to 2014.

Mean = Sum/N

$$= (33.4 + 26 + 22.6 + 16 + 25 -6 -7 -16.8 + 25.3 + 3 - 0.6 + 16.3 + 6.4 - 34 + 19 + 11 + 5.5 + 7 + 26.5 + 7.5)/20$$
$$= 186.1/20$$
$$= 9.3\% \text{ yearly average gain}$$

3.10.2   Mode

Mode is the most commonly occurring value in the dataset. Let us round the yearly gain to the nearest whole number and then arrange them from the lowest to the largest.

-34, -17, -7, -6, -1, 3, 6, 6, 7, 8, 11, 16, 16, 19, 23, 25, 25, 26, 27, 33

In this case, there is no mode, as there are two 6s, two 16s, and two 25s.

3.10.3   Median

Median is the middle value in the data set. Nearly 50% of the members of the dataset fall below the median value, and 50% fall above the median value. The median of DOW yearly gain from 1995 to 2014 is $(8+11)/2 = 9.5$. In this case, there are two values in the middle (8 and 11). Hence, the average of the two values is the median in this case.

3.10.4   Range

Range is the difference between the largest value and the smallest value in the dataset.

-34, -17, -7, -6, -1, 3, 6, 6, 7, 8, 11, 16, 16, 19, 23, 25, 25, 26, 27, **33**

The range is this case is 33% - (-34%) = 33% + 34% = 67%

3.10.5   Standard Deviation

The standard deviation (SD or σ) measures how spread out the members of the dataset are. It is the square root of the average of the **squared** differences from the Mean. It, basically, tells how far or close the members are from the mean.

The square root of the variance of a set of N values is the sample standard deviation.

$$\sigma = \sqrt{\frac{\sum_{i=1}^{n}(x_i - \bar{x})^2}{n-1}}$$

$\sigma^2 =$ $((-34 - 9)^2 + (-17 - 9)^2 + (-7 - 9)^2 + (-6 - 9)^2 + (-1 - 9)^2 + (3 - 9)^2 + (6 - 9)^2 + (6 - 9)^2 + (7 - 9)^2 + (8 - 9)^2 + (11 - 9)^2 + (16 - 9)^2 + (16 - 9)^2 + (19 - 9)^2 + (23 - 9)^2 + (25 - 9)^2 + (25 - 9)^2 + (26 - 9)^2 + (27 - 9)^2 + (33 - 9)^2)/19$

         $= (1849 + 676 + 256 + 225 + 100 + 36 + 9 + 9 + 4 + 1 + 4 + 49 + 49 + 100 + 196 + 256 + 256 + 289 + 324 + 576)/19$

         $= 5008/19 = 264$

$\sigma = \sqrt{264} = 16.25$

In this dataset, standard deviation (16.25%) is much higher compared to the mean (9.3%). This means that the yearly DOW gain varies widely. **In a given year, you cannot reasonably guess how much the yearly gain would be.**

Chapter

4

4 Everybody Loves Economics

Believe it or not, we are all economists in some sense. We use the basics of economics every day in our lives. We live through the laws of demand and supply every day. Economics and its functioning have deep bearing on the stock market. We will expand the concepts to a level that is interesting but not highly academic. Our goal is not to go to the level of professional economists but know the basics to become a better investor.

4.1 What is Economics?

Economists differ, but I believe, most will agree that Economics is a branch of social science that studies the allocation of *scarce* means of production to satisfy the *unlimited* wants of people. Two things to note are the words scarce and unlimited. If the resources or means of production were infinite or the wants of people were limited, Economics would not be challenging at all. Everyone would get everything he or she wants which is an ideal situation but not realistic. Given limited means of productions and unbounded human wants, there has to be wise, efficient, and innovative ways to produce goods and render services to meet the human wants as much as possible.

The means of production or resources are **Land, Labor, Capital, and Entrepreneurial Ability**. Land on earth is limited, but mainly, it is limited where most people want it. If you want to build a factory in New York or San Francisco for example, it may not be economically viable as the cost of land would be prohibitive. You probably have to go to the outskirts or a little farther. Labor is required to produce any service or goods, and labor is not free or unlimited. Before making a decision about what kind of product you want and where to produce, you need to have the skilled labor force and the right cost structure. Otherwise, the product is not going to be competitive with other offerings on the market and is not going to be economically viable. The third means of production is the capital. To start a company or make a product, you need money or capital. It will take a few months to a few years before you can generate revenue and profit to breakeven. We need the banks, the venture capitalists, the start-up angels, friends and family, and in some cases, the government to fund a new product or business. Without money or credit, the whole economy would come to a standstill. Remember the credit scare of 2008-2009 economic crash; the credit market and flow of money dried up. Even the big banks were scared to lend to one another.

The fourth and the final means of production is the entrepreneurial ability. Having land, labor, and capital is not sufficient to be successful in business. Entrepreneurial ability is the risk taking ability, dedication to succeed, and managerial skill to get things done. Without this fourth means, the other three are likely to be wasted or utilized sun-optimally; and, business is likely run into losses. For any business to be successful and viable, it should be able to produce and sell goods or services at a cost that people are willing to pay. This is where the Entrepreneurial ability plays the vital role.

Economics is broadly divided into **microeconomics** and **macroeconomics**. As the names suggest, microeconomics deals with behavior of individual consumers. It deals with supply/demand, consumer behavior, and types of competitions (perfect competition, monopoly, Monopolistic Competition, and Oligopoly). Macroeconomics deals with the aggregate behavior of the economy. It involves areas, such as GDP, banking, monetary and fiscal policy, business, role of government, international trade, inflation, and unemployment.

4.2 Why Study Economics?

I strongly believe that it is essential to have a good working understanding of microeconomics and macroeconomics concepts, as the performance of a company and the stock market is heavily dependent on the economy. The price of a stock is highly sensitive to consumer demand for the product, labor cost, government rules and regulations, overall health of the US economy (boom, recession), health of international economy, interest rate, Federal Reserve monetary policy, government fiscal policy and taxation, inflation, unemployment rate, exchange rates, and many other factors. Unless you are an economist by profession, you do not need to be an expert in these areas, but a sound understanding of the concepts will be very helpful and come handy to be a successful investor. You can build the knowledge base over time. As you get experienced and comfortable, you will be able to read a piece of news, analyze a set of data, digest an economic event, and quickly connect the dots as to how it is likely to affect the whole stock market or a particular stock. Our goal is to introduce the basic concepts in two chapters early on that will be the foundation for your investment edifice.

4.3 Laws of Demand and Supply

The law of demand and the law of supply are the two fundamental concepts that govern free market economics. The laws are nothing but common sense and can be applied to explain why certain things behave the way they behave in almost anything in economics, life, or anything for that matter. The demand of certain product or service is sum of the demands from all the people that want to buy at certain price. Similarly, supply is sum of the all the things that producers want to offer while still making a profit. As we will see shortly, the demand and supply of certain product and service is not a fixed value, and these change based on the price of a product.

4.3.1   Law of Demand

The law states that, other factors remaining same, the demand of a product goes up when the price is reduced, and demand goes down when the price goes up. It makes sense, as a product gets cheaper, people will buy more of it, or more people will buy it. The shops use this principle all the time to increase sales. They bring down the price of a product by offering discounts, and more products get sold. We can illustrate the law of demand (relationship between demand and price) in a simple graph.

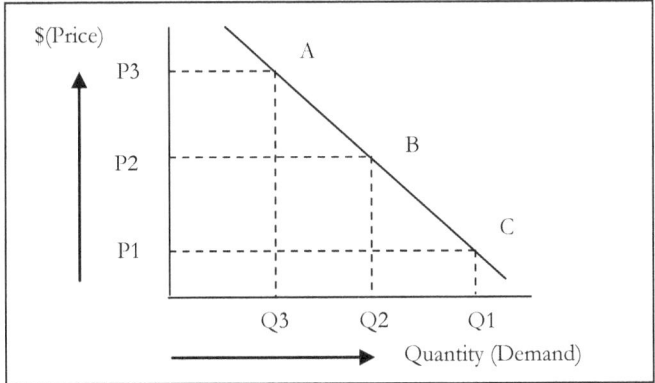

Fig. 4.1 Law of Demand

Let us look at point B on the graph, where quantity of a product demanded by the users is Q2 at price P2. If the price increases to P3, the demand will go down from Q2 to Q3. Similarly, if the price is reduced from P2 to P1, the demand will go up from Q2 to Q1.

4.3.2   Law of Supply

The law of supply specifies the relationship between supply and price. When the price of a product goes up, more suppliers come into the market, as they could make profit with higher price. Similarly, when the price of a product goes down, some of the suppliers will stop producing, as it does not become economical for them to produce and still make a profit. A perfect example is shale oil production in 2014-2015. As the price of crude was around $100 per barrel, many shale oil producers came in and made good profit for some time. However, when supply went above the demand and stayed in oversupply condition for some time, the price of crude oil crashed to below $50. As the price went down, some shale oil producers went out of business, as they could not be profitable at sub $50 price.

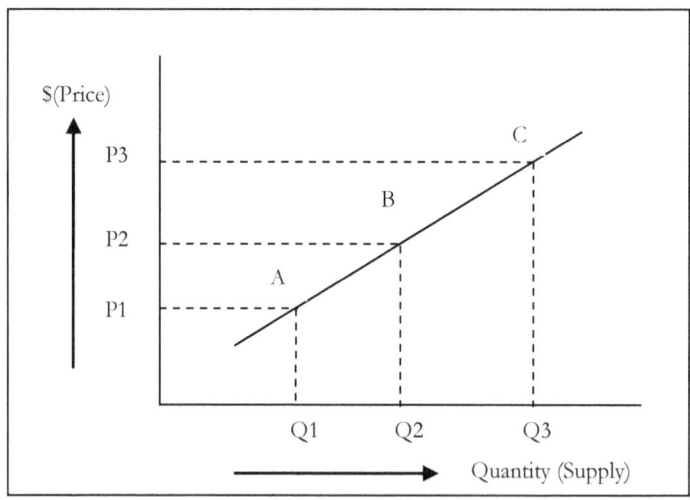

Fig. 4.2 Law of Supply

At point B on the graph, the quantity supplied is Q2 at price P2. If the price goes up to P3, the supply will go up to Q3 (point C). On the contrary, if price goes down to P1, the quantity of supply will decrease to Q1 (point A). In next section, we will use the law of supply and demand together to find the equilibrium.

4.3.3   Supply, Demand, and Equilibrium

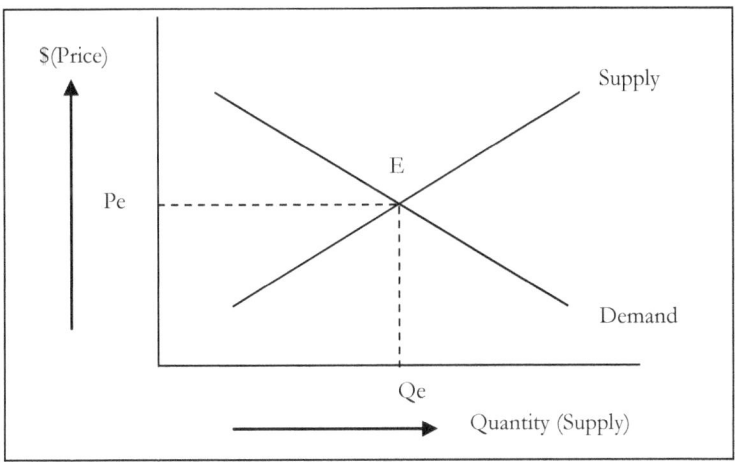

Fig. 4.3 Law of Demand and Supply

We can draw the demand-price line and supply-price line into one place to find out how price, supply, and demand are related. The point where both lines intersect is the equilibrium point (E). The price is the equilibrium price (Pe), and the quantity is the equilibrium supply (Qe). At this price, the supply and demand of a product have matched or reached equilibrium. However, in real market, things do not stay in equilibrium for long. They move based on change in supply or demand.

Oversupply

More producers have entered the market, or existing producers are producing more. The price will move down due to excess inventory, and for them, it is better to make some profit at a lower price than not being able to sell. When the price goes down, more buyers will come into the market increasing demand for the product. At some point, the supply and demand will match at a new equilibrium point (at higher quantity and lower price). When there is oversupply of oil, it pushes the price down.

Undersupply

When price is relatively at a lower value, some suppliers will not produce or go out of business. This will cause a under supply condition. Another example would be one large egg producer shut down due to contamination issues. The supply of eggs in the market will go down. This will cause the price to go high, which in turn will reduce the demand. The supply and demand will match at a new equilibrium point (lower quantity, higher price).

Increase in Demand

The demand for houses goes up with low interest rate as people now can afford bigger loans. If there are not many houses on the market, home price will go up. As the price goes up, there will be more existing homeowners willing to sell, or more houses will be built. This will move to a new equilibrium point (higher price and higher quantity).

Decrease in Demand

When the demand decreases, the producer has to reduce price to attract buyers to come to the market. When there is excess inventory of houses and housing market is cooling off, the builders or sellers often cut their prices. This house price will meet in a new equilibrium point (lower price, lower quantity). In the graph below, the arrow indicates the direction, the new equilibrium point will move from the current equilibrium point based on changes in supply and demand.

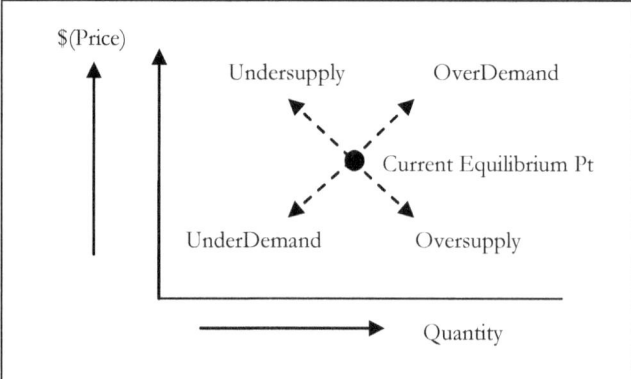

Fig. 4.4 Demand and Supply Equilibrium

4.3.4   Application of Demand/Supply

The law of demand and supply can be applied to understand many economic events and trends. The exchange rate between dollar and another freely-exchangeable currency can be explained by the law of demand. When more people want to buy or have dollars, the value of dollar goes up, and dollar appreciates against the foreign currency. There could be many reasons why people want to buy or have more dollars. During a war or turmoil, dollar provides stability and becomes a safe haven. Another scenario is when the US government bonds provide higher yield and inflation is lower compared to other currencies. The US dollar becomes attractive. The exchange rate turns the other way when there is less demand for dollar.

After a good quarterly result, there are more people who want to buy than people who want to sell at the current price. This pushes the price up. As the price goes up, the number of sellers goes up, and the number of buyers goes down. At a higher price, more people are willing to sell to make a profit, and fewer people are willing to buy as it has become expensive. At some higher price, the number of sellers and buyers would match, and the price stabilizes at that price. Similar things happen after a bad quarterly result. People want to dump the stock, and there are few buyers. This pushes the price down. As the price keeps falling, it becomes attractive for many investors. Also, fewer sellers are willing to sell at a lower price. At some point, the number of sellers and buyers match, and the price stabilizes at a lower value.

When the Fed executes QE, it pumps money into the economy and buys government bonds. This pushes down the bond yield. As there are more buyers for government bonds, the demand for the bonds goes up. With higher demand, the price of the bonds goes up, and the yield goes down. Government can pay lower interest rate for the bonds it sells, as there are more buyers for these bonds.

4.4 Market – Invisible Hand

The invisible hand, originally coined by famous Economist, Adam Smith, means the free market economy where the buyers and sellers decide what to produce and how much to produce without any imposition or restriction from the government. It is the invisible hand (producers and consumers) that decides the price of a product. It is the free market force and the law of demand and supply that decide the economy. If there is a large demand for a product, more producers or suppliers will step in to increase production. If there is not much demand, the suppliers will reduce quantity to match demand.

4.5 Marginal Utility

Marginal utility is the incremental or additional satisfaction (utility) a consumer gains by consuming one more unit of a good or service. You are hungry and have pizza to eat for lunch. The first slice will give the most satisfaction. By the time you are on to your third slice, the satisfaction has decreased - you are most likely to say no for the fourth slice. Marginal utility is used in production decisions. As a producer, you want to maximize profit. You can maximize your profit by making the price cheaper that will sell more number of units. However, after a certain point, the consumer will not buy any more (for example, many households won't buy more than two or three TVs even if the price of the TV goes down further). It is also referred as, **"Law of Diminishing Returns."** As you keep adding units, the value or returns from an additional unit diminishes compared to the previous unit.

4.6 Opportunity Cost

It is a very important concept that we encounter almost every day in decision making including its frequent use in investing. It is the cost of passing over or foregoing the second best option and going for the best option at a particular point. When the first option or alternative is far superior to the second best, it is an easy decision and opportunity cost is not huge. However, when both the alternatives are equal, it becomes a difficult decision – you have to give up something big to gain something of equal or higher value. When we say, "I am torn between this and that," it is opportunity cost on display.

Here is an example. You are deciding whether to join a company after finishing your bachelor's degree or continue on to a master's degree. This is a difficult choice. If you decide to go for the master's degree, you are losing two years of salary and benefits. Not only that, you would miss out the returns on the investments for next 30-35 years for the investments you would have made during these two years. On the other hand, if you get a master's degree, it could help you in your professional career, and there is potential of making more money down the road due to the master's degree. The opportunity cost of choosing the option of pursuing master's degree is the loss of 2 years of salary and potential gain from investment.

Here is another example. I am writing this book while working part time. The opportunity cost for me is foregoing part of my salary and compensation. I love writing and want to produce the best book possible. I want to devote quality time in producing the best contents for my readers. For me, the benefit of finding a few days for uninterrupted writing time every week and producing a great book outweighs the cost of losing out part of my salary. Opportunity cost comes very frequently in stock investing. You have shortlisted several good stocks in a sector that you want to buy. However, you have a fixed amount of money, and you cannot buy all of them. Then you rank them based on your selection criteria, such as fundamentals, dividend yields, and stock buyback history. Finally, you make your best judgement and pick one or two from the shortlist. When you are selecting one or two, you are foregoing the potential gains from the others in the shortlist.

4.7 Competition and Market Structure

Competition is broadly divided into four types – Perfect Competition, Monopoly, Monopolistic Competition, and Oligopoly. Perfect Competition and Monopoly are at the two opposite ends of the competition spectrum.

4.7.1   Perfect Competition

In a perfect competition, there are many sellers or producers. The three main characteristics of a perfect competition are a) there are many sellers, b) they sell same products, and c) there is no barrier to enter the market. Many sellers means a large number of sellers without any seller having a disproportionate share of the market. This means no seller has the leverage or scale to affect supply and price of a product or service because of its large market share. Same product means similar product in a category but not identical. No two products from two companies are ever going to be identical. However, for most practical purposes, we can treat them as same products if they meet most of the requirements of the consumers. An example would be cooking oil where there are many products with very similar compositions, such as fat contents, cholesterol content, and other things. The third characteristic is the ease of entering to market. Farms can enter or leave the market based on their business decisions rather than any outside restriction or constraint.

4.7.2   Monopoly

In a monopoly market, there is only one seller or supplier. This is the opposite of Perfect completion, which has a large number of sellers. Monopoly has three defining characteristics, a) Control of essential resources, b) Government ownership, and c) Being the first. Due to lack of competition, the price of the product tends to be higher, the product quality inferior, and there could be disruption of supply if something goes wrong. If a company has exclusive rights to any kind of resources including mineral resources, it results in a monopoly. Government can have monopoly over certain industries. In some countries, government owns many industries and does not allow private companies to compete. The third part is being there first and creating a large barrier of entry. The barriers of entry are created by patents (though patents are essential for recouping investment dollars), knowhow, and large capital requirements to enter.

The US government has antitrust laws that look into companies that are monopolies or could become monopolies. One of the key tests in company merger is whether the new entity will become a monopoly or reduce competition significantly. The government also looks at if the services or products are essential to people, and it can break a company into multiple smaller companies. In 1982, ma Bell was divided into many smaller telephone companies (baby bells) as government deemed that telephone is an essential service and telephone industry was a monopoly.

4.7.3   Monopolistic Competition

The perfect completion is an ideal scenario, and Monopoly does not stay longer. Monopolistic Competition is as real as it can get in real life. In real life, most of the businesses are monopolistic competitions. It is closer to perfect competition as there are many sellers or providers in a monopolistic completion. However, these companies are monopolies in their own regards. Even though they produce similar products or services, they differentiate within that category to become a sought-after product or a monopoly in a sense. Some examples are restaurants, grocery stores, SPAs, and many companies that provide essential daily products and services. Not all the people in a town may go to a particular restaurant all the time. However, the restaurant offers something unique that attracts certain section of the population who goes to the restaurant on a regular basis.

4.7.4   Oligopoly

Oligopoly is defined as an industry that has only a few farms or companies. In an Oligopoly, at least one farm is large enough, compared to others, to influence price of a product. It is closer to a monopoly than to a perfect competition or a monopolistic competition. Since only a few companies dominate the market, there could be inclination in an Oligopoly to set price with a wink and a nod. There are laws against price fixing and collusion, and the companies can be penalized for being involved in price fixing and collusion to defraud the consumers. Sometimes, the collusion and price fixing go undetected for long before finally being caught.

Chapter

5

5 The Big Picture-Macroeconomics

In the last chapter, we discussed many aspects that are part of Microeconomics. In this chapter, we will discuss the big picture - the Federal bank, the commercial banks, the government and its role, fiscal policy, GDP, inflation, and international trades. All these come under the branch of economics called the Macroeconomics.

5.1 Federal Bank and Monetary Policy

When we talk about monetary policy, the Federal Reserve, or shortly the Fed comes to our mind. Monetary policy is about supply of money, credits, and interest rates. The counterpart of monetary policy is the fiscal policy, which is about taxation. We will discuss fiscal policy in a later section.

Federal Reserve was founded by Congress in 1913. The Fed is an independent body with the authority to set policies without influence from other branches of governments. Here is the mission statement from Federal Reserve web page, which summarizes its role. Fed's policy impacts not only the American citizens but the rest of the world as well.

> ➢ Conducting the nation's monetary policy by influencing the monetary and credit conditions in the economy in pursuit of maximum employment, stable prices, and moderate long-term interest rates
> ➢ Supervising and regulating banking institutions to ensure the safety and soundness of the nation's banking and financial system and to protect the credit rights of consumers
> ➢ Maintaining the stability of the financial system and containing systemic risk that may arise in financial markets.

> ➤ Providing financial services to depository institutions, the U.S. government, and foreign official institutions, including playing a major role in operating the nation's payments system

As we all know, the only entity in the country that can create money is the Fed - not even the congress, the treasury, or the president can create money. Money and the availability of money play a very critical role in the economy. Depending on the current economic conditions (GDP growth, inflation, and unemployment), the Fed decides whether to increase money supply or withdraw money from the system. Higher money supply is intended to increase growth and is generally applied to bring economy out of recession. However, too much of it or prolonged oversupply could lead to high inflation. On the other hand, money supply is reduced by the Fed to fight high inflation. However, as a side effect, it could slow down the economy and could cause recession. Apart from controlling the supply of money, the Fed sets short-term interest rate and influences long-term interest rates.

The Fed has three tools to affect money supply that we will discuss next.

- Discount rate – affects short-term interest rates
- Open market operations – affects supply of money
- Reserve rate – affects supply of money

5.1.1   Discount, Funds, and Prime Rate

Discount rate is the rate that the Fed charges the commercial banks and other financial institutions for borrowing money from it. Each bank is required by law to maintain certain percentage (typically 10%) of the deposits at the Fed. If the bank has deposit of $500 billion dollar, it needs to maintain $50 billion dollar with the Fed as reserve and can lend out the rest. When the amount falls below the requirements, they usually borrow from other banks and as a last resort, from the Fed. The Fed sets the discount rate every two weeks. The discount rate as of April 2016 stands at 1.00%, which is historically on the very low side.

What is Federal Funds Rate?

Federal **Funds Rate** is the rate that the banks charge to one another. As described earlier, each bank has to maintain the required reserve. The banks keep the reserve money with the Fed, which is called the **federal funds.** At the end of a day, if the money they have with the Fed falls short of the reserve requirements, they can borrow money from another bank or from the Fed if not available from another bank.

The Fed does not directly set the funds rate but sets the desired or target rate established by the Federal Open Market Committee (FOMC). The funds rate is lower than the discount rate. FMOC meets eight times a year to set targets for the funds rate. As of April 2016, the federal funds rate is 0.50%, and discount rate is 1.00%. In summary, the Fed sets the discount rate, which in turn, drives down the funds rate to a target value lower than the discount rate.

Why Funds Rate (Discount Rate) is important?

It affects many other short-term interest rates that we are concerned with - interest rate we get with our bank deposits, prime rate, short-term mortgage rates, Money Market Funds rate, and rate for Home Equity Line of Credit.

Why do the interest rates on saving accounts, money market funds, and short-term CDs go down as interest rate goes down?

The banks borrow money at a cheaper rate and loans out at a higher rate. They make a profit by the difference in the rates. Banks play a very important role of connecting the lenders to the borrowers. When the banks can get the money from Fed at lower rate, they will not need your money at a higher rate. The interest rate you get will automatically track the federal funds rate – it will go down when funds rate go down and vice versa. The Fed lowers the target funds rate so that money is cheaper to borrow which is intended to increase economic activities. The downside is that people relying on fixed income, mainly older or retired people, do not get much on interest from their bank deposits. They are less likely to invest significant portion of their money in stocks, as stocks could lose value when time horizon for investment is short. After the 2009 market crash, the Fed aggressively lowered interest rate close to zero and has kept the rate at this level for the last 7-8 years.

The rate cuts generally follow a pattern (downward or upward) over a period of time that spans years rather than months. When the Fed wants to increase rate, it would exercise the rate hikes in a series of steps of 0.25% to 0.5% rather than increasing in one big swoop. Generally, it does the same thing when it reduces rate - by going in steps.

What is Prime rate and why is it important?

Prime Rate is the rate that bank charges to its most credit-worthy (high FICO credit scores or AAA ratings) customers. The Prime rate is tied to the federal funds rate and is typically 3% higher than the funds rate. Currently (April of 2016), the prime rate is at 3.50%. The prime rate directly affects the short-term rates, such as rates for credit card loans, short-term ARM (Adjustable Rate Mortgage), Home Equity Line of credits, and other short-term loans. It does not affect the long-term mortgages, such as 15-yr or 30-yr fixed loans. These long-term mortgage rates are driven by the Fed's 10-yr Treasury note interest rate or yield.

What is LIBOR and how does it affect us?

LIBOR stands for London InterBank Offered Rate. It is a short-term (overnight to 1-yr) benchmark rate that the international banks charge one another. The rate is published by Reuter every day at 11 A.M. Among other things, LIBOR is used in setting ARM mortgage rate and base price of Credit Default Swaps (CDS). CDS are forms of insurance against default of loans.

2008 financial crisis explained in simple terms

- US housing boom started around 2001-2002, and by 2006-2007, the housing market was very hot. The housing bubble was fueled by cheap loan with little collateral. These loans are also known as subprime loans. Usually when a bank issues a loan, it asks for collateral in the form of reasonable down payment. With many subprime loans, the down payment requirements were much lower which allowed more people to take out loans and engage in speculative purchase of real estate properties. The subprime loans also had much smaller initial monthly payments that accelerated the boom and much higher payments a few years later that caused the crash.
- The banks sold these mortgages to agencies, such as Fannie Mae, Freddie MAC, or other private institutions (Lehman Brothers, one of them). These institutions then securitized these loans as MBS (Mortgage Based Securities) and sold them like bonds to other investors. The yield from MBS is typically higher than government bonds, which made it attractive to many buyers. When homeowners pay monthly mortgage payments (principal and interest), the money goes to the MBS holders.
- The buyer of these MBS also bought credits default swap (CDS) which is a form of insurance against default of MBS issuer. This gave them the so-called "protection" against possible default.

- The housing boom could not sustain forever as it usually happens with any bubble. The number of buyers started to fall below the number of sellers. Many speculative buyers, who bought houses to make a quick profit, could not sell in time and could not afford higher mortgage payments as initial low payments came to an end. This caused many homeowners to default – they could not pay monthly mortgage payment. There were foreclosures, and many of the mortgage-based securities lost most of their values or could not be properly valued. As these assets could not be properly valued, banks were unwilling to lend money that led to severe liquidity crunch. Many investors started to withdraw their support and were unwilling to inject fresh cash. Lack of running cash forced many companies into bankruptcies. Stock market crashed, and there were widespread layoff. This is one of the major economic crises of modern times. As many lost jobs, more homeowners defaulted on their mortgage payments. It was like a chain reaction, one feeding into the other.

5.1.2   Fed Open Market Operations

The Fed performs open market operations (buying or selling short-term government securities such as treasury notes of maturity one-yr. or less) from the secondary bond market to increase or decrease money supply in the economy. When it wants to inject more money into the economy, it creates new money and uses this money to buy securities in the open market. When it wants decrease money supply, it sells back these securities in the open market and takes the money out of the economy.

How is Open Market Operation different from Discount Rate?

One is a pull model, the other one is a push model. Discount rate works as a pull model. By reducing the rate, the Fed makes it cheaper for people to borrow money. More people are willing to take out loan at a cheaper rate. The banks can borrow money from the Fed at a cheaper rate and consequently, loan out the money to people and business at a cheaper rate. The Fed is not pushing money directly but is creating an environment such that banks can pull the money from the Fed and pass it to people and business.

Open market operation is a push operation by the Fed. It is directly pushing the change in money supply (injecting or reducing) by engaging in buying and selling short-term securities. The money is directly entering or exiting the economy (bond market). Apart from changing the money supply, it also affects the short-term interest rate. Next, let us walk through the steps involved in buying securities.

Fed wants to increase money supply:

- The Fed, at its FOMC meeting (held 8 times a year), decides to increase money supply by buying short-term US government securities.
- It instructs New York Fed to carry out these operations.
- New York Fed contacts some 30 approved primary dealers that it wants to buy securities.
- The dealers put a competitive bidding, and the Fed selects the winners.
- The primary dealers may already own some of these securities, or they buy them from the secondary bond market.
- The Fed then collects the securities and deposits money in form of checks to the primary dealer's commercial bank partner's account at New York Fed branch. Let us say the primary dealer's partner bank is BoA. Remember that each commercial bank maintains reserve account with the Fed. The Fed deposits the money to BoA account at the New York Fed branch.
- The money went to primary dealers, and then it goes to people or entities that sold the securities – more money in the economy.

Where does the Fed get the money?

We know that the Fed can print money to create new money as much as it wants. In this case, it actually does not print paper money but creates money by just crediting the BoA account (remember money is not just hard cash but includes checks as well).

How does buying securities increase money supply, and what does it intend to achieve?

In the secondary bond market, there is regular buying and selling of bonds. Some people are buying, and some are selling – no net change in money supply. However, when the Fed put new money and bought some of the bonds from secondary market, two things happened. As there is more demand for these bonds, it will increase the bond price higher and push the yield lower, making short-term borrowing cheaper.

The people who did not buy from the secondary bond market because of lower yield have the money available to be invested elsewhere in the economy. This money will percolate to other parts of the economy, resulting in lower mortgage rates, lower home equity rates, lower margin rates, and many more. As the money becomes cheaper (lower interest rate), people will start thinking of borrowing money to open new businesses, buy houses, or invest in stocks. They can avail home equity loans, home equity line of credit, or other loans at cheaper rates. Suddenly many things became possible, and economy would start to grow.

Bond buying by the Fed increases money supply in another way. When the Fed deposits the money in the reserve account of the bank, its reserve amount goes up, and the bank can now create new loans that was not possible before. An example - prior to this, the bank had $1B in reserve, and the loan, it had issued, was $10B (with 10% reserve requirement). Now let us say the reserve became $2B, which will enable to hold $20B of loan – it now can create a $10B of new loan. More money in the economy means more economic activities.

What happens when the Fed sells bonds instead?

The process works exactly the opposite of buying bonds. There is one difference though - it cannot create bonds as it could create money. It is the government that creates the bonds. The Fed sells bonds that it had bought in the past. When it sells bonds, there is more supply of bonds, which lowers the price and increases the yield. Some of the money, that used to circulate in the economy, is now diverted to the Fed. It results in contraction in money supply, and borrowing cost goes up. This brings down inflation and occasional recession along with it. The Fed usually sells bonds to decrease money supply and fight inflation.

We discussed the two important tools (Discount Rate and Open Market Operations) that the Fed employs to affect monetary policy. The third tool is the **Reserve rate**. It can affect money supply by changing the reserve requirements. When the reserve requirement is decreased, the banks have to maintain fewer dollars as reserve at the Fed. In other words, for the certain amount of reserve, they can loan out more money now. This increases money supply in the economy. If the reserve requirement is increased, banks have to decrease corresponding amount of loan from the market. This results in decrease or contraction of money supply. The Fed rarely plays with the reserve requirement, as the effect on money supply is much bigger than the other two. It is more of a coarse method that is used rarely.

5.1.3   Quantitative Easing (QE)

Quantitative Easing is a form of bonds and assets buying program by the Fed to increase supply of money in the economy with an intention to spur economic growth and lower unemployment. After the 2008-2009 economic crisis, the Fed lowered interest close to zero and engaged in heavy bond buying programs through open market operations. The unemployment rate was still high and growth was tepid. It was running out of options and wanted to do more. It performed a series of QEs (QE1, QE2, and QE3) starting from end of 2008 until 2014. It was a massive infusion of money into the economy in a short span of time.

How is QE different from conventional bond purchase through Open market operations?

Both are tools to increase money supply. Conventional open market operations focus on short-term (less than a yr.) bond market, whereas QEs were targeted for specific sections of the economy. It bought Mortgage Based Securities (MBS) from the banks so that banks can get the toxic MBS assets off their balance sheets and use the new money to give out more loans. The goal was to bring the housing market out of depression. The Fed also bought long-term bonds instead of short-term bonds. It was called **operation twist** that brought down the long-term US bond yield to very low (2%) level. The money was cheap for short-term loans but now became cheap for the long-term loans as well. This helped to bring down long-term mortgage (15-yr. and 30 yr.) rate to historically low levels. The Fed continued to buy MBS and long-term bonds until Oct'14 when it announced that it was ending the QE purchases. Fed's assets increased to $4.4T from $2T.

There have been many debates about the effectiveness of the massive QEs that the Fed undertook. This is unprecedented in the sense that this has never been done in history in such a massive scale. Some believe that it helped decrease unemployment and increased growth, and some believe that monetary policy is not the cure-all, and it has its limit. There has to be other reforms in fiscal policy along with monetary policy to spur strong economic growth. Nobody knows the long-term effect of the huge QEs. How is the Fed going to handle if the economy falls in to recession despite this huge injection of cash? Is it going to do more of QEs to keep things from falling further? Is it going to make interest rate negative? When it increases interest rate at some point in future and starts selling these bonds back to market, is the economy going to fall into depression? How is it going to increase interest rate without causing slowdown in the economy? There are many questions, and, it seems, there are no easy answers. Another aspect of quantitative easing is that it is not limited to the Fed; other central banks (European Common Bank, Bank of Japan) are undertaking such measures as well.

What is Next?

It is possible that the central banks will reverse course and start increasing interest rate but very slowly. The short-term and long-term interest rates are likely to stay low for more years down the road. In a global economy, the US economy and the US stock market are not solely influenced by the Fed's action and the events in the US. These are dependent on other economies (UK, Europe, Japan, and China to large extent) as well. When the US stopped its QE in 2014, Europe was coming out with its own form of quantitative easing program. The dollar appreciated significantly. When there is more supply of a currency, the value of it goes down. So, when the US stopped the growth in supply of Dollar and Europe started growing supply of Euro, the Euro became cheaper in comparison to the Dollar. This has implication for investors. For the US companies that generate significant portions of their revenue in Europe, the goods will now be more expensive in Europe, and revenue from Europe would fall. Their stock price would fall. On the contrary, the imports from Europe will be cheaper. The same analogy holds with respect to Japan, China, and other major economies in the world. It is a constantly changing scenario; the US economy is more linked to the world economy than ever before. As an investor, you need to keep an eye on what is happening not only in the US but also in other economies around the world.

What affects the Home mortgage rate?

The short-term mortgage rates are influenced by Feds discount rate (funds rate). However, the long-term mortgage rate (15-yr, 30-yr) are mainly influenced by 10-yr Treasury note yield. The institutions that are lending money (bond funds, pension funds, insurance funds) have two major choices, among others, to lend money. They can lend their money to government by buying safe long-term bonds or to relatively riskier homebuyers as loans. Because the home loans are riskier (could default) compared to government bonds, the lender would require a premium (called risk premium) compared to the government bonds. It is usually a few percentage points above the government bond yield. When 10-yr yield goes down, the long-term mortgage rate also goes down and vice versa. With several QEs, the 10-yr yield is very low (2%) which has kept the long-term mortgage rate at historically low level as well. The other aspect that influences the long-term mortgage rate is the future expectation of inflation. If inflation were expected in future, lenders would demand higher yield for their money, meaning higher long-term mortgage rate.

Macroeconomics

5.1.4   Fed's Impact on Investment Decision

By now, it is very clear that the Fed plays a very critical role in the economy, mainly anything to do with money. We may not always agree that the Fed's action produces the desired results in the economy or is the best course for the economy, but we could not refute the impact it creates. With sustained low-interest rate, close to zero and large amount of money pumped into the economy, a lot of money is available in the system. Some of it went toward creating new jobs, and a good amount went to stock market and housing market. With very low yield on fixed-income assets and more money available for investing, the stock market became the default choice for many. Dow, from the bottom of 7,000 in 2009, skyrocketed to 18,000 by 2014 surpassing the previous high of 14,000. The Fed's policy (expansion or contraction) does not change quickly; it stays for some time before it changes direction. Knowing Fed's intention to increase money supply, it would not have been wise to go bearish on stocks during this period. It is not possible to time exactly what the Fed is going to do, but the trend stays and does not reverse suddenly. There is a saying, "Don't fight the Fed." Whether we like it or not, it has the power to move things in certain direction - we can align our overall investment strategy with the Fed.

1995: Feb	6.0%	Raised in February.
Dec	5.5%	Lowered in July and December.
1996: Jan	5.25%	Lowered in January.
1997: Mar	5.5%	
1998: Nov	4.75%	Lowered in September, October, and November.
1999: Nov	5.5%	Raised in June, August, and November.
2000: May	6.6%	Raised in February, March, and May despite stock market decline in March.
2001: Dec	1.75%	President George W. Bush took office. Rates lowered 11 times to fight recession.
2002: Nov	1.24%	
2003: Jun	1.00%	
2004: Dec	2.25%	Raised 5 times starting in June.
2005: Dec	4.25%	Raised 8 times starting in February.
2006: Jun	5.25%	Ben Bernanke became Fed Chair. Raised rates 4 times to cool housing market.
2007: Dec	4.25%	Lowered 4 times starting in August.
2008: Dec	0.25%	Lowered 7 times. LIBOR started rising in April.
2009:2015	0-25%	
2016 -	0.25 -0.5%	

5.2 Commercial Banks and Their Roles

As mentioned before, the banking system consists of the central bank (Federal bank) and hundreds of commercial banks. The role of commercial banks is to facilitate borrowing and lending of money to individuals, corporations, and other organizations. Banks make money by borrowing (our deposits) at a cheaper rate and lending out at a higher rate (mortgage loans, home equity, and other loans). In the process, they make profit for the bank shareholders, but more importantly, they facilitate flow of money (credit) and act as intermediaries and undertakers of financial transactions.

How do banks operate?

The banks procure money through checking deposits, savings deposit, and CDs from customers. They also get money by issuing bank shares to investors or borrowing money from the private market. They pay interest on these accounts. Why do banks solicit money from outside? Because they can loan it out in forms of home mortgage, home equity loans, commercial loans, or any other loan at a rate, higher than they borrow. They make a profit by the difference between the lending and borrowing rates. However, there is cost associated with paying salary, operational expenses, and other expenses that the banks have to pay. Typically, banks keep 300 basis points (or 3%) margin between lending and borrowing rates to be profitable.

How much margin between lending rate and the borrowing rate do banks keep?

To cover the expense of running the banks, they need to keep the margin at least 3%. The banks would like to keep the margin as high as possible (5%, 10%) to maximize their profit. However, competition from other banks keeps the difference between lending and borrowing at around 3%. Competition from other banks drives down the lending rate and drives up the borrowing cost for the banks.

How many loans a bank can create?

Banking sounds like an easy business model to make money. The more number of loans a bank can create, the more money it will earn. The banks would like to have no limit, but there are government requirements, regulations, and market forces that determine how many loans a bank creates. First, a bank has a **reserve requirement** to meet which is usually 10% of deposit liabilities. Suppose the total demand deposit in the bank is $100M. They have to keep $10M as reserve money with the Fed. They can loan out the rest ($90M). Second, they cannot push more loans than the economy can absorb. Certain factors in the economy create more demands for loan and more loan creation opportunities for banks. When the Fed lowers the discount rate and keeps the target funds rate low, it helps the bank to issue loans at lower rate. Also, when Fed carried out massive QEs, it brought down 10-yr treasury yield to a very low value. This, in turn, brought long-term mortgage rate lower. With lower rates, more people are likely to take loans and do something with the money.

In addition, there are many commercial banks that are competing among themselves to win the customer loans. In this process, the rate they charge for loans goes down, and the cost of raising capitals goes up. It causes the margin to shrink, and, at some point, the loans would not be profitable. This puts a brake on how many loans they create. Another important aspect is the risk with each loan. There is always risk that the loan could default where the banks would lose good part of the loan. This happened during sub-prime lending crisis in 2007-2008. Many loans were issued by banks without much collateral (down payments). When housing market crashed, there was not much equities left in the houses (went negative in many cases), and the banks lost a lot of money. There is another regulatory requirement called the capital requirement that we will discuss next.

What are capital requirements for banks?

Using the accounting equation: Assets = Liabilities + Equity (or Capital). The bank's capital or equity is the difference the assets and liabilities. The banks need to maintain a minimum capital to assets ratio. The banks go through stress tests by the Fed periodically to ensure that they have the minimum capital or equities for the assets they hold. The lower the ratio is, the higher the leverage a bank is using. The idea is that if a bank loses money (some of the loans default), they should have enough capital or equity to absorb the loss rather than failing. After the financial crisis of 2008, the banks are now required to have higher capital to asset ratio. Actually, not the entire asset is included in the calculation. Different asset classes have different risk levels associated with them. For example, cash, treasury securities that a bank holds have no risk, whereas home loans have high risk. The capital ratio requirement is with respect to the risk asset, not the total asset. Sometimes we hear about banks going through capitalization to pass stress test. They sell some of the risk assets and convert to risk-free assets to bring down risk assets or issue new shares to increase capital.

Assets and Liabilities of a bank: A walkthrough example

- A new bank was created by selling shares in public worth $10K. The $10K will be entered as asset (cash), and equity (capital) will be $10K.

- Bank collected $100K as deposits from the public. Now Assets = 110K (cash), Liabilities is $100K, and capital is $10K. At this point, risk asset is zero, and capital requirement is easily met.

- The banks cannot afford to keep the deposits sitting idle with them. They need to loan out to make profit. For 100K deposit liabilities, the bank needs to keep $10K at the Fed as reserve. They loaned out rest 90K as loan. At this point, the balance sheet looks as:
  - Assets (110K cash and 90K loan paper)
  - Liabilities (100K + 90K)
  - Capital (10K).

An interesting thing to note is that cash is still 110K, and there is a new asset of 90K loan paper. The liabilities also increased by 90K. At the instant the loan was created, the bank deposited the money in the homebuyer's account that got the loan. However, the money is still in the bank, hence cash still shows as 110K, and liability shows as 190K.

- The buyer wrote a check of 90K to the seller. The seller of the house deposited the 90K check in another bank.

- When the check arrived at the issuer bank (our bank in this example), it has to pay 90K to the seller's bank. The money was transferred to the other bank through their Fed account. Now the balance sheet looks as:
  - Assets (20K cash and 90K loan paper)
  - Liabilities (100K)
  - Capital (10K)

- Let us calculate the capital to risk asset ratio. Risk asset is the $90K loan, and capital is $10K. Capital to risk asset ratio is 10K/90K = 1/9, which is fine.

- The bank borrowed another $200K from private market. The balance sheet looks as:
  - Assets (220K cash and 90K loan paper)
  - Liabilities (300K)
  - Capital (10K)

- The bank kept another $20K at the Fed for the reserve requirement for $200K it borrowed and loaned out another $180K. After the seller of the house encashed its check at another bank, the balance sheet looks as:
  - Assets (40K cash and 270K loan paper)
  - Liabilities (300K)
  - Capital (10K)

- The equity or capital has not changed - still at $10K. However, the risk capital has increased to $270K. The bank is leveraging higher or taking higher risk. The capital ratio is 10K/270K = 1/27 = 3.7%. This falls below the leverage or capital ratio requirements, which is 4% at this time. The bank has to raise additional capital by issuing new shares or sell some of the loans to bring down the leverage ratio or capital ratio to the required level.

5.3 Fiscal Policy

Fiscal policy is the counterpart of monetary policy that we discussed earlier. Fiscal policy involves taxation and spending by the government. Monetary policy is carried out by the Fed, whereas fiscal policy is carried by the government (congress and the president). The government influences the economy by changing taxation and government spending. When government wants to rev up the economy to bring out of recession, it adopts expansionary fiscal policy by increasing government spending, reducing tax, or combination of both. When there is high inflation and high asset valuation, the government adopts contractionary fiscal policy by reducing spending, increasing taxation, or a combination of both. To understand how spending and taxation influences the economy, let us use the Aggregate Demand equation:

Aggregate Demand = Consumption + Investment + Government Spending + Net Exports

5.3.1   Expansionary Fiscal Policy

When the economy is in recession, the government can employ expansionary fiscal policy. It can increase government spending, reduce tax, or do both. When government spends more, it increases the aggregate demand of the economy. When tax is cut, people have more money with them and spend more that leads to higher consumption. Both of these factors increase aggregate demand and the GDP.

5.3.2   Contractionary Fiscal Policy

When inflation is high, the government can reduce spending, increase tax, or do both. When spending is less, the aggregate demand falls. When tax is increased, people have less money to spend which reduces consumption and aggregate demand. The result is slowdown in economy and reduction in inflation.

5.3.3   Pros and Cons of Fiscal Policy

It usually takes two consecutive quarters of GDP contraction to declare that economy is in recession. By the time expansionary fiscal policy is employed, it may be a little late. The other aspect of expansionary fiscal policy is that it could create budget deficit due to increased spending and reduced tax revenue. Deficit, occasionally, is OK to fight recession when the national debt is low. Some people and Keynesian economists believe that government is the only entity that can spend money in a scale required to fight deep recession such as the economic crisis of 2008-2009. Other people believe that economy can recover by itself, and government spending only prolongs the recovery. The reality may be in between. However, with the very high level of current government debt (19+ trillion dollars), there is not much room for government to add on to the debt.

The effect of taxation is also received differently by different people. In the short run, reduced taxation can add to the deficit due decrease in revenue. However, some economists believe that when tax is reduced, people keep more money that is ploughed back into the economy. Also, this will incentivize people to work, save, and invest more. This creates more jobs and more tax revenue for the government. Economist Laffer pointed out that total tax revenue would increase with tax rate, but after a certain point, the revenue would fall. It is represented by Laffer curve, named after him.

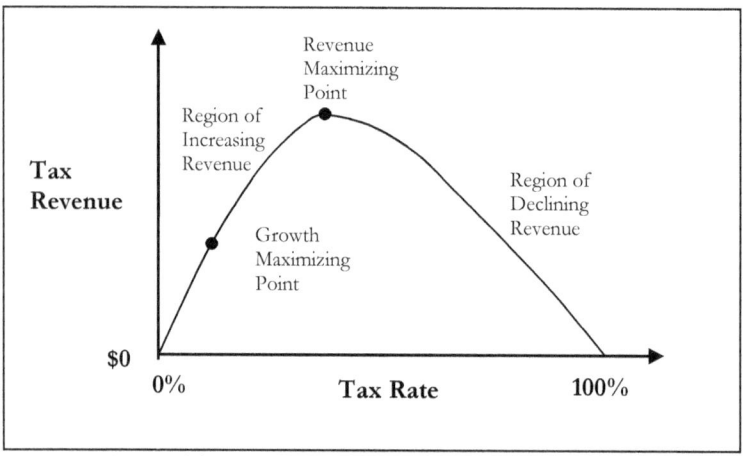

Fig. 5.1 The Laffer Curve

We know that with 0% tax rate, revenue will be zero. Similarly, at 100% tax rate, the revenue will be zero as no one will work - they will lose 100% of their income to the government. Therefore, the max revenue point has to be somewhere in between. The revenue will go up with tax rate and reach the point of maximum tax revenue before coming down. Based on this curve, the revenue will increase by increasing tax rate if it is operating in the region of increasing revenue. Similarly, the overall revenue will increase by cutting tax rate when it is operating in the region of declining revenue. Most agree on this concept, but people do not agree on the exact tax rate at which revenue is the maximum.

5.4 Role of Government

The role of government in the economy is a highly debated topic and often a political one. The views lie from no involvement of government on one end to majority or complete ownership of the business and economy by the government on the other end. It varies from countries to countries. The US is a capitalistic economy where government involvement or ownership of business is on the minimal side.

The US Economy is mostly a free-market economy where the free market forces rather than any outside influence or government decree drives the economy. The consumers and the producers decide what to produce, how much to produce, and the law of demand and supply decides the price. The government acts as the referee with many established laws (antitrust laws, for example) to make sure the business are run in a fair and legal manner. However, government indirectly influences the business and economy through its fiscal policy (taxation) and monetary policy (interest rate). Under extenuating circumstances, the government takes more involved role in the economy. After a recession or a depression, it generally initiates spending programs, such as building roads, bridges, and infrastructure. During the 2008-2009 economic downturn, the US government provided loans to auto industry and insurance industry that were under severe duress. The government also plays an active role in the defense industries and space/exploration industries. For any new technology that does not attract private investments, government either provides direct funding or provides various incentives to encourage adoption of new technologies.

It is not an easy decision and often becomes a political one. Some argue that these dire situations need government's direct involvement in the economy or a section of the economy to survive. The government should get out after the situation has become normal. Others argue that, let the free market forces deal with the situation. It is the very nature of the free market economy where it goes through highs and lows. It will take out the weak players and let the strong companies survive. They argue that intervention by government only prolongs the malaise instead of solving the real problem. I believe, the reality lies somewhere in the middle.

5.5 Gross Domestic Product (GDP)

GDP (Gross Domestic Product) is the total amount of goods and services produced in a country, measured over a period of time, usually every quarter. It is the most important and the most widely watched economic indicator of the health of the economy. We would not be wrong if we say that it is the quarterly results of a country. When the GDP growth is positive, everybody is happy, and the economy is performing well. When the GDP growth is negative, the economy is not doing well, and the economic activities are contracting. When it is negative for two consecutive quarters, it means things are getting bad, and we hear about the dreaded R word, the Recession. Next, let us discuss the precise and quantitative definition of GDP and a get a close feel for it.

5.5.1   Quantitative Measure of GDP

Quantitative Measurement of GDP is defined as:

$$GDP = C + G + I + NX, \text{ where}$$

C is the total consumer spending,
G is the total government spending
I is the total Investments into the economy, and
NX is the net exports, which is exports minus the imports.

Let us look at the typical breakdown of the different components that contribute to the GDP. In year 2014, US GDP was $17.4 trillion of which,

- Lion share was consumer spending: 69% ($11.93T)
- Government spending: 18% ($3.2T)
- Investments: 16% ($2.86T)
- Net exports: -3% (around half trillion dollars)

The imports were more than the exports in 2014.

As we can see, the US economy is dominated by consumer spending.

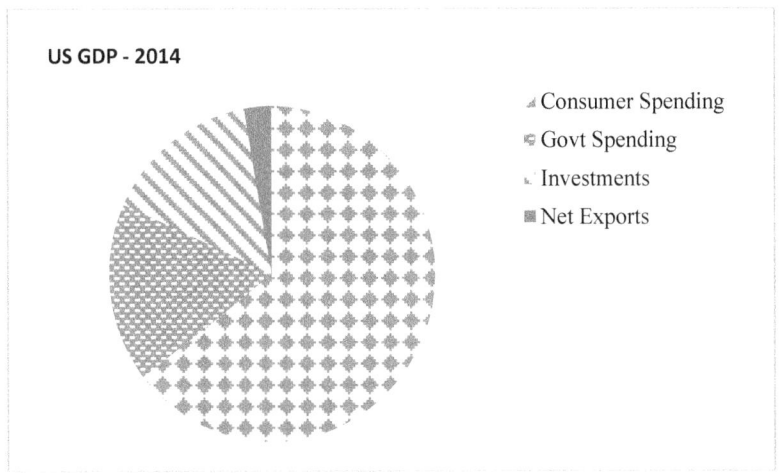

Fig. 5.2 US GDP Components in 2014

5.5.2   US GDP Growth, Last Twenty Years

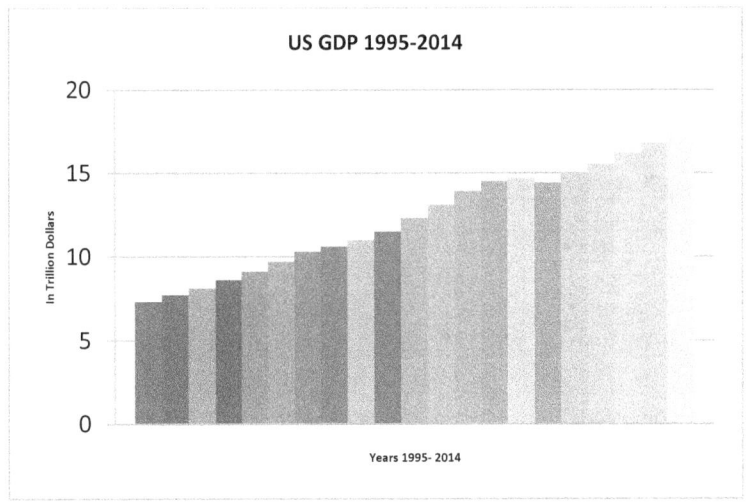

Fig. 5.3   US GDP 1995 to 2014 (source World Bank)

The US GDP was $7.3T in 1995 and $17.4T in 2014, with an annualized growth rate of 4.44%. The GDP contracted during major economic downturn of 2009.

5.5.3   What is Real GDP?

The nominal GDP or simply the GDP does not account for inflation and may not give a true indication of how it is faring over the years. Real GDP is the GDP adjusted for inflation and provides real measure of how the GDP is performing.

5.5.4   GDP of World Major Economies

The world GDP (combined GDP of all countries) was $77.87 trillion dollars in 2014. The USA and China were at the top with $17.42T (22.37%) and $10.36T (13.3%) respectively. Here are the top 15 major economies in the world in terms of GDP in 2014.

Country	GDP	Percentage
USA	$17.42T	22.37%
China	$10.36T	13.3%
Japan	$4.62T	5.93%
Germany	$3.86T	4.96%
UK	$2.95T	3.79%
France	$2.85T	3.66%
Brazil	$2.35T	3.02%
Italy	$2.15T	2.76%
India	$2.05T	2.63%
Russia	$1.86T	2.39%
Canada	$1.79T	2.3%
Australia	$1.45T	1.86%
Korea	$1.42T	1.82%
Spain	$1.41T	1.81%
Mexico	$1.29T	1.66%

As the international economy is highly inter-dependent and the USA is a trading partner with most of these countries, the US economy and the US stock market get affected when other economies slow down. Similarly, any change in the US economy gets reverberated around the world. Many times, you will see the stock markets around the world moving in tandem in a 24-hr period, the US leading the change sometimes and Asia or Europe leading the change other times.

5.5.5   Why GDP Figures are Revised Sometimes?

GDP is a very important parameter to gauge the health of the economy and is used to shape monetary and fiscal policy to correct the underlying problems and get the economy back on track. For example, if the economy is contracting, monetary policy is loosened to encourage investments and consumer spending. Fiscal policy is adjusted by increasing government spending, cutting tax, or both to boost GDP. The sooner we get the GDP figure, the sooner the corrective action can be started. Determining the GDP number is a complex task where not all the data may have been available by the end of a quarter. Estimated GDP data is released with the information available at the time of release. However, sometimes, when the real data becomes available later on, the numbers may be different, and the GDP figure is revised accordingly. Sometimes, the revised GDP number shows better than original or not as good as the original in other times. However, most of the times, there is not much change. The funny thing is that stock market gives up gains when the revised numbers turn out to be not as good as the original numbers were. Also, the stock market gains when the revised numbers are better than the original.

5.5.6   GDP Growth and Stock Market

The link between GDP growth and the stock market is one of the most researched topics, and, it seems, there is no definitive answer to it. However, there are some common sense approaches we can talk and strategize our investment plans accordingly. A bull market starts from a deep crash and pessimism, when things are at the lowest level. When things start to turn around with GDP growth, the stock market also starts to pick up. However, the stock market does not wait for the whole GDP growth to happen. It starts climbing up with some proof and mostly in anticipation. As economy continues to grow, the stock market continues to do well. When the GDP is growing steadily and strongly, many companies are doing very well. Their revenues and earnings are on the rise. In such a scenario, most stocks do well. Apart from strong GDP growth, there are other factors that affect stock performance.

If the stock market has built a bubble (it has moved far ahead of the real economy), the stock market can crash despite good GDP growth but with a hint of slow down. On the other hand, during a low-interest rate period, the stocks become the default choice for investment by elimination. There are no safe options available that can provide reasonable returns. The stock market can flourish even with slower positive growth when other alternatives for investments provide poor returns, and companies can borrow money inexpensively to fund buybacks and buy other companies.

5.6 Deficit/Surplus and Debts

Every year, the government collects revenue, mainly through taxation, and spends money on various categories. When the expenditure is less than the revenue, it results in surplus, and, when the expenditure is more, it results in deficit for that year. For 2015, the US government revenue and expense were $3.25 trillion and $3.69 trillion respectively, with a deficit of $440 billion.

National debt is the cumulative deficits over the years. If there is surplus for a year, the debt is reduced by the surplus amount; if it is a deficit for a year, it adds on to the national debt. The US government funds the debt by selling treasury securities (treasury bills, notes, and bonds).

Source: http://www.treasurydirect.gov

Debt in Billions of Dollars

Year	1990	1991	1992	1993	1994	1995
Debt	3,233	3,665	4,064	4,411	4,692	4,973

Year	1996	1997	1998	1999	2000	2001	2002	2003	2004	2005
Debt	5,224	5,413	5,526	5,656	5,674	5,807	6,228	6,783	7,379	7,932

Year	2006	2007	2008	2009	2010	2011	2012	2013	2014	2015
Debt	8,506	9,007	10,024	11,909	13,561	14,790	16,066	16,738	17,824	18,150

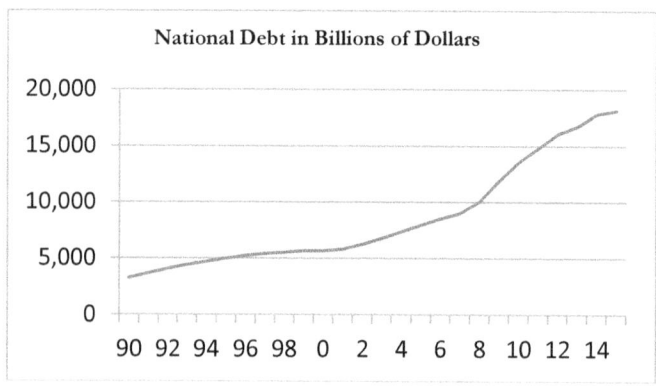

Fig. 5.4 US National Debt 1990 – 2015

5.7 Money and Wealth

> Money, money, money,
> Brighter than sunshine, sweeter than honey;

You woke up one morning and found that there are no dollar bills, coins, or banks. They simply vanished. Can the society function without money? Will the economy run at all? Probably yes, but, it would be very painful and very restricted. Before money was invented, society functioned through barter exchange. People would trade one good for another. I will give you two chickens in exchange of five gallons of milk. You would accept a dozen of banana in exchange for half a dozen of mango. Things would work in a crude way but would be very painful.

Money was invented at some point but not the paper money we see now. In history, people have used different things, such as, cattle, salt, iron, and gold coins as money. So what is money really? Money is something that acts as a medium of exchange, is a unit of value, and can store value for future. Something, that can be used as money, should be easy to carry and exchange, difficult to counterfeit, and inexpensive to produce.

We all know dollar bills and coins as money. But, is that all or something more to it? Apart from the currencies (bills and coins), money includes traveler's checks and demand deposits, such as checking accounts against which check can be issued. All these forms of money together are called **M1**, which is the most liquid form of money. **M2**, a broader definition of money, includes all forms of M1 money plus savings deposit, CDs, and money-market funds. M3 money is the broadest definition of money that includes all forms of M2 money plus large time deposits, institutional money market funds, and other large liquid assets. **M3** includes all the money supply in an economy. When we hear about expansion or contraction of money supply in the economy by Fed's monetary policy, it talks about the broadest definition of money, the M3. Wealth includes money (M3) and all assets (gold, houses, factories, intangibles, and all physical goods) that have some value.

How are money and wealth created or destroyed?

Money is created by Federal Reserve. Refer to section 5.1.2 on how the Fed creates money to expand money supply and removes money to contract money supply. Wealth is created by producing finished goods (houses, boats, TVs, etc.), creating intangibles, and providing services. Wealth is also created when assets go up in value. When the price of a home appreciated from $300,000 to $350,000, the homeowner's wealth increased by $50,000. When the stock market goes up, stockowners' wealth increases. Similarly, when asset value goes down, wealth is destroyed. We hear wealth creation and destruction all the time when the stock market goes up or goes down.

5.8 Inflation and Unemployment

High inflation and high unemployment are two major problems that have plagued American economy from time to time. Before we discuss the effect of inflation, let us talk about no inflation or deflation (negative inflation). During deflation, things become cheaper as they cost less than before. This, on the surface, looks good and should be welcome by people. However, deflation has much more negatives than getting things cheaper. Deflation depresses the economy. The revenues of companies fall, the economy and the GDP contract, and everything looks backward instead of going forward. People tend to spend less or postpone buying goods as they are not in a hurry - the price is expected to fall further in future. Consumer spending is the lion share of the American GDP. The shrinkage of GDP leads to job loss. It is a downward spiral with one thing leading to another. Government tries to fight deflation at any cost by reducing interest rate so that money becomes cheaper to borrow. Government fights this by adopting fiscal measures, such as tax cuts, additional government spending, or any other measure that would encourage people to spend more.

Having established that deflation is a bad thing for the economy, does it mean that we should have inflation? In fact, a little bit of inflation is good for the economy. The target is to have 2% to 3% but not more. Like deflation, high inflation is bad for the economy. It has many downsides. The cost of everything goes up too much, too quick. It hits people with fixed income the most. It is bad for business as well. It becomes difficult for business to plan and budget with a quickly shifting baseline. This is mostly true when the inflation is unanticipated. Anticipated inflation is somewhat manageable, as everybody is expecting it and can plan around it. On the contrary, unanticipated inflation is very detrimental as nobody is sure what to do, and too much uncertainty is bad for the business and the economy.

The causes of inflation can be attributed to two types of occurrences, demand-pull inflation and cost-push inflation. Demand-pull inflation is caused when demand far exceeds the supply. It is the traditional definition of inflation, too much money chasing too few goods. This can happen if the money supply quickly goes up compared to the goods produced. It also happens during war or big calamities when there is large disruption of supply. The other form of inflation is cost-pushed. When the cost of production (raw materials, other ingredients, and wages and salary) goes up, the companies increase the price of their products to maintain their profit margin or just to remain profitable.

When the unemployment level reaches the theoretical minimum (around 5%), it starts driving up the wages. Five percent unemployment is considered full employment in the economy. The remaining 5% of the population just do not want to work or are between jobs. When the economy reaches full employment level, there are no more people available to hire. The employers have to bid up to displace workers from a company and hire them. This leads to higher wages/salary and higher inflation. Government fights inflation by increasing interest rate that makes it expensive to borrow. The net effect is reduction in money supply aimed at bringing down inflation. The government also sells bonds with the net effect of sucking money out of the economy and moving it to the Fed's balance sheet.

5.9 International Trade and Multinationals

International trade has rapidly expanded in last two decades. Many US multinational companies now derive substantial revenues and profit from countries outside the US. Similarly, many non-US multinationals have increasing presence in the US with product development and manufacturing. Apart from the traditional developed countries, highly populous countries like China and India play increasingly important role in the international market. Both these countries together have 30-35% of world population with a large rising middle class. These are huge markets for the US multinational companies that normally lead the world with innovative products and services. On the other hand, the US has seen steady decline of manufacturing jobs that are moving to other countries where labor is cheaper. This has been a highly debatable topic as things are changing rapidly. As we can see, countries have become highly dependent on one another, and it is likely to continue in that direction. One way to make the process fair for all countries is to make the trade balance between countries neutral so that each side has equal amount to sell with the best products it can produce. On a bilateral basis, both countries work together to export goods and services with equal amount so that it becomes a balanced give and take.

6 Accounting Basics

6.1 Accounting Equation – Balance Sheet

The fundamental **"Accounting Equation"** is a simple equation that categories everything into one of the three groups - assets, liabilities, and equity. It goes like this:

A (Assets)   = L (Liabilities) + E (Equity)

At any point of time, the equation should hold good. Assets are things that a company owns, such as cash, factories, buildings, investments, accounts receivable, inventory, patents, and goodwill. Liabilities are the things that a company owes to others such as accounts payable, rents, and short-term and long-term loans. Equity or the stockholders equity is the value that remains after you deduct the liabilities from the assets. If we rearrange the accounting equation, it will read like this:

E (Equity) = A (Assets)   - L (Liabilities)

One of the important things to consider before buying a stock is to evaluate its fundamentals – how strong its balance sheet (assets and stockholder equity) is and what the quality of the balance sheet is. We will study balance sheet in details in section 12.4. Here, let us build the concepts with a real example. Here is the real balance sheet of Cisco Systems as of July 25, 2015: Source Yahoo Finance.

Accounting

Balance Sheet (All numbers in thousands)

Period Ending	Jul 25, 2015
Cash And Cash Equivalents	6,877,000
Short Term Investments	53,539,000
Net Receivables	12,750,000
Inventory	1,627,000
Other Current Assets	1,490,000
Total Current Assets	**76,283,000**
Long Term Investments	3,858,000
Property Plant and Equipment	3,332,000
Goodwill	24,469,000
Intangible Assets	2,376,000
Accumulated Amortization	-
Other Assets	3,163,000
Deferred Long Term Asset Charges	-
Total Assets	**113,481,000**
Accounts Payable	4,215,000
Short/Current Long Term Debt	3,897,000
Other Current Liabilities	15,511,000
Total Current Liabilities	**23,623,000**
Long Term Debt	21,457,000
Other Liabilities	3,335,000
Deferred Long Term Liability Charges	5,359,000
Minority Interest	9,000
Negative Goodwill	-
Total Liabilities	**53,783,000**
Misc Stocks Options Warrants	-
Redeemable Preferred Stock	-
Preferred Stock	-
Common Stock	43,592,000
Retained Earnings	16,045,000
Treasury Stock	-
Capital Surplus	-
Other Stockholder Equity	61,000
Total Stockholder Equity	**59,698,000**

Let us plug the number in the accounting equation and check it ourselves.

Assets ($113,481,000) = Liabilities ($53,783,000) + Equity ($59,698,000).

Generally, assets are divided as current or liquid, Long-term investments, and plants and properties. Other forms of assets are intangible assets and goodwill that are very subjective and should be taken with a grain of salt. Liabilities are also broadly divided as current (immediate) and long-term liabilities.

Are employees assets or liabilities?

> In accounting terms, the salary and benefits are counted as current liabilities as the company needs to pay salaries to the employees, at least for the short run. However, I would count the employees as one of the most important assets (not in accounting terms) of a company any day. They are the real value for a company. The companies pay them salaries and benefits, but the employees create value much more than that.

6.2 Figuring out Your Net Worth

We always hear about net worth. What is the net worth of a person? We will talk about only the tangible value, such as checking and savings account balance, stocks, and other properties but not the intangibles. Every human being is priceless and worth a lot. Let us bring the accounting equation back:

Equity (Net worth) = A (Assets)   - L (Liabilities).

Let us work out a fictitious example - list all the assets and liabilities in a table and then find out net worth.

	Assets	Liabilities
Current/ Liquid	• Checking Account: $5,000 • Savings Account: $10,000 • 1-Yr CD: $10,000 • Stocks: $50,000	• Credit Card: $2,000 • HELOC*: $15,000
Long term	• 10-yr Bond: $10,000 • 401K: $50,000	
Others	• Home: $400,000 • Automobile: $20,000 • Other goods: $20,000	• Home Loan: $300,000 • Automobile Loan: $15,000 • Home Equity Loan: $20,000
	Total Assets: $575,000	**Total Liabilities: $352,000**
	Net worth is $575,000 – $352,000 = $223,000	

Fig. 6.1 Personal Net worth Worksheet

Accounting

*HELOC (Home Equity Line Of Credit): Include only the amount you have drawn, not the limit. If you have a line of credit for $50,000 and have drawn up $15,000, your liability is $15,000, not the whole $50,000.

Note: Home and Cars are both assets, but home is an appreciating asset, where value usually goes up in the long run. Car is a depreciating asset, where the value goes down rapidly in the first two years and then steadily onwards. Car is a personal choice where one considers safety, personal image, and satisfaction. There is no clear-cut rule here, but be aware that a $40,000 car would probably be worth only $15,000 after 10 years.

6.3 Double Entry Accounting

Most of us probably will not be involved in book keeping in accounting, but it is good to understand the concept of double entry book keeping. When any of the item in the equation (assets = liabilities + equities) changes, it results in two entrees. For example, when a company raises cash by selling corporate bonds, the cash value (assets) goes up, and long-term debt (liabilities) also goes up by equal amount – both sides still match in the accounting equation. In this case, both asset and liability went by the same amount. Let us look at a few more examples:

Example:

> The company used up $25,000 dollar to buy furniture. The current asset (cash) went down by $25,000, and property assets (furniture) went up by $25,000. The total assets of the company remained the same, and nothing changed in liabilities or equity. The furniture will depreciate over time, but at the time of buying the furniture, it was worth $25,000.

More Examples:

- The company sold additional shares and raised $50M. In this case, the cash asset went up by $50M, and equity went up by $50M.

- The company made a net profit of $10M for the quarter. The assets (cash) went up by $10M, and equity went up by $10M.

- The company had a quarterly loss of $2M. The assets (cash) went down by $2M, and so did the equity.

- The company paid out $5M as dividends to shareholders. The cash asset went down by $5M, and the equity went down by the same amount.

When two entries are made for any transactions, the accounting equation still holds good. There are multiple ledgers for cash, accounts payable, receivable, and equity. After a transaction, entrees are made to two of the books. It helps to not only keep the equation balanced but also spot error easily if mistake happens somewhere.

6.4 Other Important Accounting Concepts

Accrual vs. Cash-based Accounting

In accrual-based accounting, revenue is counted when earned, and expense is counted when incurred, even if the actual cash comes in later or expense is paid later. In cash-based accounting, the revenue is counted when actual cash is received, and expense is counted when it is paid out.

Amortization

In mortgage, it refers to the schedule of how a home loan, for example a 30-yr loan, is scheduled to be paid off. Part of the monthly mortgage payment goes toward the interest payment on the outstanding loan balance, and remaining goes toward principal reduction. As years pass by, the principal balance keeps going down, and an increasing portion of the mortgage payment is applied toward principal reduction.

In business, amortization is used for intangible assets, such as patents, licenses, and intellectual properties. Intangible assets typically get to the balance sheet during acquisition of another company. Each year, part of the intangible assets value is amortized (expensed) until it carries no asset value in the balanced sheet. It is similar to depreciation except depreciation is done on tangible assets (factories, computers) whereas amortization is done on intangible assets. Since it is an expense, the net income is reduced by the amortized amount. Amortization does not affect cash flow value, except to the extent of reduction in tax payment.

Note: When analyzing balance sheet, carefully look at the intangible assets and goodwill values. Since these are hard to evaluate and can suddenly lose value, a balance sheet, where a significant percentage of stockholder equity consists of intangibles and goodwill, should be discounted. Most of the balance sheets usually report two values - total stockholder equity and the net tangible assets. While evaluating the strength of assets, consider only the net tangible assets.

CHAPTER 6 — Accounting

Cash Flow

It is the difference in money coming in and going out. If more money is coming in than going out, it is positive cash flow. If it is the other way, it is negative cash flow. Cash flow is one of the important parameters to watch for a stock. Is the dividend sustainable? Is it generating enough cash to pay out dividends, or is it dipping into the cash reserve quarter after quarter. This would be a sign that dividends could be cut or suspended in the future. However, the most important aspect of cash flow is its impact on staying solvent. If the company is steadily having negative cash flow, it may run out of cash leading to layoff or possible bankruptcy. Revenue is vanity, profit is sanity, and cash is king.

Depreciation

Depreciation is the decrease in value of an asset. Every asset has a useful life period, after which it has no useful value or has minimal value (salvage value). Depreciation is an expense for the company. Take the example of a car rental company. A twenty thousand dollar car will be worth $12,000 after 5 years. The asset lost $8000 value in five years.

Two of the commonly used depreciation methods are the straight-line method and the accelerated method. In straight-line method, the depreciation amount is evenly distributed for each year. In accelerated method, the depreciation amount is more in the beginning years and less in the later years.

In cash flow statement, you would see the depreciation as a positive cash flow entry. Why? Because, it is an expense, but the company did not really spend that money. The final profit for the company is reduced by the depreciation amount, but the money or cash, equal to depreciation amount, is still with the company.

GAAP (Generally Accepted Accounting Principles)

Generally Accepted Accounting Principles (GAAP) are a collection of standard accounting rules and guidelines issued by Financial Accounting Standard Board (FASB). When the companies report quarterly results (Balance sheet, income statement, and EPS), they adhere to the GAAP standards, which make it easier for investors to evaluate company performance in a consistent manner.

Another form of quarterly results reporting is non-GAAP or adjusted earnings. One time charge due to restructuring cost or write down of some non-performing assets results in lower EPS as per GAAP reporting. Non-GAAP or adjusted earnings reports the EPS excluding the onetime charge, which reflects more accurate performance of the company. In most quarterly results, you would see both GAAP and non-GAAP EPS.

Impairment

Impairment of assets (both tangible and intangible) occurs when an asset suddenly loses a lot of value due to change in market conditions or other factors. The difference between in the current book value and the fair market value is the impairment charges. In a balance sheet, it results in reduction in asset value as well as reduction in stockholder equity.

How is impairment different from depreciation and amortization?

Depreciation and amortization are gradual planned reduction in asset value whereas impairment is sudden drop in asset value. For example, a company has intangible asset of $5B in the balance sheet from an earlier acquisition. Five years later, another company invented a superior technology that made the existing technology worthless. This results in a big impairment or a write-off on the intangible asset.

Note: When a company has a large impairment, it results in a big loss for that quarter and reduction in stockholder equity. Look at companies with a great deal of suspicion that have a history of big acquisitions only to write off a significant portion of the acquisition a few years down the road. They are throwing away cash or incurring debts to finance questionable acquisitions – neither one is good.

Intangible Assets and Goodwill

Intangible assets include patents, copyrights, trademarks, licenses, intellectual properties, customer database, and goodwill. Goodwill, a form of non-identifiable intangible asset, is acquired during buying another company. It is the difference between the purchase price and the fair market value of the company. Goodwill is not amortized (expensed) but tested for impairment annually.

Accounting

Revenue vs. Income

Revenue is the total amount of money that comes in. It is also called the gross income. When you take away the cost of revenue (cost of goods) from the gross income, you get the gross profit. When you further deduct the operating expenses (research and development and sales and administrative cost), you get the operating income or loss. After you take the income tax from the operating income, you get the net income on which earning per share (EPS) is calculated.

- Gross Income or Revenue = Total money coming in
- Gross Profit(Loss) = Gross Income - Cost of Revenue
- Operating Income(Loss) = Gross profit - Operating Expenses
- **Net Income(Loss)=** Operating income - Income tax

7 Ignorance isn't Bliss

7.1 Know the Laws

There are a few things one need to be cognizant of so that he or she does not get into troubles knowingly or unknowingly. One of the most important things is insider trading that some people have engaged in, including celebrities. The stock market is expected to operate in a fair way so that people who are privy to information do not take advantage of it in an unfair and illegal way. The other important thing is the wash sale rule where certain losses are not counted as loss for tax purposes. We will cover some of these topics in this chapter.

7.2 Insider Trading

Insider trading is buying or selling stocks or bonds based on information about a company that is not public yet. An insider is a person that is privy to this information. For example, the quarterly result of a company is known to the CEO, CFO, and other top people of the company several days or weeks before the announcement. If the results are strong, the stock is likely to move up significantly or may go down significantly if the results are terrible. It is illegal for the insider to use this information to buy or sell the stock and make a profit. He or she would land up in jail. Another instance is, where two companies are talking about merger or one company acquiring the other company. After the announcement of the merger or acquisition, the stock price could gain significantly. It is illegal to buy or sell stocks based on this information prior to the public announcement of such merger or acquisition.

How about an insider passing the information to a friend and the friend acting on the information? It is still illegal for both, and both the insider and the friend could end up in jail. How about an insider casually disclosing the information in a party without seriously thinking about it and a friend or friends act upon it to make a tidy profit? It does not matter; it is still illegal. If you have access to non-public information about a company, it is your responsibility to not divulge it, deliberately or inadvertently. Also, it is your responsibility to not act upon such information if you become a recipient of such information, no matter how it happened.

Can an insider (typically director and above) still trade his or her company stock? Yes, but there are restrictions. They are required to file their transactions with SEC (Security and Exchange Commission) in advance using form4. Can the SEC really catch insider trading with so many people buying and selling stocks in so many places? The SEC has smart algorithms and people to monitor trading patterns (unusual volume or large profit) to find out such illegal activities, and they have caught many such incidents.

7.3 Antitrust Laws

Antitrust laws are a group of laws (The Sherman Antitrust Act, The Clayton Act, and The Federal Trade Commission Act) that are designed to prohibit business practices that unreasonably deprive the consumers of competition in the market. If there is less competition, it could result in higher price for consumers. It also outlaws all contracts, combinations, and conspiracies that unreasonably restrain interstate and foreign trade, including fixing price by competitors, rigging bids, and allocating customers, which are punishable as criminal felonies.

Companies in similar fields merge, or one company buys another company to reduce overlapping cost and produce economy of scale. However, the FTC reviews these cases such that the merger does not limit consumers' choice, and there is still enough healthy completion out there.

Why is it important to you? If you are the CEO of one of these companies involved in the acquisition or merger talk, you want to make sure that there is a strong possibility of the merger going through; else, it could create chaos and loss of focus for both companies, negatively affecting shareholder values. If you are an investor, it also has financial implications. Many times, you would hear about possible merger or acquisition in the news or blog posts. When this happens, the stock price generally moves up significantly. You need to watch these events carefully and make informed decision about buying or selling stocks of these companies. Sometimes, the news or rumor may not come true or the FTC does not approve the deal; the stock price would come down quickly. If you already own these stocks, you may want to sell and lock profit when the price went up. If you do not own stocks of these companies, it may be risky to buy after the price has popped. You could be stuck with a big loss if the merger fizzled out.

7.4 Wash Sale

When someone buys back a stock within 30 days after it sells the same stock at a loss, it results in a wash sale. The tax loss is not allowed under IRS wash sale rule. It also results in wash sale if one buys a stock 30 days before selling the same stock at a loss. A loss is a loss, and why shouldn't it be allowed? The rule was created so that people do not defer tax gain by manipulating buy and sale timing.

However, if you sell a stock at a loss and buy back a similar (not same) stock in that category even within 30 days, it won't result in wash sale. An example would be; you have some Chevron (CVX) stocks that have a big loss for the year. You can sell CVX to offset some of the capital gain from other positions and buy Exxon Mobile (XOM) stock on the same day. You have to make that judgement that the upside potentials for both CVX and XOM are fairly identical at this point. The danger of selling at a loss and waiting 30 days to buy back is that things could move up quickly and your loss with CVX would be permanent, missing the sudden jump after you sold at a loss. Since CVX, and XOM are in the same business class and things are likely to affect both companies equally, it makes sense to sell CVX and buy XOM. The example could have been the other way as well – selling XOM and buying CVX. It can be a good strategy to take the loss for this year from one stock and still not miss sudden upside jump by buying a similar stock at the same time in that category.

7.5 Uptick Rule

Uptick rule involves short sale of stocks. The rule requires that one can short a stock only at a price higher than the current bid price. This was designed to prevent short sellers from putting further downward pressure on a stock that is going down. However, uptick rule is not applicable for certain types of highly liquid financial instruments, such as futures and currency trades.

In February 2010, SEC adopted a new short sale price test restriction, which is commonly referred to as the **"alternative uptick rule."** The alternative uptick rule is designed to restrict short sellers from further driving down the price of a stock that has dropped more than 10 percent in one day compared to the closing price on the previous day.

7.6 Online Safety

We all know and read about accounts being hacked and think it is someone else. I had the same view until I got a call early morning (5AM) from my on-line broker, "Did you place these trades." To my horror, I woke up and found that there were large buy orders placed for some little known stocks in my account. Fortunately, the broker had already frozen my account before the trading opened and then called me. With some research, I found that, hackers coordinate large buy orders so that stock opens with a big jump in price. Then they dump the stocks with a big gain for them and big loss for these hacked accounts. Also, came to learn that online brokerage companies use software where they watch for unusual activities and automatically alert or take necessary actions to prevent such unlawful activities from taking place.

I believe, there are protections from frauds, and liability, as a consumer, is probably limited. However, it is better to take upfront safety measures to reduce the possibility of such occurrences than to fight and spend time to clean up after things happen – not to mention the trauma one has to go through. Here are some safety measures that would go a long way.

- Get a hardware device (dongle) from your broker. It generates a new code every 30 seconds or so. You append this code after you type your password every time you log onto your trading account. Since it is a physical device and you only see the code, it would be very difficult (probably not impossible) for someone to get into your account. It is like a new password every time you log on.

- Have a strong password and have different passwords for different financial accounts.

- Have a dedicated computer (desktop or laptop) that you use for all your financial transactions. Do not use this computer for other activities, such as emails, surfing web, or anything else. This reduces the chance of virus, worms, Trojan horse, or malwares getting into your computer from other sites or as attachments from emails. My son laughed at me when I said I use this computer only for financial transactions, but it is a good way to keep troubles at bay.

- Have an antivirus and anti-spyware software that runs regularly on this computer.

- Set up two accounts – an administrative account and a user account. Log on to your computer through the user account, not the admin account. It protects from inadvertent installation of software that you do not want. Before a program gets installed, it will ask for administrative password, and you can decline it. This acts as another layer of safety.

- Go to the website by typing website address into the address bar rather than clicking a link. These look-alike links will take you to the fraudulent sites directly.

- Do not use public computers, such as at airport, library, and restaurants to log on your financial accounts – these could very well be infected with malwares that will capture your username and password.

- Do not leave the computer ON while connected to the internet. Once done, logout and switch off the computer.

- These may sound like extremes but are easy-to-adopt measures that will reduce the possibility of on-line hacking.

Chapter

8

8 Of the People, by the People,..

8.1 Our Government

All of us, as active citizens and residents, are interested in the political system of our country, because the policies (and many times the politics of it) play a critical role in the functioning of the country and the economy. Moreover, directly or indirectly, it affects our personal finances and investments. As active investors, we need to have an eye on what is going on out there – who is in power, what kinds of policies are going to be passed, and how is it going to affect the economy. The policies may be to our likings or different from ours, but we, as investors, need to be on top of our personal finances and investments. We all are very familiar with budget impasse, debt-limit crisis, and the stock market gyrations. As citizens, we have our political opinions, and it is healthy to have opinions on important policy matters. However, it cannot be denied that it affects our investments, may be temporarily; and, it can offer investment opportunities if we understand the process and stay calm. Let us briefly refresh our understandings of the different branches of governments and discuss how laws and policies are passed.

8.2 US Constitution

The US Constitution, adopted in 1789, is the supreme law of the land. It is the law book based on which the country is governed. The first 10 amendments to the constitution, known as the Bill of Rights, offer important fundamental rights, such as freedom of speech, freedom of assembly, and right to fair trial. The constitution established three branches of government – legislative, executive, and judicial, based on the doctrine of separation of powers among the branches.

8.3 Branches of Government

The US has three main branches of government:

❖ The Legislative branch – The House of Representatives and the Senate
❖ The Executive branch – The President, the Vice-president, and the federal workers
❖ The Judiciary branch – The supreme court and the lower courts

The founders of the nation thought through this hard and divided the power among the three branches so that one acts as a check and balance against the others, and power is not concentrated in one branch. The president is the most powerful, but other branches also have a lot of powers.

The Legislative Branch

It consists of the House of Representatives (or just the House, in short) and the Senate. Both the House and the Senate together are referred as the Congress. There are 435 voting members in the House and 100 members in the Senate. Each term of House is for two years. Every two years, all the seats of the House are up for reelection. However, there is no term limit for members of the House. The senate, on the other hand, is intended to have less frequent changes. Each member serves for six years after winning election. The election for the Senate is staggered such that one third of the seats in Senate undergo election every two years. Each of the 50 states in the US elects two Senate members, with a total of 100 Senate members.

The Executive Branch

The president is the top of the executive branch. The presidency is up for election every four years, and a person cannot be the president for more than two terms. The president is the CEO of the country and has tremendous power and responsibility. He is the final authority who signs a bill into a law - we will discuss this later in more details. The president is also the commander-in chief of the defense department.

The Judicial Branch

The Supreme Court is the highest court in the country and the final authority on legal matters. There are nine permanent members (justices) in the Supreme Court, headed by the chief justice. The president appoints justices to Supreme Court. Most of the legal issues are resolved in lower courts in the country.

However, things, that have wider implications or that affect the whole country, usually end up in the Supreme Court. The majority opinion (five or more justices) is the final verdict on a matter, and everyone has to abide by the verdict.

8.4 How are the Laws Formed?

Any member of the Congress (House or Senate) can initiate a bill. When it is presented in House, it goes to the House committee; and, when it is presented in the Senate, it goes to the Senate committee. When the bill passes in one chamber of the congress, it goes to the other chamber for voting. To clear the House, it needs a simple majority. Similarly, for Senate, it usually requires a simple majority except for some cases where it requires 60 out 100 votes to pass a bill. If it is a tie (50-50) in the Senate, the Vice President casts his vote to break the tie.

Sometimes, both chambers of the congress have their own versions of a bill. In such cases, the bill goes to a "conference committee," represented by members from both chambers. In the conference, they resolve their differences and send it back to both chambers for approval. Though a bill can be presented in any house, there are some cases where each chamber has some unique powers. Only Senate can reject a treaty signed by the president or block a supreme-court nominee, initiated by the president. Any bill that involves taxation can be introduced only in the House. When a bill passes in both the chambers, it goes to the president's desk.

The president has three options. He can pass the bill, and it becomes the law of the land. He can veto (reject) the bill and send it to the House giving the reason for the veto. The House can reintroduce the bill, and if it passes with two-third majority in both chambers, it becomes the law overriding the President's prior veto. The third option is when the President does nothing on the bill. In this case, if congress is in session, the bill automatically becomes law after 10days.

As we discussed, the president has the power to pass a bill into law, but he himself cannot introduce a bill. There are several political parties in USA, among which, the Democratic and the Republican are two main parties. When the house, the senate, and the presidency belong to one political party – typically happens after a presidential election, it becomes easier to make policy changes. Sometimes, president belongs to one political party, and one or both branches of the congress belong to the other party. In such instances, it becomes difficult to enact big policy changes.

When the presidency, the house, and the senate are divided, it is not necessarily the case that there is always difference in opinions on everything. However, in many instances, both parties do not agree on important policies completely. It becomes frustrating to the other side, but what it is saying that both sides feel strongly about certain issues. In such cases, it acts as a check and balance, and there is no easy solution to move things forward. Both sides need to objectively look into the issues and come up with practical solutions focusing on things where both sides agree and take series of baby steps. Due to uncertainty, the stock market goes through big ups and downs during these times. Stay calm and look at the big picture. It may look scary but could be buying opportunities for fundamentally strong stocks.

8.5 What is the Budgeting Process?

The President submits a detailed budget request for the coming fiscal year that starts on Oct 1. The budget then goes to both house subcommittees on budget – House Committee on the Budget and the Senate Committee on the Budget. Both the committees pass their Budget Resolutions. Budget resolution is a non-binding resolution that forms the framework for budget decisions. The budget resolution does not specify the specifics of the spending but specifies the limit for spending. Then the budget resolution moves to the appropriation committees of both houses. There are multiple subcommittees where each subcommittee discusses the requirements of each department with the department head and comes up the specifics of spending within the limit set by the budget resolution. Each subcommittee votes on the subcommittee appropriation bill. When it passes the subcommittee, it goes to the full Appropriation Committee. The full committee reviews it and sends it to the full house and senate.

The full house and senate independently debate on their appropriation bills from the 12 subcommittees. After both the house and Senate passes their version of the appropriation bills, they meet over the conference committee to resolve the differences. The end result of the conference is one bill that goes back to the house and senate for voting again. When the bill passes both houses, it goes to President's desk. The President can sign it or veto it. If president signs, it becomes the law. If the process could not be completed by Oct 1, congress can pass a temporary measure called Temporary Resolution. The governmental departments continue to receive money until the budget is passed. If the congress does not pass a Temporary Resolution, it can result in government shutdown.

CHAPTER 8   Off the People, by the...

8.6 Debt Limit and its Significance

The national debt limit or ceiling is the maximum amount of debt the government can have. Every year the government gets certain amount of revenue through taxation and spends certain amount of money on various heads. When the expenses are more than the revenue, the government borrows money by selling securities (treasury notes and treasury bonds). The deficit is added to the existing debt. However, the treasury cannot borrow money that crosses the debt ceiling without approval from congress.

The US national debt currently stands at $19T, which is very high by historical standards. It is a hot-button topic among the political parties and a major concern for many citizens. We have seen the debt ceiling issue several times recently when the debt reached the limit. There are two sides to the argument – one side wants to limit government spending as the debt has become large; the other side does not want to limit the debt ceiling so that government doesn't run out of money. Both sides are correct – The debt is huge, and there should be ways and efforts to stop growing it. It should also be done in a smooth way without causing sudden dislocations and shutdowns. However, the urgency to find practical solutions to this issue by both parties has never been more urgent than now.

Section II

Savings Accounts
CDs
Bonds
Stocks

Chapter

9

9 Investments, the Safe Route

- In investing, what is comfortable is rarely profitable." - Robert Arnott
- On the contrary, a bird in hand is worth two in the bush.

Checking accounts, savings accounts, and CDs come under fixed income category as the returns are fixed – they won't go up or down unlike stocks where the returns could be high, low, or negative.

9.1 Checking Accounts

Checking accounts are not investment accounts. These are current accounts, used almost as cash. We use checking accounts to write checks for recurring monthly expenses or use the checking account for auto payment. Since a checking account does not earn any meaningful interest, there is no point keeping a large amount of money other than keeping a minimum balance to avoid service charge and overdraft. You can have two checking accounts in a bank as a security measure. You can use one account for more established companies and the second one for occasional purchases or smaller transactions. This just limits the amount of fraud if it were to happen. There is usually no penalty or restriction for withdrawing money from checking account, except in some cases, where the bank imposes maximum number of transactions per month. You still need to be mindful of overdraft as the fines are big.

9.2 Savings Accounts

Savings accounts earn a little better interest rate compared to checking accounts. However, the interest rates on savings accounts have been less than half percent for some years now. Generally, there is no penalty or waiting period for withdrawing money from savings accounts. Savings accounts are typically not treated as investment accounts. For the amount of money that you would earmark as emergency money (6-9 months of living expenses), some goes to checking account, some goes to savings account, and some goes to 6-month and 1-yr CDs.

9.3 Money Market Accounts and CDs

Money market accounts are offered by banks and financial institutions, and they typically offer slightly better rates than checking and savings accounts. You can write checks against a money market account. They typically impose restrictions on number of withdrawal and require larger minimum average balance to maintain.

CDs (Certificate of Deposit) have been used for current needs as well as for investment purposes. They offer higher interest rates compared to checking and saving accounts. However, they are not as liquid as the checking and savings accounts. CDs are drawn for a fixed length of time (6 months to several years, for example). If you need the money before the CD matures, you have to break the CD. There could be big penalty for breaking it early that would annul a significant portion of your gain. Keep a portion of emergency fund in 6-month or 1-year CD.

CDs used to provide reasonable returns and were used as investment vehicles by many. However, the returns have been meagre for almost a decade now. Still many people use it as an investment vehicle – something is better than nothing. It depends on personal risk tolerance, comfort level, age, and other considerations. As an investor, you have to take a serious look if CD is the right investment choice or you could do better with stocks and other high-yielding investment options. Even if you decide to go for CDs, stagger them with different maturity dates than having one large CD. Staggering helps to get the money without breaking if you need the money. With staggering, you can also go for a longer maturity period, as you have not committed the whole thing to one maturity date. Specially, when the current rates are low, there is a good chance that it could be better in a few years.

10 Bonding with Bonds

10.1 Bonds Basics

Bonds are fixed-income vehicles that involve two parties - the issuer (or seller) and the buyer of the bond. The buyer of the bond loans the issuer certain amount money for a certain period. In exchange, the issuer is expected to return the principal at the end of the period and pay interest (or coupon in bond lingo) at periodic intervals. There are many entities, such as the US government, state governments, municipalities, local governments, and corporations that issue bonds.

The US government needs money to funds its operation. It sells bonds of different durations (less than a year to 30 years) to meet its short-term to long-term needs. The state government and municipalities sell bonds to meet their short-term and long-term needs as well. The corporations use the proceeds from bonds to expand operation or shore up cash reserves.

Example of Bond: You bought the US 10-yr bond for $5000 that gives 2% coupon. What this means is, you will get your principal of $5000 back at the end of 10 years (maturity). You will also receive $100 of interest payment or coupon per year. Actually, the government pays interest twice year, and you will receive $50 every six months. When you buy newly issued bonds, you are buying from the primary market. You can keep the 10-yr bond until maturity and collect coupon payments along the way. Finally, you redeem the principal after 10 years. Or, you can sell the bond in the secondary market before the maturity date.

In the secondary bond market, one can buy or sell bonds freely everyday as one can buy or sell stocks in the stock market. If the price increases after you bought, you make a profit when you sell it. Likewise, if it falls, you incur a loss when you sell it. The price of bonds keeps changing in the secondary market in reaction to the supply/demand and Federal interest rates. The price of bonds is highly dependent on the interest rate – they move in the opposite direction. When the interest rate goes up, bond price goes down, and when the interest rate goes down, bond price goes up. In the next section, we will explore this in closer details.

10.2 Bonds and Interest Rate

You always hear about bond price going up when interest rate goes down and vice versa. Interest rate and bond price are inversely related - if one goes up, the other goes down and vice versa. This looks counter-intuitive, isn't it? It is the price of bond in the secondary market that moves opposite to the interest rate. If you are buying newly issued bonds from the primary market, higher interest is good news, as it will fetch better yield. It is the secondary market where the relationship is inverse and seemingly counter-intuitive. Let us take an example to understand this better.

You bought a 10-yr US bond for $1000 last year that pays 2% interest. Now, the interest rate has gone up, and one can buy newly issued 10-yr US bond paying 3% interest. If you want to sell the bond in the secondary market that you bought last year, no one will buy it at its face (original) value of $1000. They have a better choice. They can buy 3% yielding bond from the primary market.

You need to reduce the price so that it becomes attractive for someone to buy. He will make less money from the interest payment (at 2%), but he is going to make up the difference from the discount in the principal. He will buy the bond from you for less than $1000 but is going to redeem for $1000 at maturity. We will leave out the exact math as to how much it needs to go down from $1000, but it is clear that it needs to go down to be attractive. The overall money he would make buying the 2% paying bond from you would have be equal to or more than the money he would have made by buying the 10-yr bond at 3% rate. **When the interest rate goes up, bond price goes down in the secondary market.**

What would happen if the current interest rate were 1%, instead of 3%? A person can buy the bond from the primary market yielding at 1% or buy the bond from you in the secondary market that pays 2%. He would love to get it from you at $1000. But, you have a higher-yielding bond, and you can ask for a premium. Your bond of $1000 will go for higher value in the secondary market.

As interest rate goes down, the price of existing bonds goes up in the secondary market.

Apart from the interest rate, the other thing that determines the price of an existing bond in the secondary market is the time left to maturity. If a bond has lot of time left (ex: still 9 years left to maturity for a 10-yr bond), the difference in interest rate will have a higher impact on the price. As a bond moves closer toward maturity, the bond price is less influenced by the interest rate differential. The time value of a bond decreases as it approaches maturity. If only one year is remaining to maturity, there are not many interest payment instalments left. The bond price will be very close to $1000 in the secondary market.

Actually, we can explain the relationship between bond price and interest rate with the law of demand and price. When interest rate goes up, your lower-yielding bond has less demand, and the price has to drop to match demand. When interest goes down, your higher-yielding bond has more demand, and the price will go up to the point it matches the demand.

10.3 Are Bonds Safe Investments?

It depends. It depends on the issuer of bonds. Even if the issuer of the bonds is contractually obligated to pay the principal and ineptest, it could go bankrupt, and one can lose money. When Enron went bankrupt, the bondholders got back only 53% of their value and lost 47% of their holdings. The most critical risks associated with bonds are Credit Risk/Default risk and Interest-rate risk.

Credit/Default Risk

It is the risk of the issuer going bankrupt and defaulting on its obligation to pay back the principal. The bonds from the US Government, states, municipalities, and blue-chip companies are generally safe. The default rate is low. The US government is deemed as the safest as it has never defaulted on its obligations. The next in the category are blue chip companies that have solid balance sheets and long track record of maintaining solvency. The least safe are smaller companies or risky companies without long track records. These are also called junk bonds.

Why would then someone buy these risky (junk) bonds instead of the US government bonds? It is because of the higher yield or rate of interest payment. It is a risk-reward tradeoff. The goal of the issuer is to raise capital from the market at the lowest interest rates they could sell the bonds. The higher the perceived risk, the issuer has to pay higher interest rates to be able to raise capital. That is why the risky or junk bonds pay higher interest rates compared to the US government bonds. As a buyer of the bond, you are looking at the highest yield (interest rate) you could get with the risk you want to take. If you want the least amount of risk, US bonds will be the best choice, but it comes with the least yield. If you are willing to take the highest risk, you can buy junk bonds that give the best yield but could lose your principal if the company files for chapter 11.

Interest Rate Risk

If you are planning to hold the bond until maturity, there is no interest-rate risk. You are going to collect interest payments and get back the principal at maturity. However, it is a different case in the secondary bond market. The bond price in the secondary market is dependent on the prevailing interest rate. If the interest rate goes up in future, the bond price will decrease. If you need the money and have to sell it, you will get a lower price when interest rate goes up.

10.4 Safety Assessments of Bonds

We talked about relative safety of different types of bonds. Is there a more objective way of assessing the safety of bonds? There are credit rating agencies (Moody's, Standard and Poor, and Fitch) that provide credit rating starting from AAA to C or D. Below is a table of credits ratings notations from three credit agencies. AAA is Prime or the best, and the risk goes up with the Alphabet where C and D are close to default or at default. As a bond investor, look at the credit ratings to evaluate risk. Are the agencies always right? Mostly, but they also could be wrong from time to time. Example: Mortgage Based Securities in 2008-2009 were incorrectly given triple 'A' ratings where these securities contained highly risky sub-prime loans.

Moody's		S&P		Fitch		Rating description
Long-term	Short-term	Long-term	Short-term	Long-term	Short-term	
Aaa		AAA		AAA		Prime
Aa1		AA+	A-1+	AA+	F1+	
Aa2	P-1	AA		AA		High grade
Aa3		AA−		AA−		
A1		A+	A-1	A+	F1	
A2		A		A		Upper medium grade
A3	P-2	A−		A−	F2	
Baa1		BBB+	A-2	BBB+		
Baa2		BBB		BBB	F3	Lower medium grade
Baa3	P-3	BBB−	A-3	BBB−		
Ba1		BB+		BB+		
Ba2		BB		BB		Non-investment grade speculative
Ba3		BB−	B	BB−	B	
B1		B+		B+		
B2		B		B		Highly speculative
B3		B−		B−		
Caa1	Not Prime	CCC+		CCC+		
Caa2		CCC		CCC		Substantial risks
Caa3		CCC−	C	CCC−	C	
Ca		CC		CC		Extremely speculative
		C		C		Default imminent
C		RD		DDD		
/		SD	D	DD	D	In default
/		D		D		

Fig. 10.1   Credit Ratings: Wikipedia

As of April 2016, USA has AA+ (S&P), Aaa (Moody's), and AAA (Fitch) credit rating. Below is a table of some of the largest economies in the world with their credit ratings.

Source: http://www.tradingeconomics.com/united-states/rating

Countries	S&P	Moody's	Fitch
USA	AA+	Aaa	AAA
Germany	AAA	Aaa	AAA
Japan	A+	A1	A
UK	AAA	Aa1	AA+
China	AA−	Aa3	A+

10.5 Bonds versus Stocks

Stocks, over a longer period, provide better return compared to bonds. Bonds provide safer but lower returns. However, bonds are not completely risk free. You could lose money in bonds when the issuer goes bankrupt, especially with junk bonds. The risk is low with high-grade bonds, such as the US government bonds or blue-chip corporate bonds.

Why should one invest in bonds that provide lower returns compared to stocks? The answer is; it depends. Even if Dow provided 11.2% annualized returns from 1996-2015, one could lose money in the stock market let alone making a profit. One can lose money by buying at the wrong time, selling at the wrong time, or buying wrong stocks. There are many ways one can lose money in the stock market. To make money in the stock market, one has to spend time to understand how stocks work, be disciplined, and gain real-life experiences from the market over a period of time. However, once you become a savvy investor and are willing to put some time, the rewards could be much higher. With compounding effect, it will be very attractive in the long run. In the beginning, you need to put more time, but slowly, it will become your second nature, and you can figure out how to invest in the stock market spending a smaller amount of time per day or per week. This is the main goal of the book – to provide all relevant information so that you can come up to speed quickly and make informed investment decisions.

Another important factor for deciding between stock and bond is the time horizon. How soon are you going to need the money? If you are saving money for a down payment for your house and need the money in next 1-2 years, investing in stock could be risky. During major crash, stocks could lose 30-40% value, and stock market boom and bust are regular occurrences. If you are retired and need the money in the next few years, investing in stock could be risky. A person at age 25 has much longer time horizon compared to a person at age 60-70, and he or she can take much higher risk. Overall, stock market is a much better choice, provided he or she understands the stock market well.

10.6 Federal Government Bonds

The treasury sells bonds starting from small durations (less than a year) to very long durations (30 years). The federal government collects various taxes from individuals and corporations, which forms the revenue for the government. Also, the government spends money on various heads (Social Securities, Medicare, interest payments on existing loans, defense, and many other) that constitutes the yearly expenses.

Why does the Government sell bonds?

> One of the reasons is to get money for meeting short-term obligations while it collects tax. However, the main reason for selling bonds is to pay off maturing bonds and to cover expenses when yearly expenses are more than the revenue. When the revenue matches the expense, it is called **balanced budget**. When the revenue is more than the expenses, it results in **yearly surplus**, and when expenses are more than the revenue, it results in a **yearly deficit**.

In general, fixed-income Treasury securities are classified according to the length of time for maturity. These are the three main categories – Treasury Bills, Treasury Notes, and Treasury bonds. You can buy these securities through TreasuryDirect, bank, or broker. The interest is exempt from state and local income taxes.
http://www.treasurydirect.gov/ - The link provides more details on the products.

Treasury Bills (T-bills) – These are short-term debt securities maturing in less than one year. They are available with maturities of 4wk, 13wk, 26 wk, or 52 wk. They are sold as zero coupons meaning you pay less than the face value when you buy them and collect the face value upon maturity. T-bills are sold in increments of $100, and the minimum purchase is $100.

> **T-bill Example:** You bought a treasury bill that matures in 52 weeks for $980 and has a face value of $1000. Upon maturity, you will collect $1000. The yield is 2.04%. On Oct'15, yield of 52-wk T-bill stood at 0.31%, which is very low by historical standard.

Treasury Notes (T-notes) – These are medium-term securities maturing in two to ten years (2, 3, 5, 7, and 10 year maturity). Since they are of longer duration, they usually offer higher yield compared to T-bills. They, unlike T-bills, are sold at face value when newly issued. The government pays the face value upon maturity along with coupon (interest) payments twice a year until maturity. Notes are sold in increments of $100, and the minimum purchase is $100.

The 10-yr note is the most widely followed of all securities. It is used as the benchmark for the Treasury market and the basis for banks' calculation of mortgage rates.

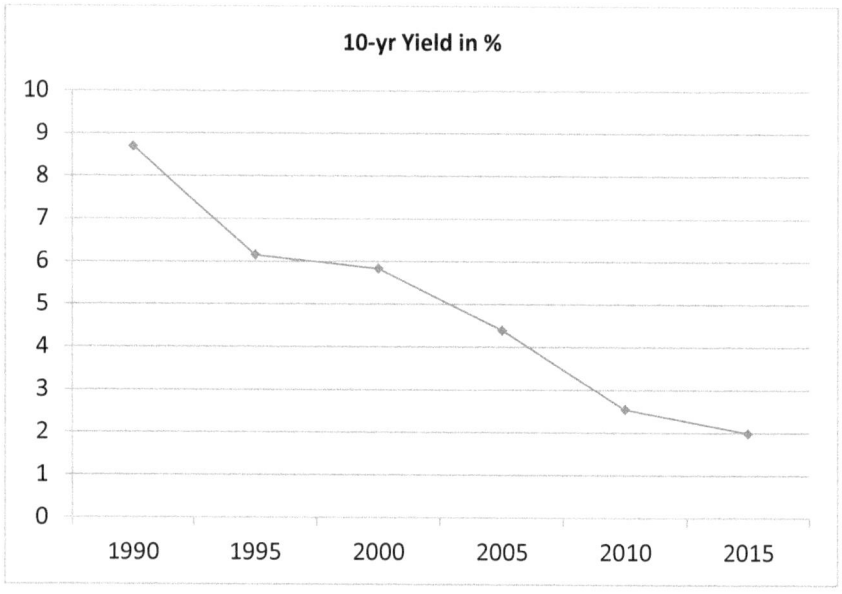

Fig. 10.2   **10-yr Yield (1990 -2015)**

Treasury Bonds - Treasury bonds are issued in terms of 30 years and are offered in multiples of $100. They are similar to T-notes as they pay back the face value upon maturity along with interest payments twice a year until maturity. The main difference is the duration. They usually pay higher rate compared to T-notes because of longer duration.

10.7 Municipal Bonds

Municipal bonds or Munis are bonds issued by states, counties, and local governments to fund various projects, such as high-speed rail, colleges, schools, and roads. They typically offer a little higher yield compared to Treasury bonds. The interest income is exempted from federal tax and in some cases, from state and local taxes as well.

10.8 High-yield or Junk Bonds

High-yield bonds are below investment grade bonds that provide higher yields but come with higher risks. In the current low-interest environment, where government and other high-grade investment bonds offer very low yield (2% to 4%), many turn into high-yield bonds. Make sure you understand the associated risks, and do not put a large part of portfolio in such risky assets.

10.9 Tax Benefits of Bonds

When you are comparing different investment vehicles (government bonds, municipal bonds, and stocks), look at the tax benefits as well. Interest incomes for some of the bonds are exempt from federal tax, and some are exempt from state and local taxes. For example, a municipal bond is offering yield at 3% is free from federal tax. Short-term gains in stocks, on the contrary, could be taxed at 33%. This means, the return on stocks has to be at least 4.5% to match the post-tax returns (3%) from federal tax-exempt municipal bonds.

Treasury Securities

The interest income from Treasury securities are counted as taxable income for federal tax but exempt from state and local taxes.

Municipal Bonds

Municipal bonds or "Muni" bonds are issued by state, municipalities, and local administration. The interest incomes from municipal bonds are exempt from Federal tax. The interest is sometimes exempt from state and local tax. However, the interest income may be taxed under AMT. The interest incomes of state bonds are exempt from state tax.

10.10   Yield Curve

Yield curve is the graphical representation of yield offered by the various Treasury securities (from short-term bills to 30-yr bond). The x-axis represents the duration, and the y-axis represents the yield in percentage.

Friday Oct 2, 2015: http://www.treasury.gov/resource-center/data-chart-center/interest-rates/Pages/TextView.aspx?data=yield

1 mo	3 mo	6 mo	1 yr.	2 yr.	3 yr.	5 yr.	7 yr.	10 yr.	20 yr.	30 yr.
0.00	0.00	0.06	0.25	0.58	0.85	1.29	1.67	1.99	2.44	2.82

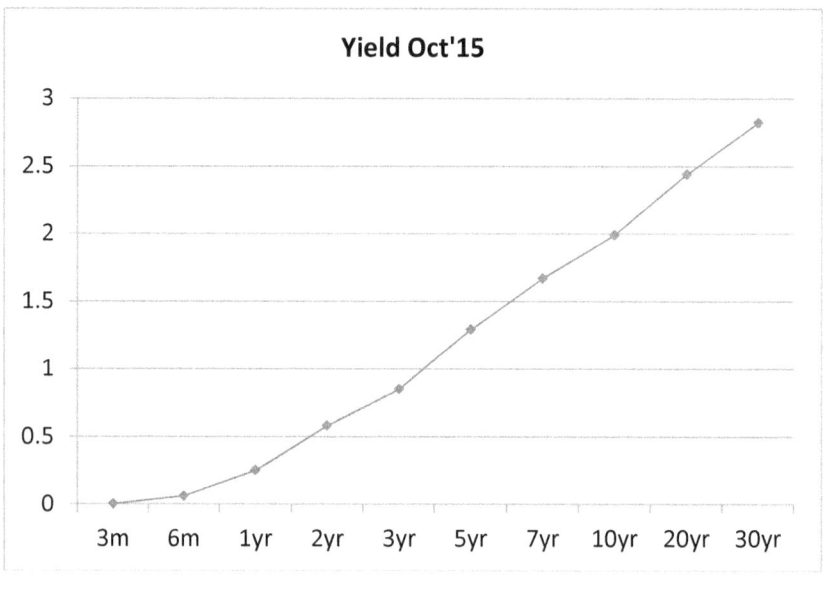

Fig. 10.3   **Yield Curve – Oct'15**

It is a very important graph, and many use it as an indicator of how the economy is going perform in future. It is a leading indicator meaning it tells about the future. The yield curve can be categorized as a) normal or upward sloping curve, b) flat curve, and c) inverted yield curve or down-slopping yield curve.

A normal or upward slopping curve is where the yields for the longer-duration securities are higher than the shorter-duration securities. This makes sense, as people, who are tying up their capital for longer durations, want a better yield.

This type of yield curve indicates that the economy is going to expand in future, and nothing alarming is expected in the future.

When the slope is downward, it means the yield on shorter-duration is higher compared to the longer-term securities. This seems counter-intuitive as why someone would lend his or her money at a lower yield. An inverted yield curve indicates that the economy is expected to contract, and recession is expected in future. Investors are willing to accept a lower long-term rate as things might become worse in future. When government fights inflation, it increases the short-term interest rate that makes it costly for people to borrow money. Reduced money supply fights to bring down inflation. This also makes the yield curve inverted. When the short-term yield and the long-term yield are same, the shape of the curve is flat. This is generally a transient period at the beginning phase of a recession. People accept the available longer-term rates as the rates are on the way to decline more in future. The figure below illustrates the flat/inverted nature of the yield curve in Aug'07 – The big recession of 2008-2009 followed it.

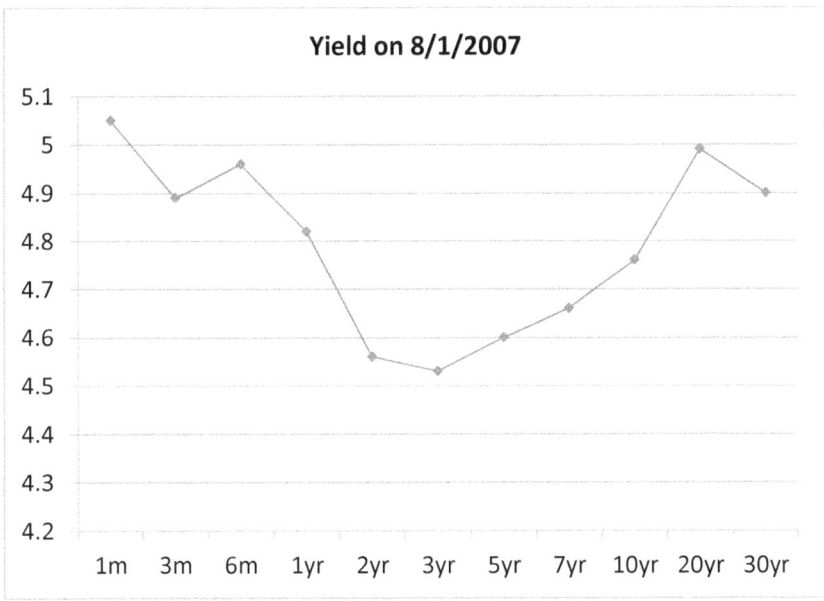

Fig. 10.4   **Inverted yield curve before 2008 recession**

10.11 Historical Yield Curves 1995-2015

Let us compare the yield curve in the 1st week of Oct for 25 years at 5-yr interval to get an idea how the treasury yield has been historically.

Date	1mo	3mo	6mo	1yr	2yr	3yr	5yr	7yr	10yr	20yr	30yr
10/02/15	0.00	0.00	0.06	0.25	0.58	0.85	1.29	1.67	1.99	2.44	2.82
10/01/10	0.15	0.16	0.19	0.26	0.42	0.63	1.26	1.9	2.54	3.4	3.71
10/03/05	3.22	3.61	4.02	4.09	4.21	4.23	4.25	4.31	4.39	4.67	N/A
10/02/00	N/A	6.27	6.33	6.06	5.98	5.92	5.86	5.95	5.83	6.18	5.93
10/02/95	N/A	5.53	5.64	5.65	5.82	5.89	5.98	6.1	6.15	6.61	6.48
10/02/90	N/A	7.41	7.55	7.61	7.92	8.1	8.35	8.6	8.69	N/A	8.84

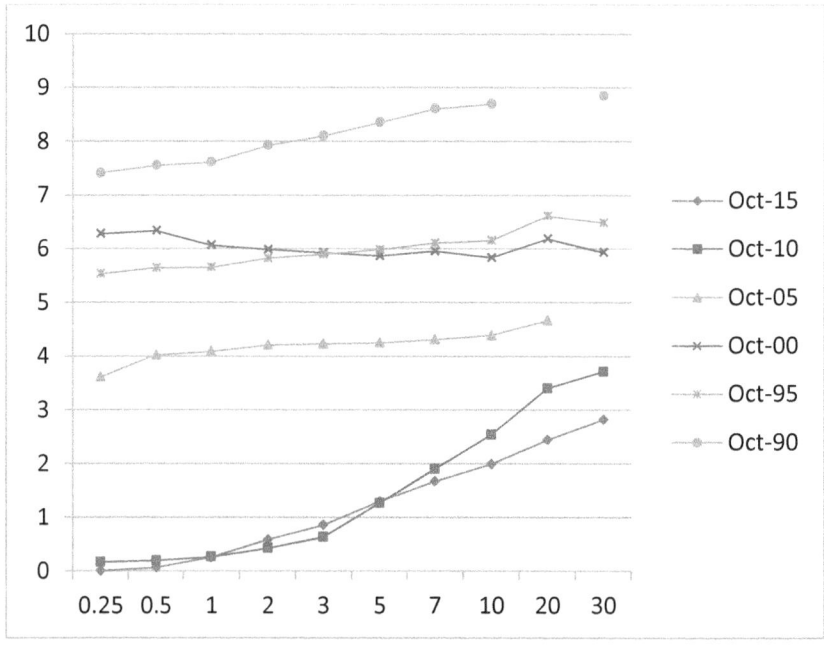

Fig. 10.5   Yield Curves: 1990 - 2015

10.12   Yield Spread

Yield spread is the difference in yield between two types of investments, typically bonds. For example, it can be the difference in yield between no-risk 10-year Treasury note and junk bonds. In the bond market, there is an historical expected spread between no-risk bonds and high-risk bonds. Let us look at an example when the 10-yr Treasury is yielding at 2%, and the high-yield junk bonds are yielding at 6%. The spread is 6% minus 2% or 4%. If the spread widens to 6% where the yield on junk bonds goes up to 8%, it would indicate that market is anticipating higher risk of defaults on the high-yield junk bonds. This indicates problem for economy in future. The yield spread is often an indicator of future economic health. If the yield spread widens, economic slowdown or recession is expected. If the yield narrows, economic expansion is expected.

10.13   Where can you Buy Bonds

Many financial institutions sell and buy bonds. Fidelity, for example, has the following on their website:

Types of Bonds: Source: https://www.fidelity.com/fixed-income-bond

U.S. Treasury	Direct debt obligations issued by the U.S. government, which uses the revenue from the bonds to raise capital and/or make payments on outstanding debt
Agency	Debt obligations issued by agencies of the U.S. federal government or by private agencies, called government-sponsored enterprises (GSEs), which are federally chartered but publicly owned by their stockholders
Municipal	Debt obligations issued by states, cities, counties, and other public entities that use the loans to fund public projects, such as the construction of schools, hospitals, highways, sewers, and universities
Corporate	Fully taxable debt obligations issued by corporations that fund capital improvements, expansions, debt refinancing, or acquisitions that require more capital than would ordinarily be available from a single lender
High yield	Debt securities rated below investment grade[2] based on the issuer's weaker ability to pay interest and capital, resulting in the issuer paying a higher rate to entice investors to take on the added risk

11 The Promised Land - Stocks

11.1 Investing in Stocks

As we discussed in the beginning of the book, stocks have historically provided very good returns. DOW Jones stocks produced an annualized return of 9.3% over the last twenty years (1995-2014). If we include average 2% dividends, the returns come to around 11.3%. As the number shows, the returns have been very good over the long run. There were years when the index went negative and years when the returns were higher than the average. If someone invested in the DOW index for specific years or a smaller number of years, the returns could be different. For example, if someone invested in Oct'2007 at the market peak and got out at the bottom (Feb '2009), he would have lost roughly 50% of the investments. If someone invested in 2009 and stayed until 2014, his gain would have been around 125%.

As we see, stock market is inherently risky and rewarding as well. There are many strategies in investing, long-term, medium-term, short-term, and passive investing such as investing in stock indices. I have devoted the next ten chapters to focus on investing in stocks. Investing in indices over a longer horizon is definitely a good strategy to achieve good returns. However, as an individual investor, one can achieve better returns. Nothing is guaranteed in stock market, but I truly believe, it is possible to do so. We will discuss how to evaluate a company for its true worth or intrinsic value through fundamental analysis. I buy stocks based on fundamental analysis that provides safety and room for appreciation. There is a chapter on technical analysis, which can be used along with fundamental analysis.

We will discuss how the news and economy affect stock price and how the indicators can be used to gauge market direction. We will discuss different strategies to be successful in the stock market. We will discuss how psychology and personal discipline play critical roles for success in the stock market. Psychology (fear and greed) becomes critical during interesting times (market crash and boom), and it is easy to get swayed by these poignant emotions. In the end, I have discussed my personal experience in investing in stocks from 2011 to 2016 - how I pick stocks, my investment strategy and philosophy, my personal view and experience in using leverage, and areas for improvement. I firmly believe that there is always something to learn and room to grow to be a better investor tomorrow than I am today.

12 A Thorough Physical Checkup

12.1 Evaluating a Stock (Company) - Fundamentally

When you buy a stock, you are buying a part of the company, not just a piece of paper. The good thing about owning a stock is that you are a part owner of the company without the responsibility, and you participate in company's success through stock price appreciation and dividends. The bad thing is that you are putting your money where you do not have direct control (true for most investors except activist hedge fund managers who buy a sizable percentage of the company stocks and influence the direction of the company). Hence, it is very critical that you evaluate a company thoroughly so that the money you are putting to buy is at the right price, and the company is the right company. Warren Buffett aptly said, **"Price is what you pay, and value is what you get."** So, how do we evaluate a company?

In this chapter, we are going to discuss and explore the **fundamental analysis** of a company, which includes the following:

- The Management
- Balance sheet
- Income statement
- Cash flow
- P/E ratio
- Dividends
- Stock buybacks
- Growth

12.2 The Management

The top management, especially the CEO, is a critical part of the evaluation matrix of a company. If the management is strong, competent, driven, and works with integrity, you would expect that things will be good. We have seen what competent and driven CEOs can achieve and where they can take the company. Bill Gates (Microsoft), Steve Jobs (Apple), Larry Elision (Oracle), Larry Page and Sergey Brin (Google), Jeff Bezos (Amazon), Howard Schultz (Starbucks), Mark Zuckerberg (Facebook), Elon Musk (Tesla), and Warren Buffett (Berkshire Hathaway) are some of the best CEOs and visionaries that come to mind. You want your money to be with good and able hands. If they are worrying, you do not have to.

Look at the history and track record of the CEO in the current company and the previous companies he or she worked for. If the CEO does not have a good track record or the top management does not have a history of successes, the company could be at risk, and it may not be a good investment.

12.3 Market Cap

Market cap is short form for Market Capitalization, which is calculated by multiplying the share price by the total number of outstanding shares. For example, Apple on 4/4/2016 had per-share price of $111.12, and there were 5.54B outstanding shares. The market cap is $615B (111.12 times 5.5B). Based on their market cap, the companies are divided into large cap (generally above $10B), medium cap (between $2B and $10B), and small cap (less than $2B) stocks. Market cap by itself (small, medium, or large) is not a part of fundamental analysis, and large-cap companies are not necessarily better or worse than small-cap companies. However, large cap companies, in general, are stable companies and do not grow that much, whereas small cap companies have much more room to grow. The share price usually does not fluctuate in wide range for large cap companies. On the other hand, share price for small cap stocks can fluctuate in a much wider range.

12.4 Balance Sheet

When I am studying a stock, the first few things I look at are the balance sheet, income statements, and cash flow. It immediately gives a very good picture of the overall health of the company. After you become well versed in understanding these parameters, it does not take much time to figure out the overall health and strength of a company – in 15-20 minutes, you will be able to construct a mental picture of the company. The Balance Sheet is like the net worth of a person. If the company is liquidated, how much will it fetch? The line just above the last line in a balance sheet is the "Total Stockholders Equity" that includes goodwill and intangible assets as well. The last line in the balance sheet is the net tangible assets.

As a safe investor, I consider only the tangible assets that include cash, short term and long-term investments, buildings, plants etc. as the basis for net worth evaluation. I discount the goodwill and intangible assets, as these are hard to evaluate - may lose value when technology changes and may have been inflated to start with. By comparing the tangible assets with the market cap of the company, you can get an idea if the company is overvalued or undervalued. If the market cap is too high compared to the tangible assets, it indicates that the company could be overvalued. This typically happens with tech companies or any company where a lot is expected in future. It is possible that some of these companies with astronomical valuations will grow to justify these values, but many will fail. This happened during dotcom era and currently with social companies. What it tells is that there is high risk in these kinds of companies. If growth slows down, the share price could fall dramatically.

On the other hand, if the market cap and tangible values are close, it indicates that the stock price has fallen into undervalued territory. You have to carefully analyze why the stock price has fallen bringing down the market cap close to the book value (tangible assets). If it is a permanent problem with declining prospects, even a strong balance sheet won't be able to prevent the company to lose value further significantly. Nokia had a good balance sheet, but with changing phone technology, the stock lost a significant portion of its value.

Another important thing to look in the balance sheet is the cash position and short-term and long-term investments. These give a cushion for the companies to survive if business conditions change unfavorably. They will have a good cash position to wither out any storm. Without reasonable cash cushion, companies go bankrupt when business worsens or the overall economy crashes. Also important is the short-term and long-term loans. If there is a large short-term loan, it could be problematic for companies to meet short-term cash obligations.

Here is the balance sheet of Apple.

CHAPTER 12   Fundamental Analysis

Annual Data	All numbers in thousands		
Period Ending	Sep 26, 2015	Sep 27, 2014	Sep 28, 2013
Assets			
Current Assets			
Cash And Cash Equivalents	21,120,000	13,844,000	14,259,000
Short Term Investments	20,481,000	11,233,000	26,287,000
Net Receivables	35,889,000	31,537,000	24,094,000
Inventory	2,349,000	2,111,000	1,764,000
Other Current Assets	9,539,000	9,806,000	6,882,000
Total Current Assets	**89,378,000**	**68,531,000**	**73,286,000**
Long Term Investments	164,065,000	130,162,000	106,215,000
Property Plant and Equipment	22,471,000	20,624,000	16,597,000
Goodwill	5,116,000	4,616,000	1,577,000
Intangible Assets	3,893,000	4,142,000	4,179,000
Accumulated Amortization			-
Other Assets	5,556,000	3,764,000	5,146,000
Deferred Long Term Asset Charges	-	-	-
Total Assets	**290,479,000**	**231,839,000**	**207,000,000**
Liabilities			
Current Liabilities			
Accounts Payable	60,671,000	48,649,000	36,223,000
Short/Current Long Term Debt	10,999,000	6,308,000	-
Other Current Liabilities	8,940,000	8,491,000	7,435,000
Total Current Liabilities	**80,610,000**	**63,448,000**	**43,658,000**
Long Term Debt	53,463,000	28,987,000	16,960,000
Other Liabilities	33,427,000	24,826,000	20,208,000
Deferred Long Term Liability Charges	3,624,000	3,031,000	2,625,000
Minority Interest	-	-	-
Negative Goodwill	-	-	-
Total Liabilities	**171,124,000**	**120,292,000**	**83,451,000**
Stockholders' Equity			
Misc. Stocks Options Warrants	-	-	-
Redeemable Preferred Stock	-	-	-
Preferred Stock	-	-	-
Common Stock	27,416,000	23,313,000	19,764,000
Retained Earnings	92,284,000	87,152,000	104,256,000
Treasury Stock	-	-	-
Capital Surplus	-	-	-
Other Stockholder Equity	(345,000)	1,082,000	(471,000)
Total Stockholder Equity	**119,355,000**	**111,547,000**	**123,549,000**
Net Tangible Assets	**110,346,000**	**102,789,000**	**117,793,000**

Current Assets

These are cash, short-term investments, and receivables that provide stability in the immediate future. If something unforeseen happens, the company can withstand the shock without going bankrupt, having to sell assets to raise cash at very unfavorable terms, or losing leverage in business and financial transactions. We can relate this easily to our personal financial situation. We need to have a buffer (my rule of thumb is to have enough cash to cover at least six months of expenses if both spouses are working and 9-12 months of expenses if only one spouse is working) to get through if we lose our jobs. The cash cushion gives us the support to wait for a good job rather than being forced into accepting first job even if it is sub-optimal. Let us get back to the company and understand the use of cash and how much cash a company should hold.

Use of Cash and how much to hold in Cash

We agree that a company needs to hold some cash to take care of short-term needs and unforeseen situations. But, how much? In current low-interest regime, cash practically generates no returns. One can argue that cash is sitting idle and not participating in generating revenue for the company. Honestly, it is a good situation to be in with cash than to be in debt. Some companies generate tremendous amounts of cash on a regular basis, which is a wonderful thing. So how can the excess cash be used or deployed? Cash can be used to acquire assets, or companies, which can increase earnings going forward. However, the difficulty or the irony is that hot companies are very expensive, and the companies, you can buy on the cheap, are not so good after all. We have seen companies spending a fortune to acquire a hot company only to write it off in a few years later.

I am fine with acquiring smaller companies that align to the company's business strategy and that do not cost a lot. Other than acquiring smaller strategic companies, my personal preference is to rather preserve the cash and wait for the right opportunity and the right moment. Economic downturns are the best time to acquire good assets and companies at reasonable price. As a company, I would hold on to the cash to buy back my own company shares if the price drops to undervalued territory. I use the same philosophy in my investments. I always keep some cash to buy stocks cheaply at the right time. On the surface, it looks as if I am underutilizing cash. But, in reality, if I can wait for the right moment and buy good stocks at 20-30% discount, that is a big leg up for my investments.

The other option for companies is to return some of the income as dividends. If a company is generating increasing or steady income, the cash reserve or short-term investments would grow. The company can return cash to shareholders in the form of dividends with a 2-4% yield goal. Sometimes, companies return excess cash as one time dividend in addition to regular dividends. I, personally, do not favor this. A better use is to buy back shares at the right time (when stock is undervalued) and retire these shares. A one-time dividend is an unpredictable thing, and the money is gone! It is past and does not help the future stock price. Buybacks that we will explore more in details later in this chapter, on the other hand, reduce the share counts and help in higher EPS in future.

As an investor, ask yourself these questions on how a company uses its cash. Does a company use excess cash in a conservative and smart way? Or, does it have a history of using large amount of cash (sometime borrowed cash) to acquire companies and write off in a few years?

Long term Investments

Long-term investments can be treasury notes, bonds, or even investing in promising start-ups. The yield on long term investments are not that great (10 year treasury has been yielding around 2% for the last decade). However, 2% return is better than close-to-zero yield on short-term investments.

Property Plant and Equipment

Not all property, plant, and equipment are equal. Some hold value better than others do. For some companies, these are essential to generate revenue; for some others, these can be in the form of real estate and buildings that do not depreciate rapidly. It depends on the sectors and technologies. Commodities, (iron, oil etc.) for example, go through cycles, and a large part of the equity, in the form of plant and equipment, can be a liability for a company when commodities are down. The machines and equipment could be idling generating huge loss. While doing a qualitative evaluation of the balance sheet, look at how much of the net tangible assets are in machines and equipment. Even a company with a pristine balance sheet could deplete severely in a few quarters during commodity down cycle. Also, look at the long-term loan. This can be double whammy if balance sheet deteriorates quickly, and there is huge loan that needs to be serviced - it can drive a company to bankruptcy, and you could lose all your investments in that company. Recent examples are oil companies, specially, shale oils where oil downturn has driven many companies close to insolvency. But, some of these companies (that can withstand the downturn) can be attractive bargains at deep undervalued levels.

Goodwill and Intangible Assets

Treat these assets with a grain of salt. Intangible assets, such as brand name and patents are very valuable for a company. However, pay close attention if large amount of total shareholder equity is in the form of goodwill. Goodwill is typically carried over in the book from previous acquisitions. If the parent company paid huge sum to acquire a company, it will show up as large amount under goodwill for the next few years. If it turns out to be not that good or outright bad, the company will lose a lot of value, and the equity will shrink. Eventually the parent company will do impairment and remove it from balance sheet with a huge loss and a big hit on the balance sheet. I, personally, consider the net tangible assets rather than the total shareholder equity while evaluating a balance sheet. Another variable we consider while evaluating a company is the price to book value. The book value incudes the goodwill and intangible assets as well, making a price-to-book ratio low that can be misleading. Consider rather the price to tangible assets ratio for evaluation and comparison between two similar companies.

Current Liabilities

Current liabilities include accounts payable, short-term debt, and other liabilities. These are not a big deal if company is profitable. But, if accounts payable is growing steadily with increased levels of inventory, it is an indicator that the products are not selling that well. Also, if there is a large amount of short-term loan, it is a big risk, mainly for two reasons. Short-term loans can cost more to borrow, and there is an immediate need to pay back the loans. There is not much breathing room, and it can create a negative cash flow problem if the revenue and profit decline suddenly.

Long-term debts

Long-term debt is better than short-term debt, but no debt is much better than any form of debt (except when debt is used strategically and productively). Long-term debt has longer servicing window, and a company can plan better and does not have to pay back the entire loan every quarter, which is a very difficult situation to be in. It has to pay back only the interest and part of the principal on a regular basis. It is like a 30-yr fixed loan compared to a 1-yr or 3-yr ARM loan. Given that borrowing costs are very low on historical standards, it can be a good thing to borrow money cheaply as longer-term loans. It is a form of leverage that can play out well. However, it depends on how the borrowed money is being used.

Many real estate companies (REITs) use high leverage with big loans to generate larger revenue and profits. It can be a good thing when things are going well but can bite badly when things go the other way. As a business, it is difficult to say whether it is good or bad, but it increases risk; and, as an investor, you need to be aware of this. If a company is borrowing large sum of money to buy other companies, you need to carefully evaluate the prospects of the acquisition and see if the company is taking huge risk. On the other hand, if a company has been profitable, poised to be profitable in future, has a strong balance sheet without much debt, it is a smart idea to borrow money to buy back shares. However, many companies buy back shares when the share price is very high. This is a temporary gimmick to shore up EPS but comes with a huge cost. These companies can borrow money as long-term loans to buy back shares when price is down. Stock prices drop to low value regularly even for good companies. Many companies pay dividends, and with reduced shares due to buybacks, the savings from smaller payment toward dividends can offset the cost of borrowing.

Total Stockholder Equity and Net Tangible Assets

As we discussed earlier, consider the Net Tangible assets rather than the Total stockholder Equity to get a quick idea of how healthy the balance sheet is. Compare the total market cap with the net tangible assets. If the market cap is $100B with net tangible assets of $5B, it is one of the indicators that the stock could be overvalued (there are other parameters such as P/E ratio that we will discuss separately). It is typical for tech, social media, or any other companies that have innovative products to have very high market cap with very little in the form of net tangible assets. These are hot stocks that everyone is chasing. However, as a steady investor, you need to be really careful, as there is really high risk here. When the momentum stops or the company has a bad quarter, the stock price drops dramatically. If you were lucky enough or smart enough to have bought early, you will make a lot of money. But, it is difficult to pick the right ones among many that would eventually fail. Many investors buy these hot stocks at the peak and incur huge losses when the dust settles. As we will discuss later, generating steady and good returns requires a solid strategy, not a hit and miss approach.

Also, look at the net tangible assets for the last five years and for the latest quarter. It is a good thing if the net tangible assets number is growing which means it is generating steady income. If it stays at a healthy level without growing, it does not necessarily mean a bad thing. Check if the company is making steady income and where the income is going. Instead of growing the net assets, the company may be handing out larger dividends and using a large part of the income to buy back stocks on a regular basis. This can be a good thing, especially when stock is undervalued. It is bound to put upward pressure on the stock price.

12.5 Income Statement

As Larry Kudlow would say, "Profits are the mother's milk of stocks." Net income or earning is the main driver for the stock price. In a very simple term, companies exist to make money, not lose money. When a company earns profit, it grows, and it can hire more employees. When it loses money, it shrinks and lays off people. We always hear about the top line and the bottom line. The topline is the total revenue, and the bottom line is the net income. These are two most closely watched numbers in a quarterly result. When the total revenue grows quarter-to-quarter and compared to the same quarter in the previous year, it indicates that business is growing and doing good. Similarly, when earnings grow, it is a good sign for the company.

The revenue and earnings of many businesses vary among the four quarters in a year. The sales and earnings are better in certain quarters compared to others. For example, consumer goods sales are higher during the Christmas quarter than other quarters. Instead of comparing the sales and earnings to the previous quarter, a better comparison is with respect to the same quarter of the previous year. This removes the seasonality and provides a better comparison.

Many companies that are new and in growth mode sacrifice earnings to grow market share and revenue. This is fine, if that is the case and if they are growing their revenue base. It is not atypical to see these companies losing money for a few years in the beginning. But, sooner or later, these companies need to show profit with a healthy profit margin. Blindly gaining market share with much reduced margin does not sound good, as they might have to give back market share when they want to make profit. Established companies (blue chip stocks) need to show revenue and earnings growth. If one or both of these show negative growth, the stock gets severely punished. As a smart investor, you should study the company and decide if the setback is temporary and the company has a strong management team or has solid products in pipeline. This may be a good entry point to take some positions in the company. When the company turns around, you could make tidy profits with these blue chip stocks.

Another thing to watch in these numbers is the onetime gain or loss. If a company sells a division or makes some onetime profit from investments, the revenue and earnings for that quarter would be very good. However, the market discounts these onetime gains and does not reward the stock price. Similarly, if there were one-time charges, such as a big fine, impairment, or something else, the earning would drop for that quarter. Though it is not fun to lose a large sum of money even if it is one-time, the market generally discounts these onetime charges and does not punish the stock price severely.

In the beginning, I was surprised to see that stock price would drop after the quarterly results even if the revenue and earnings went up. Similarly, the stock price would go up even if the revenue declined and the company had a loss for that quarter. This seemingly ironical price moment happens not due to the absolute numbers but based on how the results performed against the expectations. Each quarter, a group of analysts, based on their models, would predict the revenue and earnings for the coming quarter, and it gets reflected (theoretically, at least) in the stock price. The stock price tries to quickly absorb any news that may affect the price favorably or unfavorably - It is also called the efficient market theory. When the results come out, all possible information has already been accounted for, and the stock is trading at the fair and equilibrium value. When the results beat the forecast value, it is a net positive for the stock, and the stock price goes up. The stock price goes down when the opposite happens. Sometimes the stock price goes down even if it beats expectations in the current quarter. It happens if the guidance for the next quarter or year is below expectations. Stock market gives higher weightage to the future health of the company than the present or past. As they say, it is not important were you came from but where you are going. Next, let us go over a real income statement of a company (Apple) and understand it in more details.

Income Statement (4/2/2016, based on Yahoo finance)

Annual Data			All numbers in thousands
Period Ending	Sep 26, 2015	Sep 27, 2014	Sep 28, 2013
Total Revenue	233,715,000	182,795,000	170,910,000
Cost of Revenue	140,089,000	112,258,000	106,606,000
Gross Profit	93,626,000	70,537,000	64,304,000
Operating Expenses			
Research Development	8,067,000	6,041,000	4,475,000
Selling General and Administrative	14,329,000	11,993,000	10,830,000
Non Recurring	-	-	-
Others	-	-	-
Total Operating Expenses	-	-	-
Operating Income or Loss	71,230,000	52,503,000	48,999,000
Income from Continuing Operations			
Total Other Income/Expenses Net	1,285,000	980,000	1,156,000
Earnings Before Interest And Taxes	72,515,000	53,483,000	50,155,000
Interest Expense	-	-	-
Income Before Tax	72,515,000	53,483,000	50,155,000
Income Tax Expense	19,121,000	13,973,000	13,118,000

Minority Interest	-	-	-
Net Income From Continuing Ops	53,394,000	39,510,000	37,037,000
Non-recurring Events			
Discontinued Operations	-	-	-
Extraordinary Items	-	-	-
Effect Of Accounting Changes	-	-	-
Other Items	-	-	-
Net Income	**53,394,000**	**39,510,000**	**37,037,000**
Preferred Stock And Other Adjustments	-	-	-
Net Income Applicable To Common Shares	**53,394,000**	**39,510,000**	**37,037,000**

Total Revenue

It is the total amount of money that comes in. In this case, it is $233.7B for the financial year ending in Sept 2015. It is also called the gross income. When analyzing revenue, study how the revenue is performing for the last five years. In this case, the revenue is increasing year over year, which is a sign of growth.

Cost of Revenue

Cost of revenue is the cost of goods to produce the end products that the company sells to generate revenue. Operating expenses, such as salary and R&D is not part of the cost of revenue. In this case, the cost of revenue was $140B for year 2015.

Gross Profit

When you deduct the cost of revenue from the gross income, you get the gross profit. In this case, the gross profit for year 2015 was $93.7B ($233.7B - $140B). Gross margin, an important indicator, is derived from the gross profit and reported as a percentage of total revenue. The gross profit was $93.7B, and the gross margin was 40% : ($93.7B/$233.7B) * 100.

Operating Expenses

The major operating expenses are R&D, selling and general and administrative expenses. Salary, wages, and benefits come under general and administrative expenses.

CHAPTER 12   Fundamental Analysis

Operating Income or Loss

After you take away the operating expenses from the gross profit, you get operating income or loss. If this number is positive, the business is making money; if it is negative, the business is losing money. It is one of the most important numbers. A company or business exists to be profitable within the bounds of rules, regulations, and national and international laws. For a business, it makes sense to maximize profit as long as it is operating legally and ethically to maximize shareholders value – it is the fiduciary responsibility of the management to do so. The hard part to evaluate is whether the companies work morally and in a socially responsible way apart from doing everything legally.

It is a hot-button topic that many US jobs are moving overseas or are being outsourced to overseas companies. This is a very difficult topic, and there is no simplistic answer to this. Since this a very important topic, let us spend some time to understand this. Companies do this to increase profit, or in many cases, they do it just to remain relevant and profitable. Today's economy is an international economy, and it comes with the benefits and drawbacks. People are losing jobs, and it is a very painful thing. Are the companies doing it legally? I believe, most are. Are these companies morally right to do so? Probably not. If these companies are given incentives and rewarded in other ways, would they reverse this trend? I guess, many will do and find ways to create jobs in the US as well.

Reducing corporate tax rate will not only encourage many American companies to stay and expand in the US but also attract overseas companies to start or expand business here. A huge amount of US corporate money is remaining outside the US, and companies do not want to repatriate back as they would lose a large part of it due to higher tax rate. Making the repatriation tax rate reasonable and tying it to job creation will help create jobs in the US.

Net Income (loss)

Every company pays tax on the net income. Net income is the remaining amount from the total income after paying the income tax. Many DOW and S&P companies make regular profit (net income), and they use the net income to grow the balance sheet, pay dividends, and buy back shares. When you analyze a stock, review the net earnings for 5 years or even 10 years. Many blue chip companies grow profits steadily which tells that they have sustained competitive advantages. They are able to generate profit (may be at a reduced level) even during tough times. Always pay careful attention to onetime gains or charges. Onetime gain inflates the earnings in a quarter, and onetime charge shows the earnings in bad light that may not be that bad in reality.

12.6 Cash Flow

When I perform fundamental analysis on a company or a stock, I look at the cash flow and study how the company is using its cash. If we call the machines, equipment, and other physical assets as the body, cash is the oxygen. Cash is the ultimate liquid asset, and without cash, the operation would freeze, or the company would be forced to liquidation in extreme cases. A positive cash flow is a very healthy sign for a company. Once in a while, negative cash flow is fine (we see the cash flow for Apple in 2014 was negative, and we will analyze why), but sustained negative cash flow is not a good sign if it is due to net loss and over expenditure. Below is the cash flow statement for Apple for 2013 to 2015.

Cash Flow Statement

Annual Data	All numbers in thousands		
Period Ending	Sep 26, 2015	Sep 27, 2014	Sep 28, 2013
Net Income	53,394,000	39,510,000	37,037,000
Operating Activities, Cash Flows Provided By or Used In			
Depreciation	11,257,000	7,946,000	6,757,000
Adjustments To Net Income	4,968,000	5,210,000	3,394,000
Changes In Accounts Receivables	(3,124,000)	(6,452,000)	(1,949,000)
Changes In Liabilities	15,188,000	13,408,000	8,320,000
Changes In Inventories	(238,000)	(76,000)	(973,000)
Changes In Other Operating Activities	(179,000)	167,000	1,080,000
Total Cash Flow From Operating Activities	81,266,000	59,713,000	53,666,000
Investing Activities, Cash Flows Provided By or Used In			
Capital Expenditures	(11,247,000)	(9,571,000)	(8,165,000)
Investments	(44,417,000)	(9,017,000)	(24,042,000)
Other Cash flows from Investing Activities	(610,000)	(3,991,000)	(1,567,000)
Total Cash Flows From Investing Activities	(56,274,000)	(22,579,000)	(33,774,000)
Financing Activities, Cash Flows Provided By or Used In			
Dividends Paid	(11,561,000)	(11,126,000)	(10,564,000)
Sale Purchase of Stock	(34,710,000)	(44,270,000)	(22,330,000)
Net Borrowings	29,305,000	18,266,000	16,896,000
Other Cash Flows from Financing Activities	(1,499,000)	(1,158,000)	(1,082,000)
Total Cash Flows From Financing Activities	(17,716,000)	(37,549,000)	(16,379,000)
Effect Of Exchange Rate Changes	-	-	-
Change In Cash and Cash Equivalents	7,276,000	(415,000)	3,513,000

Depreciation

The first line in the cash flow statement is the net income (loss) taken from the last line of income statement. The next big item is the depreciation. You will see a large depreciation amount for companies that are capital intensive such as manufacturing companies. Why is depreciation a part of the cash flow statement? All equipment and machineries have a working life when they are useful to generate revenue. After this period, they are of no use. When a company buys new equipment and pays full value to buy it, it loses some of this value every year. Depreciation is counted as expense in the income statement. Depreciation reduces the operating income, tax burden, and stockholders equity. However, the depreciation amount that was removed from calculating the operating income is still there with the company and is added back in calculating the cash flow.

Total Cash flow from operating activities

Apart from the net income and depreciation there are other adjustments, such as changes in accounts receivables, net income, inventories, and liabilities done to figure out the total cash flow from operating activities. The adjustments are done when more recent information is available, as some of the items may have been an estimate at that time. The total cash flow from operating activities for Apple was $81.2B in 2015.

Total Cash Flows from Investing Activities

The items typically include capital expenditures or short-term and long-term investments. The amount was $56.2B for Apple in 2015.

Total Cash Flows from Financing Activities

The items under this are dividend payments, share buybacks. Apple used $11B for dividends payment and $34.7B for share buyback. There is another big interesting item, net borrowings of $29.3B in 2015. Why is Apple borrowing this huge amount of money when it is rich in cash and assets? First, it can get long-term loan very cheap and use this money to buy back shares as it feels that shares are undervalued. Second, $29B is a huge amount. However, if we look at the net tangible assets ($110B), Apple has tons of cash and short-term investments; this is a very reasonable number that Apple can sleep well at night. Moreover, it generated $53B of net profit in 2015. If it feels that loans are becoming too much to bear, it can quickly payback in a few years.

Change in Cash and Cash Equivalents

This is the last line in the cash flow statement. We arrive at this figure by adding up total cash flow from operating activities (typically positive), total cash flow from investing activities (typically negative), and the total cash flow from financing activities (typically negative). We would like to see a positive number in the bottom line of cash flow statement - based on a strong number from operating activities cash flow, not due to net borrowings. Year-after-after negative cash flow or borrowed money indicates that the company might be taking bigger risks and may be living beyond means such as paying dividends that it cannot afford. Occasional negative cash flow is not an issue and may be good thing if it is done for the right reasons. Apple, in 2014, had a negative cash flow of $415M despite $59.7B of positive cash flow from operating activities. Apple stock was undervalued in 2014, and Apple used up a huge amount ($44B) to buy back its own shares, which, I believe, was a smart thing to do.

12.7 EPS (Earnings per Share)

EPS (Earnings Per Share) is calculated by dividing the yearly earnings by the number of outstanding shares. Apple's earning in 2015 was $53.4B, and it had 5.68B shares. EPS is calculated to be: $53.4B/5.68B = $9.4. EPS is an important parameter used in calculating the P/E ratio, described in the next section.

12.8 P/E (Price to Earnings) Ratio

How do we compare two stocks? Just the share price does not mean anything. A stock with $100 price is not necessarily better or worse than a stock with a price of $25. People, not familiar with stocks, assume that a stock with a higher share price is better than a stock with a lower price. Can we just compare the EPS and conclude that stock with higher EPS is a better buy as it is earning more money? The answer is again no. The stock with higher EPS may have much higher share price. P/E ratio provides a normalized value to compare two stocks. P/E ratio is calculated by dividing the price of a stock by the EPS value. Let us calculate the P/E for Apple on April 2, 2016 when Apple traded at $110. P/E was $110/$9.4 = 11.7.

What is the significance of P/E, and what does it really mean? Let us take an example of a stock trading at $25 that earns $2.50 (EPS) per each stock every year. The P/E ratio is 10. You invested $100 to buy four stocks (keeping the commission out for easy calculation). Your four stocks together would earn $10 per year. If the company were to distribute all its earnings proportionally among the shareholders for the next 10 years, you would receive $10 per year for the next 10 years. You would have received $100 in 10 years, which is basically getting your entire principal back with a 10% yearly return. You would still own four stocks at the end of 10 years. This is huge compared to 2% returns on 10-year Treasury note. Of course, a company wouldn't return all the earnings; it would return some as dividends, some as share buybacks, and use some of it to expand business which drives earning power even higher. P/E is a quick and direct measure of the rate of returns that you would expect from a stock. Everything remaining same, you would expect a stock, with lower P/E, would provide a higher return than a stock with higher P/E.

The earning (EPS) justifies why the market cap is much higher than the net tangible assets of a company. A company's net tangible assets may be $20B, but the market cap could be $100B. If you liquidate the company, you would get only $20B. But, why are you paying $100B to buy its stocks (you are not buying the whole company but percentage of the company valued at $100B)? It is the future cumulative earning power that puts the market cap many fold compared to the net tangible assets. The lower the P/E, the quicker you could get back your principal and higher the return is. The higher the P/E, the lower the return is at the current earnings level. Stock is the greatest invention to create wealth that brings the future potential into current valuation.

Does this mean that stocks are the best investment vehicles? In the example above with P/E ratio of 10, it can generate 10% return on your investments. No other form of investment vehicles come even close to that. Yes, stock provides the best opportunity to earn money as you are part owner of a company, and you are sharing the success. The answer is yes and no. If you understand a company well, understand how the stock price moves, and know what you are doing, the answer is a big yes. You will make a lot more money investing in stock than investing in bonds, CDs, or savings account. If you are trying to make quick gain with a hit-and-miss approach, the answer is no – you could lose a lot of money.

One assumption we made in the previous paragraph is that the company will maintain its earning power for the next 10 years. In fact, many blue chip companies will not only maintain their earning powers for the next 10 years but will grow it further. However, some companies will lose their earning power due to new competition, key products getting obsolete, incompetent management, or something else. As we can see, there is a big risk that something unfavorable can happen in next 10 years. There is also possibility of extreme outcome where the company may go out of business in 10 years, and you could lose your entire investments in that company. Stocks provide the highest rewards that come with the highest risks. If you are a conservative investor and buy good companies (strong balance sheet, steady income, positive cash flow) when they are down, keep your emotions in check, take advantage of market cycles, and know when to use leverage through margin account, you can make big money.

So, what is the right P/E ratio? The historical S&P average P/E ratio has been around 16. Hence, a stock that trades at a P/E lower than the average is likely undervalued, and a stock with a P/E ratio above the average is likely overvalued. New companies or hot companies typically have higher P/E ratio as they are in growth mode where earning is expected to grow significantly in coming years bringing down the P/E ratio close to the S&P average. However, one needs to be careful about companies that have P/E ratios higher than 50, 70, or even 100. Even if these stocks have good growth potential, they may flop or may not grow as expected. The stock price will nosedive even with a tiny bit of doubt or misstep in execution. If a company is fundamentally strong and P/E has fallen to be in a range of 8 to 13, it is most likely undervalued. You should consider initiating some positions. Sometimes, you will find stocks with P/E ratio of 4 to 7. Most of the cases, there is a reason why P/E has dropped to such a low value. These could be value traps. There is a big concern that the company is in real trouble and may never recover. A very low P/E ratio is trap that you should avoid in general. However, based on your analysis, if you are convinced that the problems are temporary or have been blown out of proportion and there is a good management team working hard to turn it around, this may be one of the best opportunities to make big returns when the company turns around. The stock price will pop and appreciate very quickly after that. Another parameter to look at is the forward P/E ratio as this is a better indicator of how the company is expected to perform in future.

12.9 Dividends, Yield, and Pay-out Ratio

Dividends are good sources of steady income and can be a sizable part of overall returns. Companies return part of the profits in the form of dividends on a quarterly basis. There are a few exceptions when they pay dividends on a yearly basis or twice a year. In addition, there are some real estate companies (REITs) that pay dividends on a monthly basis. What kinds of companies pay out dividends? It is mostly blue chip companies that have long records of steady income and do not need to retain the profits to grow the company fast. New companies that are in hyper-growth mode do not pay out dividends, mainly for two reasons – they need the profit to grow the business, or simply they are not making profits yet.

We have heard of dividend aristocrats that have long track records of increasing dividends over the years, and they have not missed out even during tough times. They treat dividends as something sacrosanct. They have strong balance sheets to maintain dividends during tough times. What is a good dividend yield? I see 2% to 5% dividend yield is a good number. With close to zero percent yield from short-term deposits or 2% yield on 10-year Treasury note, 2-5% dividend yield provides a better alternative. Please keep this in mind - do not buy a stock just for the dividends. You could lose more when price drops than you are making from the dividends.

What I do is shortlist 20 to 30 companies with good yield and then carry out a rigorous fundamental analysis on these companies. Then, select only those companies that are solid and do not have long-term dangers. Then, from these winners, I study their price pattern for last the ten years. Do they hold their value well, and are they at their peaks or have fallen by a sizable percent from the top? I only consider that are out of favor due to overblown pessimism. Now, I have a list of fundamentally strong and good dividend-paying stocks that have fallen to unreasonable levels. Sometimes, I find a few companies, sometimes I do not. If I do not find any company meeting my selection criteria, I wait. Believe me, there are hundreds of good companies out there that get the unfair treatment from the analysts at some point.

What I have seen is that analysts are not wrong, but they give a very short-term view of the companies. You have to really study the companies and should not lose your conviction. The stock price, in many cases, even falls after I take a position. But, if my analysis was correct and continue to be correct, I buy more. These good companies, in the meantime, are trying to fix the issues that caused the stock to fall. Many times, they do not have to do much. If they can come out with revenue and earnings that beat the already reduced forecast number, the stock pops, and analysts starts upgrading the stock. It happens time and time again. Let us save the details for stock picking strategy to another chapter and discuss more on dividends now.

What happens when the dividend yield of a company reaches 6%, 7%, or 8% all of a sudden. This means things are tough for the company. The yield skyrocketed not because the company is suddenly making a lot of money. Even if the company made a lot more money than usual, it will not increase the dividend payout in a big way. Companies do not want to increase dividend payout unless they can maintain it in coming years. In such cases, they will pay a one-time special dividend, use the windfall to buy back shares, or just add to the balance sheet for future use. So, why did the yield jumped to these juicy levels? It is mostly because the stock price has gone down considerably. Yield is basically, dividend payout divided by share price. When the share price falls while dividend payout stays at the same level, the yield goes up. **Dividend Yield = Dividends/Share Price**. In fact, many companies, in these situations, are making less profit than usual and are struggling to pay out dividends at the current levels. This is a precursor of dividend cuts or complete elimination if things do not turn around in next several quarters. During 2015-2016, when oil price crashed and stayed around $30 per barrel, we saw that many solid oil companies reduced or completely eliminated dividends.

So, what should you do in this kind of scenario? It is worth taking some risk if the company has a strong balance sheet and current share price is very attractive; things will turn around as they do in most cases. Risk is never zero in investing in stocks. However, if the downward risk from the current level is low and rewards, due to big price appreciation and steady dividends, are high, it is a reasonable bet to buy at this level.

What is Payout Ratio?

It is a very important thing to check whether the company can maintain or has room to increase dividend payments in future. Payout ratio is the percentage of net profit that a company is paying out as dividends. Thirty to forty percent is good number. It provides a solid margin of safety. If the profit falls for several quarters, they will still be able to maintain dividends without depleting the balance sheet. Also, if things continue go well for the company with increasing earnings, they are most likely to increase dividends. On the other hand, if the company is paying 60-80% of net profit as dividends, the dividends could be at risk easily. If profit falls, dividends will be cut. Also, in these cases, the balance sheet is not growing, and they do not have money to buy back shares or expand business. Many real estate companies (REITs) have dividend yields of over 10%. REITs, by law, are required to distribute all profits to shareholders. REITs look very attractive with huge yield. However, study their share price for last 5 to 10 years. The share price may be on a steady decline; so what you are making from dividends is offset by steady decline in share price – the net could be very small gain, or maybe, you are losing money overall.

12.10   Stock Buyback

Stock buyback is a form of returning profits to the shareholders. When a company buys back shares from the outstanding share pool and retires them, the number of shares goes down. What this means is that the remaining shareholders now have a larger percentage ownership of the company and will share larger portion of the profits in future. Done at the right time and right price, share buyback can be very beneficial to the remaining shareholders. Share buybacks also help in EPS growth, even at same earnings. The EPS grows due to reduced number of shares. The company also saves in dividend payment, as there is now less number of outstanding shares that it needs to pay dividend. Does it mean, buyback is always good, or could there be better use of the money?

If the profit can be ploughed back to grow revenue and earnings, it should be the first choice. However, for many stable established companies, it is not always possible to grow fast even if a company has a lot of money at hand. The share price falls when growth stalls or earnings go down. The share price, in these types of scenarios, takes a big hit. If the company has cash, making steady profit, and the share price is down, buyback is a good move by the company. But, what we see in many cases is that the companies buy back shares at peak price. Buying back shares at peak price is a move to hide slowdown in earnings. It can hide the slowdown for a quarter or two, but stock is going to fall eventually. The company wasted a lot of money by buying high which is now available 30% to 40% cheaper. Now the price is low, but company has no money left to buyback share. These kinds of share buybacks are not shareholder friendly. Also, see if the share buybacks are to cover excessive executive compensation. Executive compensation is required to keep talent, but if it is big, it is not shareholder friendly. Look at the outstanding share count for the last 5-10 years. Are they going down? Or, Are they staying same or even increasing despite the company spending a fortune on share buyback?

Let us look at buybacks at some of the companies, which I think, are shareholder friendly.

Apple (AAPL)

It had 6.55B shares in 2013 and currently (April 2016) has 5.54B shares. It has steadily reduced share count by 15% in three years, at a yearly average rate of 5%.

GAP Inc. (GPS)

It had 570M shares in 2011 and currently (April 2016) has 397M shares. It has steadily reduced share count by 30% in five years, at a yearly average rate of 6%.

Gamestop (GME)

It had 140M shares in 2011 and currently (April 2016) has 104M shares. It has steadily reduced share count by 26% in five years, at a yearly average rate of 5.2%.

12.11   Growth

Growth, more than anything else, drives stock price. Growth is the main driver for darling stocks that keep increasing their revenue and may be, earnings. Growth is still important for value stocks or blue chips stocks. Stocks that are growing rapidly, years after years, have very high P/E ratios. They are valued for their revenue growth but not as much for the earnings. The expectation is that they are either gaining market share or investing the profit to grow business rapidly. These are the stocks that everybody chases, but the difficulty is identifying them early. These have risks of losing large amount of value very quickly. The other categories of stocks are the fundamentally solid stocks that are matured to a large extent. They are growing but slowly. Occasionally, they will hit a rough patch or undergo substantial transformation before growing again. This is when the price gets hammered. Generally, these are good entry points to buy these stocks. The management, in the meantime, is working in different ways to get back to growth and profitability. It does not require a large growth for the stock price to bounce back. Sometimes all they need to do is stop the revenue fall and start turning the corner. However, the important thing is that they need to show the path for growth and show some real growth for the stock price to come back. Cyclical companies, such as staples and apparels do not need to show super growth. They need to be making steady revenue and steady income.

12.12   Alpha and Beta

Alpha and Beta respectively measure the returns and volatility of a stock. I do not consider these as part of fundamental analysis and do not put too much weightage on these as part of my stock selection process. I want to discuss them here as these two terms are used in the industry, and you may want to explore further.

Alpha

Alpha indicates the relative performance of a stock compared to the overall market (index) over a period of time. If the market return was 10% and the return of an individual stock was 20%, it has an alpha of +10. Similarly, if the return was 5%, it has an alpha of -5. I personally do not use alpha, as a tool, to make my investment decisions other than it is a number to measure the relative performance in a year.

Beta

It indicates the relative volatility of a stock compared to the overall market. Beta more than 1 means stock is more volatile than the market; beta less than 1 means it is less volatile (more stable) than the market. Established companies such as utility companies have betas less than 1, whereas speculative companies have betas more than 1. Sometimes the beta may be high for a fundamentally solid company when the price falls due to short-term issues, and it may come out as a risky investment. But, at the low price, this is likely less risky than when it was at its peak.

Chapter

13

13 Stock Market Hates Monotony

13.1 Stock Market Boom and Bust Cycles

Fundamental analysis is the very first thing you need to carry out before buying a stock, but there are other overriding events or backdrops that are very important as well. Someone said that the price of a stock depends 40% on the overall market, 30% on the business sectors, and 30% on the individual performance. Through these numbers may not be accurate like the laws of Physics, but there is a great deal of truth in it. When the indices (DOW, S&P, and NASDAQ) are moving up, many stocks follow the upward trend. When overall market is down, many stocks fall without any company-specific news. High tide lifts all boats, and low tide brings down all boats.

13.2 Chart 1985-2016 (DOW, S&P, NASDAQ)

Fig. 13.1   DOW 1985-2016 (Yahoo finance)

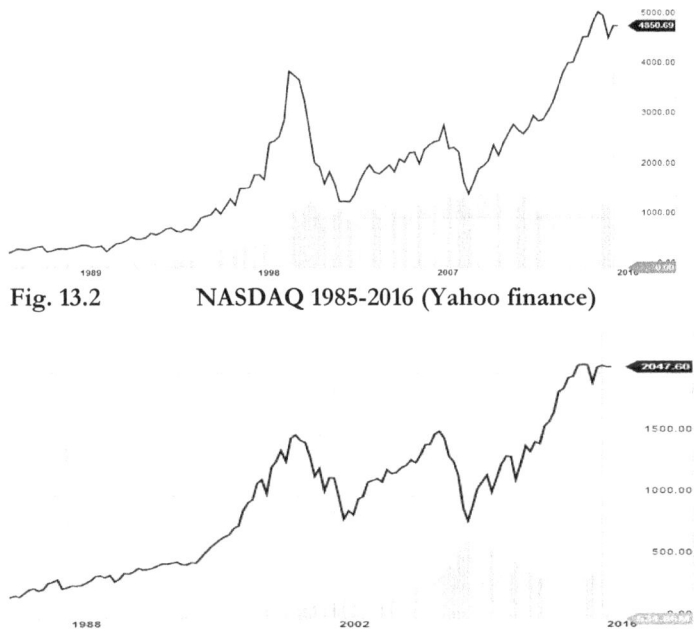

Fig. 13.2   NASDAQ 1985-2016 (Yahoo finance)

Fig. 13.3   S&P 1985-2016 (Yahoo finance)

13.3 Last Few Bull Runs and Bear Markets

We will study the last three bull runs and get some empirical data on how long a typical bull market lasts, what is the typical gain in a bull market, and how much does it fall from the top of a bull market to the bottom of the next bear market.

Bull Run 1994-2000 (Dotcom Boom)

	DOW	S&P	NASDAQ
Years of Bull run	7 years	7 years	7 years
Total gain	3900 - 11,497 (+195%)	460 - 1,499 (+226%)	777 - 4,696 (+500%)
Drop in Bear market that followed	11,497 - 7,590 (-34%)	1,499 – 815 (-46%)	4,696 - 1,172 (-75%)
Bear market duration	2.5 yrs.	2.5 yrs.	2.5 yrs.
Years to get back to previous high	6.5 years	7 yrs.	14 yrs.

Bull Run 2002-2007 (Real Estate Boom)

	DOW	S&P	NASDAQ
Years of Bull run	6 years	6 years	6 years
Total gain	7,590 - 13,930 (+84%)	815 - 1,527 (+87%)	1,172 - 2,860 (+144%)
Drop in Bear market that followed	13,930 - 7,060 (-49%)	1,527 to 798 (-48%)	2,860 - 1,377 (-52%)
Bear market duration	1.5 yrs.	1.5 yrs.	1.5 yrs.
Years to get back to previous high	5 yrs.	5.5 yrs.	4 yrs.

Bull Run 2009-2015 (Liquidity Boom)

	DOW	S&P	NASDAQ
Years of Bull run	7 years and going	7 years and going	7 years and going
Total gain	7,060 - 18,132 (+157%)	798 – 2068 (+159%)	1,377 - 5,128 (+272%)
Drop in Bear market that followed	-	-	-
Bear market duration	-	-	-
Years to get back to previous high	-	-	-

Empirical Observations
- Average bull run has lasted around 6 -7 years
- Each bull run is followed by a big drop into bear market
- The Bull Run builds slowly and stays longer. The bear crash happens quickly and does not stay long. Typical Bull Run lasted 6-7 years, and bear market lasted 1.5 to 2.5 years. There is a saying, "stocks take the staircase to go up and comes down on the elevator."

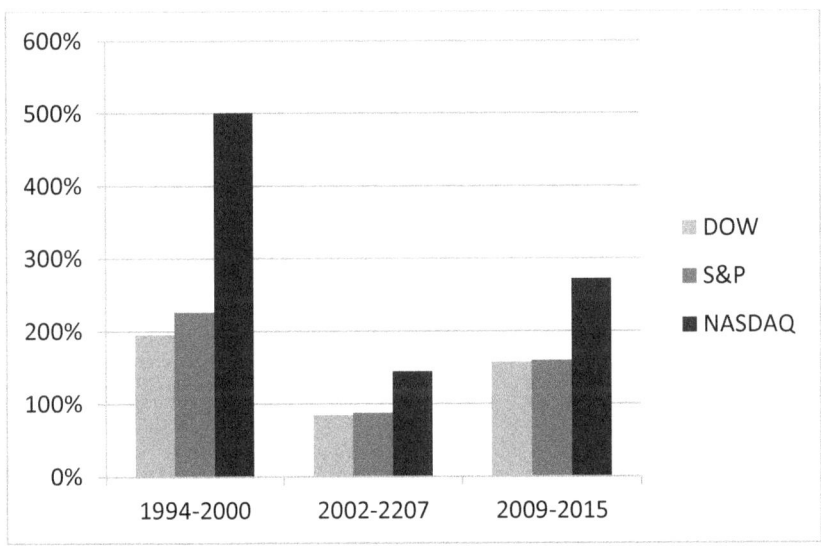

Fig. 13.4   **Percentage gain in bull runs**

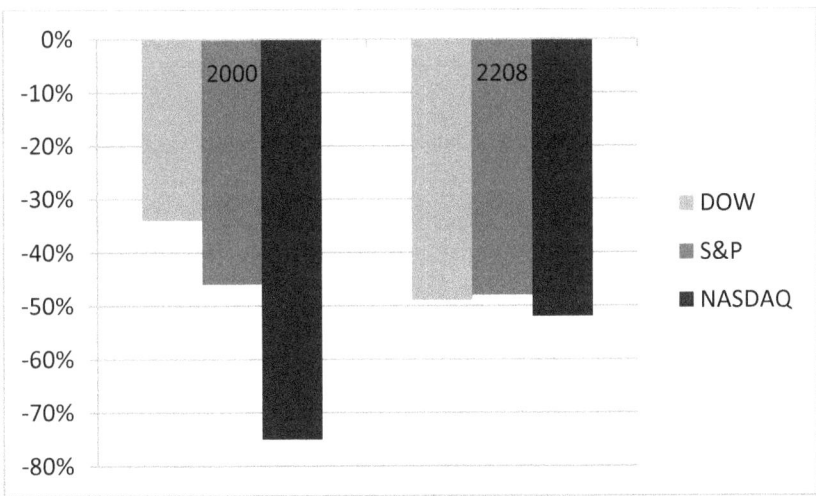

Fig. 13.5   Percentage drop in bear market

Comparison among the indices

What we observe from the three bull runs is that there is good correlation among all indices in timelines of the bull runs, market crash, and the duration of bear markets. The percentage gains during the bull runs are almost same between DOW and S&P. The percentage losses during the crashes are almost same between DOW and S&P. However, NASDAQ had larger gains during bull runs and larger drops during the bear markets that followed. The noticeable higher gain and drop for the NASDAQ can be explained by the fact that there are more technology companies in NASDAQ compared to DOW and S&P. DOW and S&P have more matured and established companies. Technology stocks go to higher overvalued territory during a bull market, and the fall is from a greater height as well. Can an investor use this discrepancy to his or her advantage to invest in one index over the others, given he wants to invest in index? The data suggests that if someone is putting fresh money at the bottom of a bear market, NASDAQ will provide better returns during the ensuing bull market. Similarly, the data suggests that, one should prefer DOW or S&P over NASDAQ at the peak of a bull market as the percentage drop would be lower in the bear market that follows. Detecting the exact peak or bottom is not very practical, but if someone can catch these points approximately, it will still make a difference. One strategy would be to put more of new money into NASDAQ at or close to the bear market, and move it to DOW or S&P as the Bull Run is ready for a change in direction.

13.4 What can be Learned from Boom and Bust?

What we observe from the last several bull and bear markets is that stock market boom and bust are normal occurrences in the long run. The pendulum swings widely in both directions. It goes into deep overvalued territory during the height of a bull market and drops to deep undervalued levels in the following bear markets. But, the thing is that, despite these wild swings, the overall direction for stock market has been upward in the long run. Does it mean that you should just invest in an index thru thick and thin and sit tight? This is probably true if you are looking at 40-50 yr. time period. But, most of us do not have the discipline and patience to wait 40-50 years to see our gain. More importantly, can we do better than investing in index? Can we take advantage of the facts that stock market go through these cycles? Nothing is 100% guaranteed, but we can strategize and position ourselves to maximize our chances of be successful. Here are some recommendations.

- It is almost impossible to forecast the exact peak of a bull market. However, we can get a sense that we are approaching the peak or getting signals that market is saturating. At this stage, do not be completely vested or use a lot of margin money. Keep some cash. But, do not get out completely either, as the market can move sideways for several years.

- Same goes for detecting the exact low of bear market – it is almost impossible. However, when the market is sufficiently down in a known bear market, start putting cash back to work. During these times, save more and generate more cash. Put off big expenses and use the cash to invest. Take the pain now and get big rewards in a few years. Use margin money, home equity line of credits or any loan that you can avail within your means. This is the time to commit and not be scared. This is of course all within the context of keeping your financial conditions stable without taking excessive risks that could destabilize your financial life.

14 All the World is a Stage

14.1 World Economies and the Stock Market

The world is a stage where all the world economies are the players. The world economies are more inter-dependent than ever before. Gone are the days when a local economy stayed locally and is not affected by the rest of the world. We recently observed how Chinese stock market crash affected the US stock market in Sept 2015. Dow fell by more than 2000 points (more than 10%) within a very short span. It happened again a few months later (beginning of 2016) when the big fall in Chinese stock market started a chain reaction around the world (DOW fell around 2000 points again).

International commerce has expanded significantly in the last 20-25 years. Other than the traditional large economies of the world (the US, Japan, and Europe), new economies have expanded with huge GDP growth. China is a major player in the world economics, and India's GDP is growing. India has the potential to be one of the major economies in future. Also, there are other economies (Brazil and Russia) that have the potential to be big. More and more companies are becoming international. Many US companies derive significant revenues (sometime more than US revenue) outside the US. It is not just the US multinationals, but multinational companies from other countries around the world generate significant revenues outside their own countries. Easy access of internet and rising standard of living in populous countries (China and India) is creating a lot of demands for products that the multinational companies are positioning to service. Needless to say, the world economies and the stock markets are not isolated or insulated any more.

What does it mean for an individual investor? It means two things. First, there are more opportunities to invest in other markets outside the US (it is a possibility but not a requirement). The second thing is that it affects the US economy and stock market significantly.

How do the world economies affect the US stock market?

Let us start with central bank interest rates in the large economies around the world. Similar to the Fed, the ECB (European Central Bank) sets the interest rate for European countries, BOJ (Bank of Japan) sets the interest for Japan, and People's Bank of China (PBOC) sets interest rate for China. Interest rate is an important thing to watch for stock market direction. Low interest rates by the central banks lower the savings and bond yields that an investor can get. Currently, the central bank interest rates around the world are close to zero in most of the large economies. The USA is trying to come off the historic near-zero rate. ECB and BOJ have negative interest rates. Without any meaningful returns from the safe assets, it forces many to move to stocks.

The other thing is that low interest rate also lowers borrowing costs resulting in lower mortgage interest rate and margin rate. Lower mortgage cost helps stock market indirectly. When mortgage rate is low, more people buy houses, and the house prices go up. With house price appreciation, people have larger equity in their houses, and they can use home-equity loan or line of credit to raise cash off the equity in their houses. They use the money to spend on goods, invest in real estate, or invest in stocks. Lower margin rates also encourage people to access money cheaply to invest in stocks. The net effect of very low interest rate is large influx of money into the stock market. It is a fact that when you supply more money into any asset, the asset price goes up; and, when you remove money, the asset value falls. Interest rate is not the sole factor in determining stock market performance, but it is a very important factor. As an investor, you need to keep an eye on not just the Fed but also the major central bank rates around the world.

14.2 World Events and the US Stock Market

Events around the world affect stock markets, mostly negatively. A regional war, turmoil in some parts of the world, natural disaster, or epidemic negatively impact the stock market. Such events create impediments to international trades with reduction in collective demands for goods and services around the world. Since many companies have multinational operations, it creates a net negative for revenue and earnings. Some of these things might be temporary, but the gut reaction of the market is to pull pack immediately. Sometimes, the stock market recovers quickly. As an investor, these pullbacks may be opportunities to buy good stocks. Here are some of the recent world events that affected stock markets negatively.

- Chinese stock market crash in late 2015 and beginning of 2016
- Greek debt crisis
- Japan Tsunami and nuclear accident in 2011
- SAR crisis in ASIA in 2003
- World Trade Center attack in 2001
- Iraq invasion of Kuwait in 1990

14.3 Exchange Rate and the Stock Market

The Dollar exchange rates in comparison to other major currencies affect US corporations that generate significant revenues from these countries. When the dollar becomes stronger compared to a foreign currency, US goods become less affordable to the people in the foreign country. This means, US companies have to either cut price or lose business. The net effect is reduced revenue and reduced margins. Normal fluctuation in the exchange rate is fine, but if there is long-term trend where dollar keeps appreciating, the stock prices of these companies take a hit. Stronger dollar is not bad for all; it increases buying power of US consumers. Goods imported from foreign countries become cheaper, and a US consumer can buy more for the same amount of dollar. Another impact of strong US dollar is that US companies fall to foreign competition, mainly in manufacturing industries. Sometimes, the manufacturing jobs move to other countries. The impact of weaker dollar is the opposite. US goods become more affordable in other countries, and it improves US exports. At the same time, with weaker dollar, imported goods become more expensive in the US. Next, we will explore what causes exchange rate to change.

What causes exchange rate to change?

There are many factors that affect exchange rate. When there is more demand for US dollar, the dollar appreciates. When there is less demand, the US dollar depreciates. The central banks interest rates of the major economies around the world are zero or negative which bring down the yield of the sovereign bonds to very low level. The US, though had interest rate close to zero for a long time, is slowly trying to increase the interest rate. Increase in Fed rate has the possibility of moving the short-term bond and 10-yr bond rate upwards. This increases demand for dollar, as more countries around the world would want to buy dollars because of higher Fed bond yield.

Another thing that affects the exchange rate is the state of the foreign economies, especially in growing countries. If the economies of the these countries stall, capital starts moving out of these countries to safe haven countries, such as the US, Japan, and Germany. This creates more demand for dollar, and dollar appreciates against the foreign currencies. Also, if there is war or turmoil around the world, capital starts moving to safe places like the US market. This increases demand for dollar that pushes dollar up.

Another factor is the process of exchange rate determination. US dollar is freely floating with some countries but not all. When dollar freely floats, the exchange rate is decided by the supply and demand in the open market. However, when a currency is not freely floating and the government can influence the exchange rate, it may not be in the best interest of the US.

14.4 Major Stock Indices in the World

US	DJIA (DOW Jones) NASDAQ S&P 500	Europe	DAX (Germany) FTSE (UK) CAC 40 (France)
Japan	Nikkei, TOPIX	China	Shanghai composite
Hong Kong	HSI (Hang Seng)	India	BSE Sensex, NIFTY 50

14.5 Chart of World Stock Indices

Here is the chart of major indices for last 10 years.

(http://www.cnbc.com)

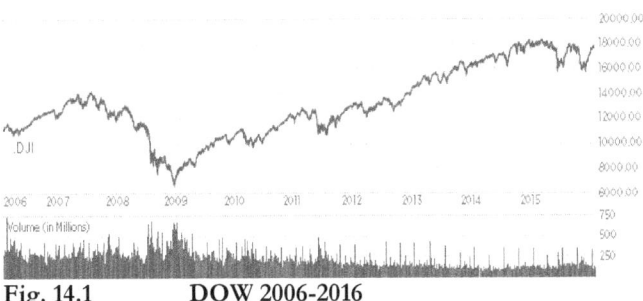

Fig. 14.1   DOW 2006-2016

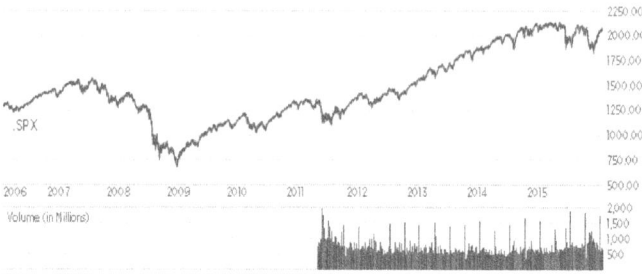

Fig. 14.2   S&P 2006-2016

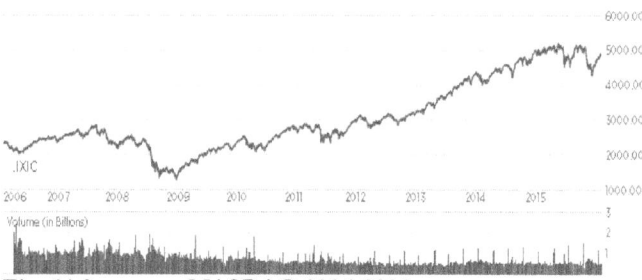

Fig. 14.3   NASDAQ 2006-2016

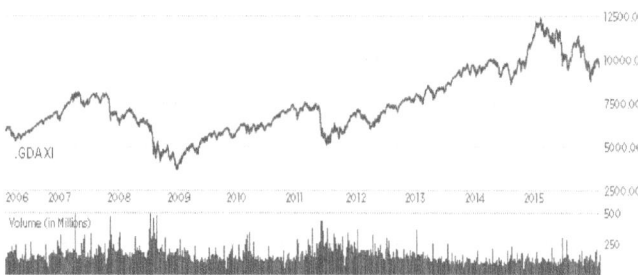

Fig. 14.4   DAX 2006-2016

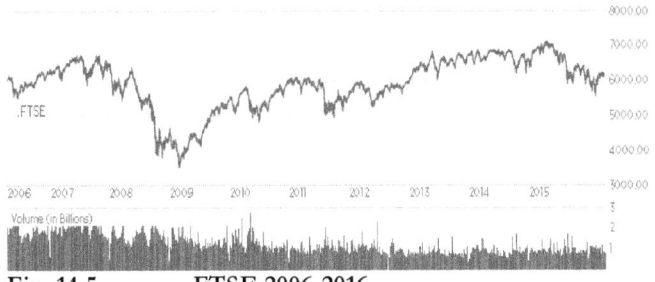

Fig. 14.5   **FTSE 2006-2016**

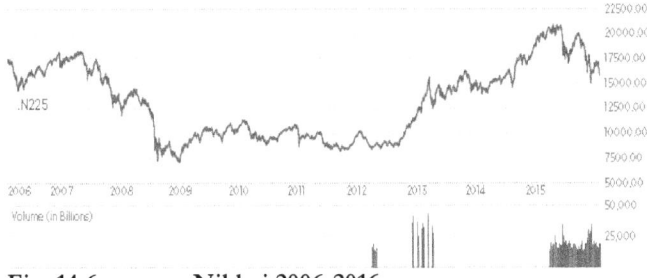

Fig. 14.6   **Nikkei 2006-2016**

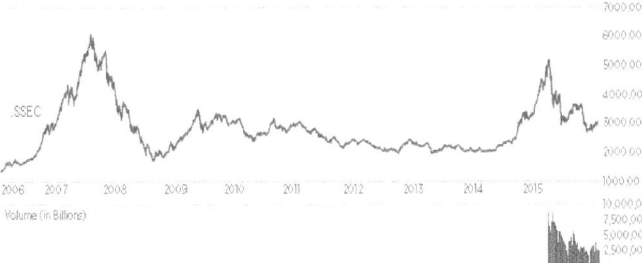

Fig. 14.7   **Shanghai 2006-2016**

Chapter
15

15 Pulse of the Market/Economy

Stock price is always reacting to the latest information available and is trying to reach the equilibrium point as quickly as possible. As an investor, you need to keep an eye and devise your strategy and tactical moves to maximize your gain. You have to keep a close eye on the tailwinds, headwinds, or no wind.

15.1 The News and Indicators

Leading indicators are things that tell what is going to come in future as opposed to lagging indicators that capture how something actually happened or confirms that something, that was thought to be happening, actually happened. Stock market performance is a leading indicator of the economy. A declining stock market is a precursor of economic slowdown in future, and an up-trending stock market indicates better economy in future. GDP is a lagging indicator for the economy as accurate GDP numbers are not available until a quarter later. As investors, if we can get an idea or indication as to how the stock market is going to behave in future, it would be of tremendous value. It is like knowing the future.

It is not an exact science, but there are many indicators that try to convey something about the future of the economy and the stock market. Our goal is to understand these important parameters; mentally construct a model, come up with our best guesses, and use the information to our advantage. Though the stock market is a leading indicator for the economy, there are many news, events, and indicators related to the economy that affect the stock market future as well. Our goal is to understand these things that affect the stock market and individual stocks and stay a step ahead of the curve.

15.2 What Causes Stock Price to Change?

The overall direction for the stock market depends on many news and developments in the economy, such as the Fed FOMC minutes, job numbers, and consumer confidence index. The market reacts to the news and updates positively or negatively. The actual effect of the news may not happen immediately, but stock market reacts quickly trying to figure out how the news is going to affect the economy and the stock market. Some of these news updates come weekly, some monthly, and some a few times in a year. We will describe some of the important news events. When you are an active investor, you need to know these news event dates so that you can make intelligent buy and sell decisions. A nice calendar of economic events is available at: http://www.bloomberg.com/markets/economic-calendar/. Another source is: https://www.briefing.com/investor/calendars/economic/

15.3 Quarterly Updates

15.3.1   GDP

GDP has two releases, advanced release and the final release. Advance release comes out four weeks after a quarter ends, and the final release comes out three months after the quarter ends. It is released by Bureau of Economic Analysis. GDP is the most important economic indicator. A strong GDP indicates a strong economy and is good for the stock market. The report can be found at: http://bea.gov/national/index.htm

15.4 Updates in Every 6-7 Weeks

15.4.1   FOMC Update

FOMC (Federal Open Market Committee) meeting minutes do not come every month but are released eight times a year, approximately every one and half months. The committee meets eight times a year and discusses the state of the economy. One of the important decisions for the committee is to decide the short-term interest rate (funds rate). They may leave it unchanged, cut it, or raise it. Fed funds rate is a very important element for the economy and the stock market. Lower rate makes it easier to borrow money that spurs economic activity and is generally good for stock market. Raising interest rate makes it costlier to borrow money. It also fights inflation and is considered a dampener for the stock market. After keeping the interest rate ultralow (close to zero), Fed has started to raise interest rate. Another thing is that when Fed starts to raise or cut, it typically does it in a series of steps. It does not go back and forth with alternate cuts and raises. The stock market typically reacts negatively to rise in interest rate. After the Fed releases its minutes (called Fed minutes), the stock market generally makes big moves (up or down). As an investor, you may want to wait for the minutes to be out before making any big buy or sell decision. The minutes of the Fed meeting are released three weeks after the meeting. Below is the list of meeting dates for 2016. The dates are not exactly same every year but close. You can find the dates from the Federal Reserve website: https://www.federalreserve.gov/monetarypolicy/fomccalendars.htm. For 2016, the meeting dates are:

- January 26-27, March 15-16, April 2-27, June14-15
- July 26-27, September 20-21, November 1-2, December 13-14

15.4.2   Beige Book

It is the report about the economy of each district, produced by each of the Fed branches. It is produced eight a times a year, two weeks prior to the FOMC meeting. This report, commonly known as the Beige book, is one of the important documents that the FOMC uses to discuss the economy and its plan of action. For more info, refer to:
https://www.federalreserve.gov/monetarypolicy/beigebook/

15.5 Monthly Updates

15.5.1   Consumer Confidence Index

Consumer spending accounts for 70% of the US economy (GDP). Consumer Confidence Index (CCI) provides an indication as to how the consumers are feeling about the economy. Are they feeling upbeat or downbeat? When they are upbeat, they are likely to spend more and engage in more economic activities, which is generally a good thing for the stock market. On the contrary, when they are not feeling excited or are worried, economic activities and consumer spending is likely to slow down. This means company earnings (specially, retails, consumer goods, tech, banking etc.) are going to slow down that puts downward pressure on stock price.

CCI is based on survey of opinions of 5,000 US households on the current state and future expectation of the economy. It is released 10 A.M. ET on the last Tuesday of the month by the Conference Board, an independent economic research organization. CCI stood at 96.2 during March of 2016 against the baseline 100 (started at 100 in 1985). The details about of CCI can be found at: https://www.conference-board.org/data/consumerconfidence.cfm

Another important indicator is the **University of Michigan Consumer Sentiment Index**. It is similar to the Conference Board index and has two components – current conditions and expectations. However, it is released twice a month:

- Preliminary data for the current month at 10 A.M. ET on the second Friday of the month
- Final data for the current month at 10 A.M. ET on the fourth Friday of the month

15.5.2   Business Outlook Survey

The Philadelphia Federal Reserve publishes the Business Outlook Survey at 12 P.M. ET on the third Thursday of each month. It is also known as Philadelphia Fed Report. It is a survey of the regional (Pennsylvania, New Jersey, and Delaware) manufacturing activities and business. A positive value indicates growth and negative value indicates contraction. The survey includes questions on employment, new orders, shipments, inventories, and price paid. Though it is a regional report, it gives an early indication of the economy and is one of the widely watched reports. It can be found at:
https://www.philadelphiafed.org/research-and-data/regional-economy/business-outlook-survey

15.5.3   Retail Sales

The retail sales number tracks the total receipt of sales of retail stores. It is a widely watched number by most economists and investors. It does not include auto sales, as auto sales can vary widely from one month to another. Auto sales are tracked as separate indicators (Auto and Truck Sales). Retails sales number does not include the service sector spending.

Retail sales report is used as a pre-inflationary indicator. It gives an early peek at the course that the Fed might take in the interest rate decision. If retail sales are slowing down, it may be indicating that recession is coming. It is released in the morning on around 13th of each month, and it contains data for the previous month. The report can be found at: https://www.census.gov/retail/index.html

15.5.4   Consumer Price Index (CPI)

It is a measure of the price level of a fixed basket of goods and services that a typical consumer purchases. It is a widely used indicator to measure inflation in the economy. The government uses this to calculate cost of living adjustments (COLA) for government programs. The Federal Reserve watches this closely to adjust interest rate. If the inflation is high, the Fed increases interest rate to reduce money supply and bring down inflation. On the other hand, if the inflation is very low or negative (deflation), the economy is contracting. The Fed reduces interest rate to increase money supply.

The data is released at 8:30 ET on the 13th of each month by the Bureau of Labor Statistics, US Department of Labor. The report contains data for the previous month. Within this, there is another indicator, called the core rate. The core rate excludes the volatile food and energy prices. Reports are available at: http://www.bls.gov/news.release/cpi.toc.htm.

15.5.5   Producer Price Index (PPI)

PPI looks at the price of goods at the wholesale or producer level. There are three main subcategories within the PPI. These are:

1.   Crude – This shows the average price change of commodities (coal, crude oil, and steel) compared to the previous month.
2.   Intermediate – It measures monthly change in price for intermediate processed goods that are used to manufacture finished products.
3.   Finished – As the name implies, this measures the monthly change in price change for finished goods.

PPI is an early indicator of future CPI as the price increase from the producers is often passed on to the consumers. The PPI report is released in the 2nd week of each month in the morning time by the Bureau of Labor statistics, US Dept. of Labor. The report can be found at:

http://www.bls.gov/news.release/ppi.toc.htm.

15.5.6   Trade Balance Report

It is the difference between the US exports and imports, measured in the US dollar. When the exports are more than the imports, it results in a trade balance. If we are importing more than exporting, it is a trade deficit. The report includes services along with goods. The U.S. is a net exporter of services and a net importer of goods. Overall, the U.S. has been incurring trade deficit with its trading partners for some time. The report is released by BEA (Bureau of Economic Analysis) around 19th of each month, and it contains data for the previous two months. The report can be found at:
http://www.bea.gov/international/index.htm.

15.5.7   Monthly Job Report

The report is out on the first Friday of a month. It is a widely watched report for getting a pulse on the job market and the economy. It also moves the stock market, positively or negatively.

15.5.8   Housing Starts and Building Permits

Housing starts are the measure of number of units for which constructions began last month, and building permits measure the number houses for which excavation can start. It is released at 8:30 ET on 16th of the month that has the data for the previous month. The report is broken down by four regions, Northeast, Midwest, South, and West. The report comes from the census bureau of the department of commerce, and it can be found at:
http://www.census.gov/construction/nrc/index.html.

This report is more useful for real estate market and investments. Continual slowdown for a few months indicates that housing market may be slowing down. You have to compare this not only month-to-month but also same month of this year to the previous year. This affects stocks, such as Home Depot, Lowes, or other chain stores that sell home upgrades and furnishing items.

15.5.9   Existing Home Sales

Existing home sales report is released by the National Association of Realtors at 10 A.M. ET around 25th of each month. It contains the data of existing homes that were sold during the previous month. Details can be found at:
http://www.realtor.org/research-and-statistics.

Existing home sales figure reports the demand as opposed to the Housing starts figure that indicates the supply of homes. Like the housing starts, it is a leading indicator and indicates how the economy is going to look in future. It also impacts housing sector stocks.

15.5.10   Auto and Truck Sales

The various auto manufactures release the auto sales data for the previous months generally during the first business day to the third business day of the month. It is a leading indicator of the business cycle. As an investor, you can get a sense where the economy might be heading but use the data for auto related stocks. Auto stocks usually have changes larger than usual after the release.

15.6 Weekly Updates

15.6.1   Weekly Jobless Claim

It provides the initial or preliminary weekly jobless claim. The weekly jobless number represents the number of people that filed for unemployment insurance for the first time. It indicates the strength of the job market and the economy. A declining claim number indicates a better job market and a positive for the economy. Increasing claim indicates slowdown in the job market and the economy. A declining trend in jobless claim and a low level of jobless claim indicate that labor market is very tight and wages could rise in future leading to inflation. Inflation or expectation of inflation can influence the Fed to increase interest rate that could negatively impact the stock market. Initial jobless claim report comes out on Thursday every week and contains data for the prior week.

15.7 Company Quarterly Results

As we discussed before, the price movement of a stock is influenced by overall economy and stock indices (40%), sector (30%), and individual stock (30%). Among all news, related to a company, the quarterly update is the most significant. It contains very important data, such as revenue, total earnings, EPS, cash flow, and stock buyback data. It also contains the revenue and earnings forecast for the next quarter or year. The stock price could move up or down significantly after the quarterly results are out. Gains or losses of 10% to 25% in a single day are not uncommon. Given the amount of change that could happen after the quarterly results, how do you position yourself?

Buy Decision

If a stock has clear expectations of good results going into the earnings, the stock price would start moving up a few weeks before the results. If you really want to buy a stock (the price is right, and you are expecting it to beat projection), buy it several weeks before the earnings. The stock price would have already moved up where the earnings beat is already priced in. If the results did not meet expectations, it could drop giving back the gain it accumulated prior to the results. In such a case, it becomes risky to buy just before the quarterly results – there is higher downside risk with low upside potential.

However, if there is no clear expectation and decisive direction in the price of a stock, it is a neutral decision. If you believe that it is the right stock and the price is right, you can buy some shares while keeping some cash to add some more if the stock were to go down after the results. Also, the best time to buy a good but beaten-down stock is right after the earnings when it drops by a big percentage (10-20%). It could bounce back in a few days, which is very good. Even if stays there or moves lower, you are still in a good position as you bought a solid stock at a cheap price.

Sell Decision

Should you hold a stock into the earnings or sell it? It depends. If your time horizon is long-term (one year to several years) and you continue to believe that company is going to grow in future and do well in future, you may hold onto it and not sell it. However, if you think the price has suddenly gone up, it is not a bad idea to take some profit.

My picks are fundamentally strong companies that do not appreciate massively over a period of years but fluctuate several times a year. This is even more true with the current overall market where it is mostly moving sideways or has stayed flat for the last 2-3 years. Most of my decisions are short term (less than a year). In such cases, if the price has appreciated with a good gain (10-20%), I sell all and realize the profits before the quarterly results. Or, in some cases, I sell half and keep half. If the stock goes up, I have realized some profit and am going to make more with the remaining positions. If it goes down, I have already locked half the gain. If the stock still looks good after going down, I buy it again at a lower price. If the stock price has not gone up much from the price I bought, I do not sell any of it. I have not made any money on that stock, and there is no point selling before the results. If it goes up after the earnings, I will decide whether to sell. If the price goes down, I will buy some more or hold the stock.

Chapter

16

16 Technical Analysis

16.1 Charts and Trends – Technical Analysis

As we discussed before, stock analysis is divided mainly into fundamental analysis and technical analysis. We discussed fundamental analysis in details in chapter 12. In this chapter, we are going to discuss technical analysis. Unlike fundamental analysis that is based on the fundamental aspects (balance sheet, income statement, and cash flow etc.) of a company, technical analysis does not consider the company fundamentals in making buy and sell decisions. Technical analysis looks at charts, trends, and patterns to make buy and sell decisions. If a chart is showing some identifiable pattern, the price could move the way it did in a similar condition in the past. For example, if the price went up with a larger than normal volume, it indicates there is an interest forming in the stock. The stock price is likely to go higher in future.

Technical analysis is based on the study of certain well-defined patterns in the stock chart. If a stock is forming one of these well-defined patterns, you can predict how the stock is going to behave based on how stocks, in general, have behaved in past. It is not a perfect science as stock price can change differently this time due overall market change or other unanticipated external factors. However, it is a reasonable guess that it is likely to follow the pattern without big external influences. Technical analysis itself is a vast field, and many people follow it successfully. However, I am not an expert in technical analysis and do not use it much in my investment decisions other than using it on some occasions (volume, double bottoms, double tops etc.). We will cover some of the basics of technical analysis in this chapter and leave the details to other books and experts in this field.

16.2 Support and Resistance

16.2.1   Support

Support is the low price level where more people are willing to buy than sell. The stock price is a constant tussle between buyers and sellers. When there are more sellers than buyers, the stock price falls. As price keeps falling, it becomes cheaper. More people want to buy, and fewer people want to sell. At some point, the stock price finds a support or floor where the number of buyers is more than number of sellers. The stock price finds a support level and does not fall further. If a stock bounces off a support level, it would continue to go up for some time. If it bounces off with a large volume, there is a good chance that it will go higher. After the stock goes back up, it might reverse trend and start falling to test support again. It may continue to bounce off the support level and stay in a range for some time. Or, it may bounce off support a few times before going up (after a double or triple bottom) or going down. When it breaks support level convincingly (with large volume) and goes down, it could go down further until it finds support at a lower level.

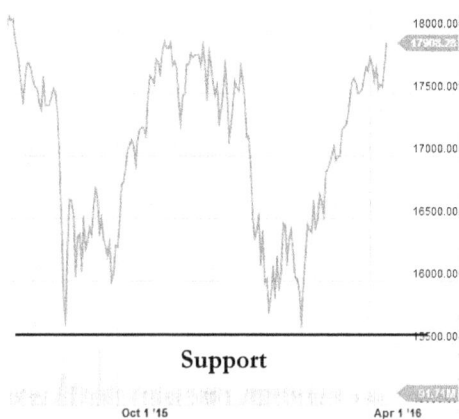

Fig. 16.1   DOW: Support at 15,660

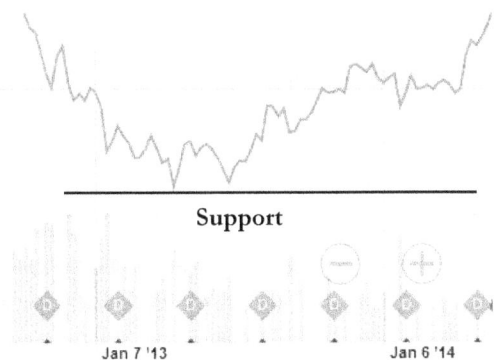

Fig. 16.2   Apple: Support at $56

16.2.2   Resistance

Resistance or ceiling is the opposite of support or floor. Resistance is the high point that the price cannot break through. It bounces off the resistance level and starts falling. When the price of a stock keeps going up, it becomes expensive, and more people are willing to sell than buy. At some point, the sellers outnumber the buyers and stock price hits a resistance and starts falling from that point. How far it will fall depends on the volume at the resistance. The stock price may continue to bounce off the resistance and stay in a range for some time. Or, it may bounce off the resistance a few times before making a downward move (after hitting double or triple top) or breaking out and going higher. If a stock breaks the resistance or ceiling convincingly, (with large volume) it could go much higher in coming months.

Fig. 16.3   Apple: Resistance at $133

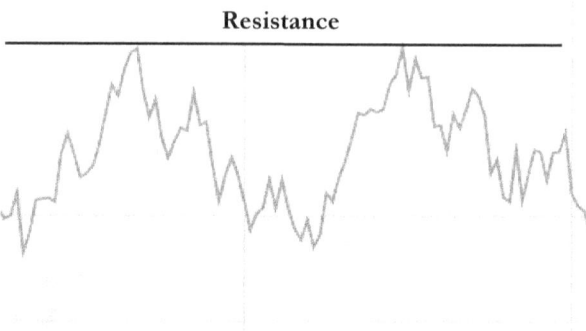

Fig. 16.4   Tesla: Resistance at $280

16.3 Volume

Volume indicates conviction and strength of a stock price move. Along with price and other considerations, volume is also a critical parameter in the final buy, sell, or hold decision. When you look up the price of a stock (in yahoo finance for example), there are two volume numbers - one is the average volume over the last three months, and the other one is the volume for the day. If the volume in a particular day is close to the average, it does not indicate a strong move. However, if the price change is accompanied with large volume (2 times to 10 times) compared to average, it indicates the start of a momentum in either upward or downward direction. If the stock moves up with high volume, it is due to large buying interest, and it is likely to move up, at least in the immediate future. This typically happens due to good news (earnings/revenue beat with good forecast, customer win, or product introduction). If price appreciation happens with normal volume or low volume, it does not indicate a strong direction. The price may go down in following days erasing the gain. Similarly, if the price drops with an unusually high volume, it indicates a downtrend. It might bounce back a little the next day (if the drop was severe and probably an overreaction). However, overall, it is likely the start of a longer downtrend.

Another thing to notice is the volume at the peak or bottom of a stock. As the price of a hot stock keeps going up with large volume, it is still a bullish sign. If you want to maximize your profit, do not sell it yet. If you want to optimize for the best selling price, look at the volume trend. When the volume starts winding down, it indicates that buying interest is slowing down, and a top is likely approaching. This is probably the time to sell. Similarly, if you want to buy at the low, look at the volume along with the price. As the price keeps falling down, the selling interest will slow down, and it is likely reaching the bottom zone.

Volume can also be used to predict overall market bottom or top. The market crash happens due to big economic events (recession, big international events, or asset bubble bursting). After the initial big drop, it may continue to fall for some time. How do you know that market has bottomed out and the pendulum has swung far to the pessimistic side? There is no definite answer to this, but capitulation (unusually large volume) is an indicator of a market bottom. In the course of a market crash, some will sell immediately, and some will sell slowly as the market keeps going down. Some people will hold on and add more as the stocks become cheaper and cheaper.

However, a sizable portion of stockholders, initially deciding to wait and ride it out, cannot take it any more mentally or financially. Mentally, it is just too agonizing to go through this, and they just want to get out. Some would be forced to sell if they need the money or had a large margin loan that they need to cover. The final selling of the stocks comes with a large volume (called capitulation). If you want to time the bottom, capitulation is one good indicator. After capitulation with high volumes occurs, most of the selling pressure has been exhausted. The only place the stock market can move is to hover around at that level or go up. You can also time the market top with unusual volume at the top. However, finding the market top, based on large volume action, is not as predictable as finding market bottom. This is because, bull markets are not sudden and happen over a longer duration (average bull market is 4 years). The bear market happens very quickly with average bear market lasting a little over a year.

16.4 Gaps

Gaps are sudden instantaneous price change (jump or fall). These typically happen after a big event or quarterly results. Most of the companies announce their quarterly results after the market is closed for the day. If the results are outstanding with a sound beat and a strong forecast, the stock price could open with a 10-20% jump in price compared to the previous day market close. This is gap up. Similarly, if the results are bad and it missed the forecast badly, price could open with a 10-20% drop next day. This is gap down. A gap up or gap down could also happen during the trading hours when a big event occurs that can impact the company positively or negatively.

Gaps are categorized as mainly there types – breakaway gap, runaway gap, and exhaustion gap. Breakaway gap occurs at the beginning of a long upward trend. Runaway gap occurs in the middle of the uptrend. Exhaustion gap occurs toward the end phase of an uptrend. Those who have been waiting on the sidelines finally cannot afford to miss it anymore and jump in. All the buyers are exhausted at this time, and it indicates a top and trend reversal.

16.5 Double Bottoms and Double Tops

16.5.1   Double Bottom

Double bottom is a reversal from a downtrend to an uptrend. The chart forms a double bottom when the stock is on a downtrend and hits two lows that are roughly equal. There is an intermediate resistance between the two bottoms. On the way up from the second bottom, if the stock breaks resistance with a large volume, it is a strong bullish indicator that stock price will continue going high with an upward trend. In the example below, Apple was on a downward trend and hit the first bottom at B1. Then, it bounced back to the resistance shown by the short line. It went down again and hit the second bottom at B2 before bouncing back again. On the way back, it broke the resistance at C. The double bottom is complete at this time. After it broke out at point C, it reversed trend and continued on an upward trend for next several months.

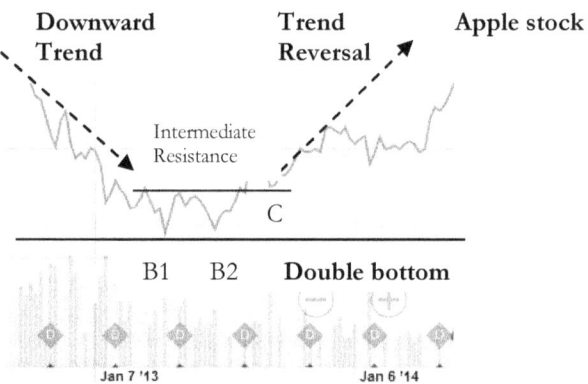

Fig. 16.5   Double bottom and trend reversal

How can an investor use this chart as it is forming?

If the fundamentals of a company are good and the investor is waiting to enter into a position in the stock, he can buy some at B1, a little at B2, and more at point C where the trend has reversed. He can hold on to gain as it continues to go up.

16.5.2   Double Top

Double Top is the opposite of double bottom. The stock is on an upward trend when it hits its first top. After hitting the first top, it goes down until it finds support at an intermediate support line and starts going back up again. On the way back up, it meets a second top before moving down toward the intermediate support line again. If it breaks the intermediate support line with large volume, it is likely to reverse trend and descend on a downward slope for the next several months. In this example, Tesla was on an upward slope when it hit the first top at T1. After hitting T1, it moved lower before finding intermediate support at the small horizontal line. It went back up and faced resistance at the second top at T2, which is roughly equal to the first top. On the way back, it broke the support at C and continued on a longer downward fall for the next several months.

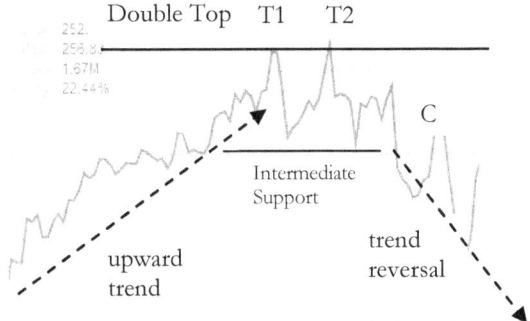

Fig. 16.6   Tesla: Double Top and Trend Reversal

How can an investor use this chart as it is forming?

If the investor is ready to sell and book profit, he may be trying to maximize the gain and is looking for the best point to sell. Instead of selling the entire position, the investor can sell some at T1, some more at T2, and finally the rest at C when price breaks the intermediate support line and starts on a long downward path.

16.6 Triangles

Triangles are a category of continuation or reversal patterns that depend on the types of triangles. There are mainly three types of triangles – ascending triangles, descending triangles, and symmetrical triangles.

16.6.1   Ascending Triangle

Ascending triangles typically indicate forward bullish behavior. We will discuss two cases of bullish behavior - first case, where it continues its bullish uptrend and second case, where it reverses trend at the bottom of a downtrend and moves higher. However, it can also indicate a future bearish behavior with trend reversal at the top of an uptrend.

Ascending Triangle: Bullish Trend Continuation

An ascending triangle is formed with a series of same highs and successive higher lows. In general, ascending triangle is a bullish indicator where the stock price could break out for higher gain toward the end of the triangle formation. The stock faces the resistance line a few times, but the overall trend is upward as the lows are higher each time. Finally, it breaks the resistance line and moves up higher.

Fig. 16.7   Ascending Triangle-Bullish Continuation

Ascending Triangle: Bullish Trend Reversal

Sometimes, ascending triangles can be found at the bottom of a downtrend that could signal a trend reversal as shown in the figure below.

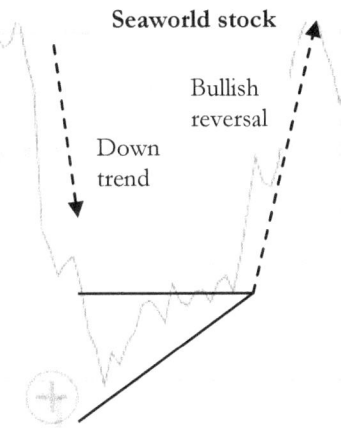

Fig. 16.8   Ascending Triangle – Bullish Reversal

Ascending Triangle: Bearish Trend Reversal

Ascending triangles are usually continuation pattern in an upward trend as shown in the figure 16.7. However, sometimes, ascending triangles form before the stock price reverses direction from an upward trend and moves lower. Below is an example of Bearish Reversal after an ascending triangle formation found in Qualcomm stock between Feb'2014 and Aug'2014.

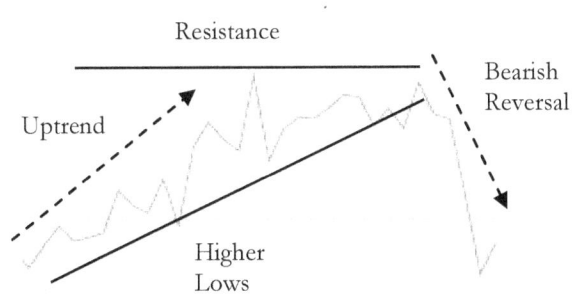

Fig. 16.9   Ascending triangle – Bearish Reversal

16.6.2   Descending Triangle

Descending Triangle: Bearish Trend Continuation

A descending triangle typically is a continuation of bearish pattern during a downtrend. What it means is that during a downward trend, it will oscillate within the descending triangle before falling sharply lower again. The bearish trend continues while it was trying to find direction inside the descending triangle. Below is an example of Bearish Continuation after a descending triangle formation found in Walmart stock between June'2015 and Sept'2015.

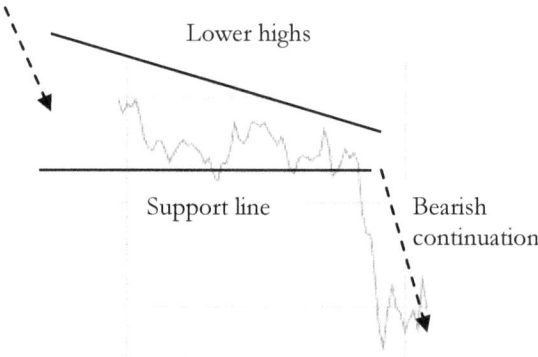

Fig. 16.10   **Descending Triangle–Bearish Continuation**

Descending Triangle: Bearish Trend Reversal

On some occasions, descending triangles indicate bearish action during an uptrend. Toward the end of the descending triangle, the stock price breaks out in the reverse direction with a sharp fall. Below is an example of Bearish reversal after Descending triangle formation showed by Facebook stock between July'2015 and Aug'2015.

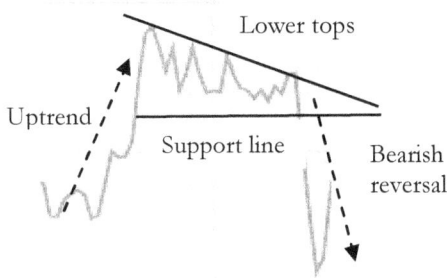

Fig. 16.11   **Descending Triangle – Bearish Reversal**

Descending Triangle: Bullish Trend Reversal

Also on some other occasions, descending triangles indicate bullish action where it does not break a strong support line. It would break out and reverse trend with a sharp rise in the upward direction.

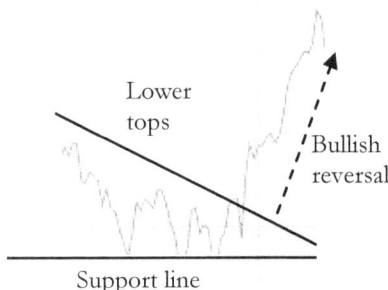

Fig. 16.12   **Descending Triangle – Bullish Reversal**

16.6.3   Symmetrical Triangle

A symmetric triangle is typically considered a continuation pattern. It is formed by two converging lines – the first line with series of lower peaks and the second line with a series of higher bottoms. It is a consolidation period where the number of buyers and sellers are roughly equal without any significant volume. If it is preceded by an upward trend, the breakout is expected to move the stock sharply higher. If it is preceded by a downward trend, breakout is expected to happen in a downward direction.

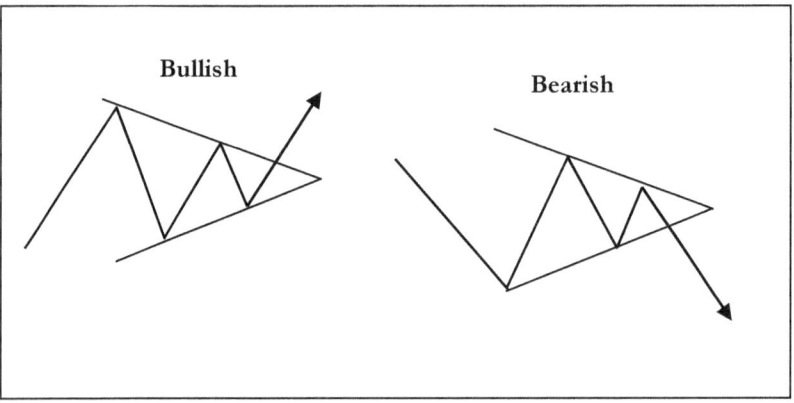

Fig. 16.13   Symmetrical Triangle

16.7 Head and Shoulder

16.7.1   Head and Shoulder

A head and shoulder pattern looks like a head (peak) in the middle and a symmetric left shoulder and a right shoulder on the sides. It is typically a bearish sign that the stock could pull back further after the completion of the head and shoulder formation. The left shoulder is formed with a big move and large volume. After the formation of the left shoulder, the stock drops to the new support line (called neckline). Then, it goes up to new high (higher than the left shoulder). Reaching the head, the stock drops back to the neckline before going up again and forming the right shoulder. The high for the right shoulder is close to the left shoulder but lower than the head. When the stock drops from the right shoulder peak and touches the neckline, it is an indication that interest in

Head

the stock is cooling down, and the stock could pull back in next several months. It indicates a sell signal at the completion of head and shoulder formation

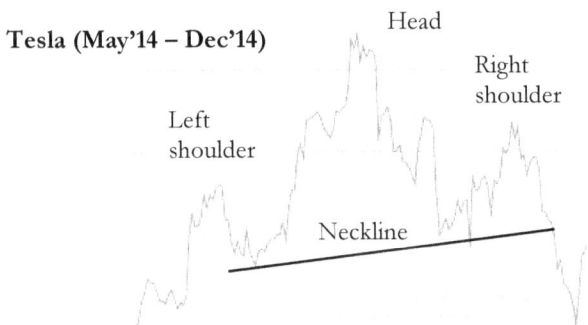

Fig. 16.14   **Head and Shoulder Pattern**

16.7.2   Inverted Head and Shoulder

An inverted head and shoulder pattern looks like the vertical mirror reflection of a regular head and shoulder pattern. It has two symmetrical local lows (left and right shoulders) and a lower low (inverted head) in the middle. Inverted head and shoulder is typically a bullish indicator. The selling pressure is getting exhausted, and buyers are stepping in. It is an indication of bottom and possibility of sizable upward movement after the completion of the pattern.

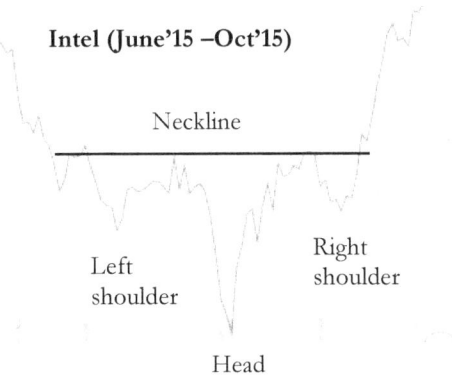

Fig. 16.15   **Inverted Head and Shoulder**

16.8 Cup and Handle

A cup and handle is a pattern that indicates bottoming out and good possibility of price breaking out on the higher side. The pattern has two parts, a cup and a handle. The left side of the cup forms when price starts to decline slowly but steadily. After reaching bottom, it starts to go back up again slowly. When it reaches the previous support level, the support acts as a resistance. The cup part of the pattern is now complete. The price goes down with a smaller drop and comes back up again to the previous support/resistance line completing the handle part of the pattern. When the cup and handle pattern formation is complete, there is a good chance that the price would go up to the projected target, the prior resistance.

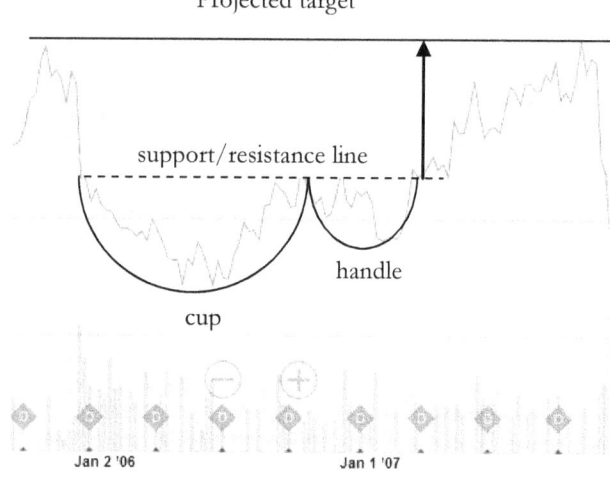

Fig. 16.16   Cup and Handle Pattern

16.9 Moving Averages

Moving averages intend to smooth out the daily price fluctuation of a stock price and provide a smoother (average) price over the last 50 days, 100 days, or 200 days. The commonly used averages are the 50-day moving average and the 200-day moving average. Average is also classified into simple average and exponential average. Simple average gives equal weightage to the price of all the days in calculating the average. Exponential average, on the other hand, puts more weightage to the price of recent days.

Moving average is a lagging indicator as it also considers the past price that may be quite different from the current price. However, it provides an overall trend in the stock price, uptrend, downtrend, or flat - the longer the average duration, the more the lag. For example, the 200-day moving average lags the 50-day moving average. The 50-day moving average is the better choice for finding out the medium-term trend; the 200-day moving average is the better choice for figuring out the longer-term trend.

16.9.1   50-day and 200-day Moving Average

Below is an example of 50-day and 200-day moving averages - Apple stock (as of April 2016).

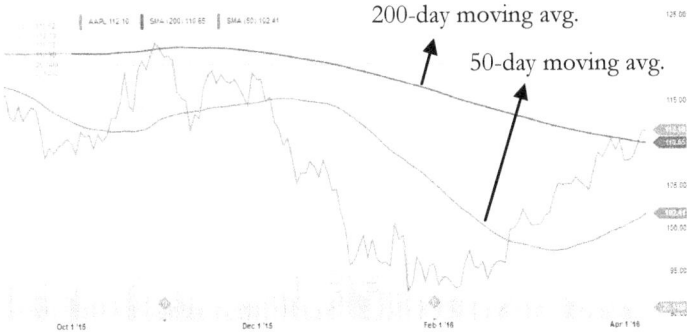

Fig. 16.17   50-day, 200-day Simple Moving Averages

16.9.2   Usage of Moving Averages

Moving averages are lagging indicators meaning they tell what happened in the past and do not directly predict future price. So, are they useful to investors to make buy/sell decisions? One of the benefits is that they filter out anomalies, such as sudden drop due to market scare (flash crash) or a rumor about a company. They establish medium-term and long-term trends of the stock price which can be useful if you are thinking medium term or long term. An interesting point is the 50-day and the 200-day average crossover. When the 50-day average crosses above the 200-day average, it is considered a buy signal, and when the 50-day moving average crosses below the 200-day average, it is considered a sell signal. As an investor, you should not make your decision based on only one indicator – it is just one of the many considerations that go into making the final decision.

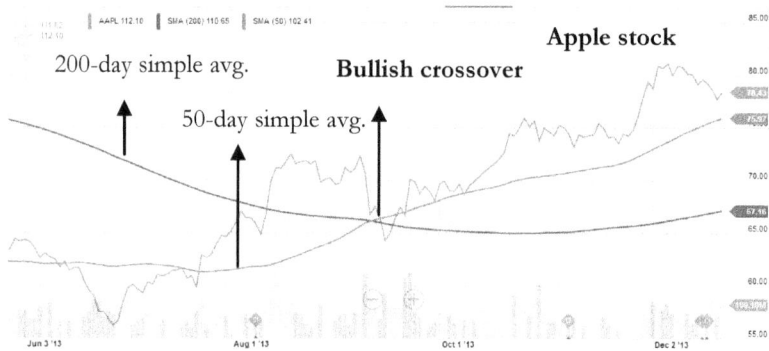

Fig. 16.18   50-day Avg Crossover - above 200-day MA

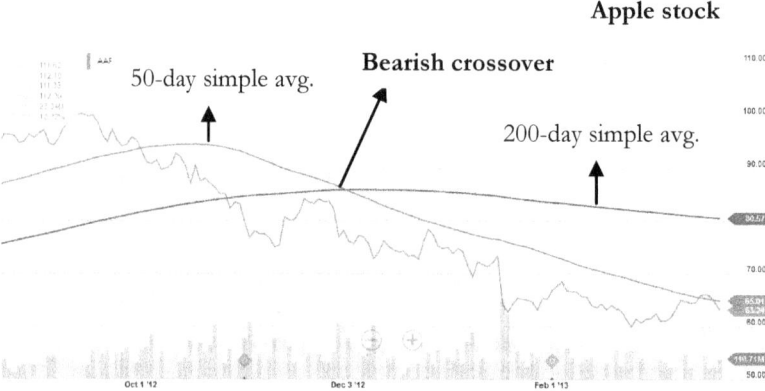

Fig. 16.19   50-day Avg Crossover - below 200-day MA

16.10   Bollinger Bands

Bollinger band was developed by John Bollinger, an American author, financial analyst, and trader in 1980s. It is a band graph with an upper line and a lower line formed by plotting points, two standard deviation away from the simple moving average stock price over a period of typically 20 days. Standard deviation is a measurement of volatility. The band widens during higher volatility in stock price and narrows when volatility abates. When the stock price touches or moves close to the upper band line, it is considered a sell signal. When the price touches or moves close to the lower band line, it is an indication of future price rise and is considered a buy signal. Like all indicators, use it with other indicators and considerations to make the final buy, sell, or hold decision.

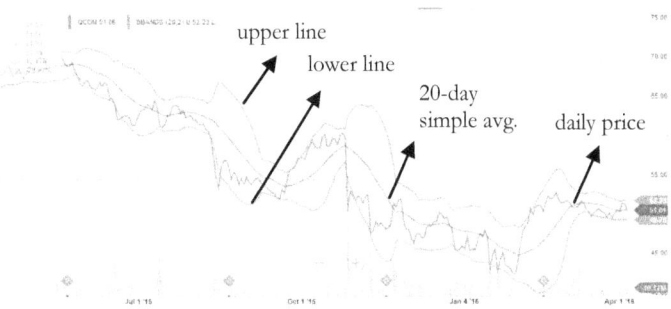

Fig. 16.20   Bollinger Band: Qualcomm

17 The Game Plan

17.1 Strategies to Make Money in Stocks

It is not necessary that there is only one or two ways to do well in stock market. We are going to explore a few of them in this chapter. But, the key is that you need understand these strategies well and use them appropriately depending on the market condition. You live through them and gain experience over the years to trust them. After a few years of working through them, you will get an idea what works and what does not. Depending on the market cycle or the phase of the market (are you at the beginning phase of a bull market or at the peak of a bull market?), you can change your strategy accordingly. For example, if it is the beginning of a bull phase after a bad bear market, you should invest all your cash, use margin and any cash you could get to buy good stocks cheaply. On the contrary, if you are in the peak phase of a bull market, you should take profits and keep some percentage in cash. You should not use margin money at the peak phase of a bull market unless you want to add more of a solid stock that has been beaten down badly and is currently screaming cheap.

17.2 Buy Low and Sell High

This is the most basic of strategies. This sounds very simple on the surface but may not be easy in real life – easier said than done. What is low, and what is high? We, generally, consider stock price low when it is well below the all-time high and consider it high, when it is at or near all-time high. If a stock was trading at $40 six months back, it must be low now to buy at $20. This may be true or may not be true. Just looking at the price is not the right strategy. If the fundamentals (management, balance sheet, cash flow, P/E, and dividends) of the company are poor, it becomes very risky to buy even at 50% of all-time high. You may have heard the saying, "catching a falling knife." It is quite possible that the stock price could move to $10 or even $5 in next several quarters. There is no floor for the price, and you could lose most of the investments in this company. It is pure speculation and cannot be a strategy for steady success.

However, if the fundamentals are very strong and the company has the staying power but is going through temporary lean phase, this is a good time to buy shares. When you start taking position in a company, always be ready to buy more if the price falls, may be another 10% -20%. I consider it as an entry point when the price has fallen 30%-40% from the recent peak. If a good stock starts falling from the peak, do not enter when it is down by just 10%-15% with a big position. If it is on a downtrend, it could fall further (30%-40%) before it starts rebounding. It is also quite possible that it will never go down by 30%-40% and recovers after falling just 10%-15%. Do not feel bad about it or sweat over it. Look for another stock, and you will find many good opportunities. You just need to be patient.

When is the price high to sell it? It is one of the most difficult decisions to make. If it is a growth stock or a momentum stock, it can appreciate very handsomely – 100%, 200%, or may be more. If you were lucky and smart enough to have bought it when it was low, you can hold it while it is going up. However, depending on overall market conditions, you should take profit, at least for part of it. If it is a stock with strong fundamentals that you bought cheap, look at the phase of the overall market before deciding to sell. If it is the beginning of a bull market, you can hold it for several years into the bull upward movement. There is a good chance that stock will appreciate very handsomely. You find these kinds of opportunities only once in six to eight years, and you do not want to let these go by. On the other hand, if you are in the peak bull phase where the market is moving sideways for several quarters or years, the stock, most likely, is not going to appreciate another 100%. It is quite likely that stock will easily bounce back 15%-25% from the low and stays there indefinitely. In this case, take this 15%-25% profit and find another stock. This 15%-25% gain can happen in a few weeks or months. Do not worry about short-term versus long-term gain – just take the profit and move on to another stock. If you wait for a year, it might be back to where you bought. It is better to pay tax at a higher rate on short-term gain than waiting to pay less tax and lose the gain in its entirety or most of it.

CHAPTER 17 The Game Plan

17.3 Buy and Hold

Let us put some of the famous quotes, and then, we will discuss what we can learn from these.

> "If you aren't thinking about owning a stock for ten years, don't even think about owning it for ten minutes." — **Warren Buffett**

> "Buy when everyone else is selling and hold until everyone else is buying. That's not just a catchy slogan. It's the very essence of successful investing." – **J. Paul Getty**

Warren Buffett, the legendary investor, buys good companies at reasonable price and holds them as long as the fundamentals justify holding them. Most good companies have done well over the years with increasing revenue, EPS, and dividends growth. It makes sense to hold them. If you sell a good stock, you have to find a better one to replace it. This kind of thinking requires that you pick your stocks based on fundamentals. For Buffett, it is a very efficient model to manage billions of dollars of investment. I call him the most efficient investor. He holds stocks for very long time and does not shuffle very often. Another advantage is that most of his gains are on paper, and he is not paying tax yet. Even when he pays, it is at lower long-term rate.

Individual investors can follow Buffett model to buy and then hold for a long time, or they can adopt some variation to this. You can hold stocks that you bought during the start of a bull phase, but you may change the strategy when bull market is at the peak. For the last several years (2014-2016), the stock market is moving mostly sideways. It has attempted to go down but has come back. The net gain is not much; it is almost flat. In this kind of environment, you could take advantage of the local ups and downs to keep making money (10%- 20%) while the overall market stays flat. In this case, holding forever does not make sense. One of the advantages for individual investors compared to big hedge funds or mutual funds is that it is easy to buy and sell stocks due to smaller number of stocks involved. For a matured stock that has gone up 15-20% in a flat market, it is unlikely to have similar gain in near future. It is time to take profit and find the next best alternative. In a flat market, holding a stock for more than a year seems like a long time. The more frequently you can achieve 10-20% gain in a year, the better your overall returns would be.

What about Paul Getty's quote above? It makes sense to pick up fundamentally good stocks when everyone is panicking. Even very good stocks become available cheaply when the overall market is down. When do you sell them to realize profit? As the bull market picks up, more people will know about it, and people will start coming back. Do not sell your stock yet! When everyone starts buying, it means there is a tremendous buying pressure that will drive the price way up. After the stock moved into deep overvalued territory, it is the time to sell and realize profit.

17.4 Invest for Growth

All companies need to have some growth to achieve good stock price appreciation. Established and large companies typically do not grow too fast, but companies with new technology, ideas, and innovating products are rewarded for their hyper-growth and future potential rather than their current earnings. The P/E ratios of such companies are very high. This generally happens in the beginning phase of a new technology. Many companies get hyper appreciation, but when the dust settles in a few years, many are gone. There are plenty of such examples. Also, there are plenty of examples where people bought early, held onto it, and made a killing. The appreciations for early investors in hyper-growth companies are sky-high, gaining several hundred percentages in a few years. Such is the allure that it pulls a lot of people into these stocks pushing the stock even higher. However, many jump in at the peak and lose a lot when the stock nosedives. So, how do we formulate a plan to hit these jackpots while not losing our shirts? I am not sure if there is such a plan out there. Is it pure luck? May be, but may be, you can increase your odds. We will take a stab at it.

When something very new or innovative is happening, research the companies thoroughly, and pick the top one or two that you believe are going to be successful. **Invest early.** Do not be the ones to get in when everyone else is taking about it. By this time, the stock price is already very high and risk increases significantly. Do not put a sizable portion of your investment into these high-potential high-risk companies. It is like risk money that could grow many fold, but you might lose it completely and still be OK. You do not want to lose a significant portion of your assets. If your picks are the top performers and you see that they are able to grow, keep the stocks, as they are likely to appreciate even more. If you think that it was a fad, there are signs of weakness, or the product is not living up to its expectations, sell the stock (at least part of it) and lock in your profits. On the contrary, if the investment turns out to be a dud, do not feel terrible about it. Think you are a sport and wanted to play the games knowing that results could go either way. At least, you will not have the lingering doubts for the rest of your life that you did not play.

17.5 Buy High and Sell Higher

This is a strategy to buy stocks that have turned around and started moving up. Inertia of motion (momentum) applies well to stock price movement. When a company has turned around after a period of doldrums, the stock price goes up and keeps going higher for some time. Before we discuss this strategy, let us put the pros and cons of "buy low and sell high" strategy to contrast both. You can buy solid companies that are beaten down cheaply while they are down and wait for turnarounds or better results. This strategy is good, as you are not going to miss the sudden price appreciation. However, downside of this approach is that you could be too early to jump in (think about the oil slump in 2015-2016), and the stock may stay low for an extended period of time. Some of your stocks could be tied up without gain or stay at a loss longer than you anticipated. Buying high and selling higher aims to avoid the wait time.

At the beginning of a turnaround, you can buy a stock and ride to higher appreciation. The main advantage is that you have not waited and have not lost time. When you are buying, the bad news is behind, and the general expectation is that it is going to be good from here until something otherwise happens. However, there is a big caveat to this. The good results become evident only after quarterly results announcement or some big news about the company. Until then, you cannot be sure that the company is doing well or about to turn around. When the stock opens after a good quarterly result or a big news, it will open with 15-20% gain, and you missed it. That is the main drawback! The other thing is that stock price could stay at that level after a pop for quite some time or fall if the perceived turnaround was immature. However, in some cases, this can be start of price appreciation phase. What happens is that as more people hear about the news, they will jump into the stock, and momentum builds up. Though I believe that this is a good strategy to be successful in stock, I have not practiced this very much except occasionally. I generally buy solid companies when they are down and wait for better results. Sometimes, I have to wait longer, and sometimes, I get my rewards shortly. If you look at the stock price of a good company, you would notice a few 10-20% changes in a year.

17.6 Dollar Cost Averaging

Dollar Cost Averaging (DCA) is an investment strategy where you buy stocks in fixed intervals (every two weeks or once in a month) with a fixed amount of money. The goal, as the name implies, is to buy the stocks at an average price over a period of time. The stock market and individual stocks keep fluctuating over time. Since it is very difficult to time the market, you could end up investing a significant amount at the peak if you put a big lump sum. DCA avoids that, and you buy when the price is high or low, irrespectively. This is a relatively safe strategy, but you should still pick your stocks carefully and with fundamental analysis. DCA is not going to protect you from incurring heavy loss if you are buying speculative stocks or falling knives. Another way to protect from buying a bad stock or stocks is to buy index funds using DCA approach.

The other thing you need to be mindful is the amount of commission. Though commissions have come down significantly ($7 per trade) in recent years, it depends on the transaction amount of your order. Even $7 commission can be a non-trivial percentage of the principal. In this case, may be, make your interval longer (every 5 to 6 weeks instead of every 2 to 4 weeks) so that you have more money. However, there is one place where the commission with respect to the transaction size does not matter. In 401K account invested in mutual funds, the commission is based on the portfolio balance, not on the number of transactions. You are going to pay the same fees if you invested $5K in ten or twenty separate transactions.

Who should follow Dollar cost averaging, and is it the best method? What I would say is that it is a middle-of-the-road approach or an average approach. It may protect you from severe downside but limits your gains to be average. While we are protecting ourselves from bad timing, we are also prohibiting from gaining from good timing. A savvy investor uses timing to his or her advantage and is not scared of it. Investing heavily during severe downturns or investing in a stock when it is badly beaten, you can generate outsized returns. It takes time to understand how the stock market works, and you need to be excited about it. If it is not something that you enjoy or have time for, dollar cost averaging is a safer and a better choice.

17.7 Averaging Down

Another form of averaging is averaging down that many successful investors do. You keep buying when the stock price goes down further. Let us say, you bought some stocks at$40. Buy some more at $35. If it goes down to $30, which is probably into deep undervalued territory, you buy even more. When the price goes up to $40, you broke even for the lot you bought at $40 but made 14% gain on the lot you bought at $35 and 33% gain on the lot you bought at $30. If it goes above $40, you even make higher gain. However, you need to make good fundamental analysis before you put more money or buying a stock for the first time.

I regularly employ averaging down strategy with fundamentally good stocks (could be large cap, mid-cap, or small-cap), and it has been my most effective strategy. Here is why and how it works. Because, I choose the stocks that are fundamentally strong and enter only when they are down 30-40%, the downside risk is very low. Roughly 50% of the time, the stocks drop further after I buy. However, before I start entering into a position, I always keep some cash to buy more if it falls. In some cases, I sell some other stocks where I am positive and move the money to shore up the temporary losers. Another important thing is that I start with a smaller percentage 2-3% of the portfolio so that I have room to add more if it goes down further. If I was convinced that the stock was good at $40, it is even more attractive at $30. I make most of my profit from stocks on the way back from the bottoms.

However, averaging down works only with stocks that are fundamentally solid with strong balance sheets and cash positions. Averaging down a bad stock is a costly mistake that many inexperienced investors do. Sometimes even with your best analysis and conviction, the stock price keeps falling. This happens if overall market is in a downtrend or short-sellers are after this stock. You need to take a breather. If you are already invested in this stock with a sizable percentage of your portfolio, the best option is to hold and not add any new shares. This is just what if, and you do not want to increase risk beyond certain point. Conviction is the greatest asset to make money, but you should have a gut feel to say no at some point.

17.8 Dogs of the Dow

This is a strategy to rebalance your portfolio every yearend. You replace the lowest dividend-yielding DOW stocks in your portfolio with the highest-yielding DOW stocks. This works as follows. Most DOW companies pay dividends and increase dividends steadily over the years. They suddenly do not have a large dividend increase in a year. Dividend yield is the amount of dividend payments divided by the share price. Since the actual dividend amount does not increase much in a year, a low dividend yield implies that stock price has appreciated significantly. Similarly, if the yield has shot up, it is most likely due to big drop in stock price.

The low-yielding stocks have appreciated handsomely but are unlikely to repeat similar performance in the next year. On the other hand, high-yielding stocks have fallen to very attractive levels and are likely to appreciate in the next year. By swapping the low-yielding, high-performing stocks with high-yielding, low-performing stocks, you are increasing the probability of better results next year.

Another benefit is that you are able to buy the high-yielding stocks at a bargain price and collect handsome dividends. While you are collecting dividends, the high dividend yield provides support and prevents these stocks from further big fall.

17.9 Investing in Index

Stocks have historically provided very good returns. There are short-term ups and downs, but the stock indices have moved up over the long run. Below is the DOW graph for 20 years (1995-2014). In this 20-year period, DOW Jones has provided annualized returns of 9.3%. If you include the dividends, it would be a couple of percent more, making the total average annual return to be 11.3%.

DOW Jones – 1995-2014

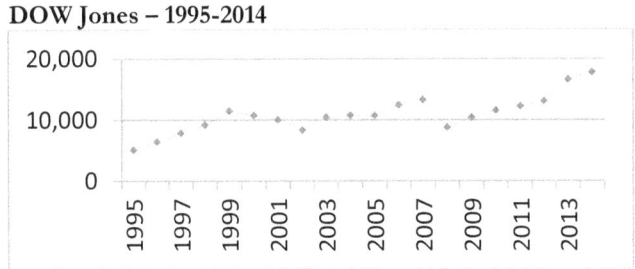

The most widely known stock indices are the DOW 30, S&P 500, and NASDAQ. There are other indices such Russel 2000 and Wilshire 5000.

DOW – DJIA (Dow Jones Industrial Average)

DOW consists of 30 stocks that represent the most important companies from various sectors of the economy. The list of companies is not fixed. New companies are added, and some companies are removed from the list from time to time. Here is the current list if DOW 30 companies.

(source http://www.cnbc.com/dow-components/)

Symbol	Name	Symbol	Name	Symbol	Name
AXP	American Express Co	HD	Home Depot Inc.	NKE	Nike Inc.
AAPL	Apple Inc.	IBM	International Business Machines Corp	PFE	Pfizer Inc.

BA	Boeing Co	INTC	Intel Corp	PG	Procter & Gamble Co
CAT	Caterpillar Inc.	JNJ	Johnson & Johnson	TRV	Travelers Companies Inc.
CSCO	Cisco Systems Inc.	KO	Coca-Cola Co	UNH	UnitedHealth Group Inc.
CVX	Chevron Corp	JPM	JPMorgan Chase and Co	UTX	United Technologies Corp
DD	E I du Pont de Nemours and Co	MCD	McDonald's Corp	VZ	Verizon Communications Inc.
XOM	Exxon Mobil Corp	MMM	3M Co	V	Visa Inc.
GE	General Electric Co	MRK	Merck & Co Inc.	WMT	Walmart Stores Inc.
GS	Goldman Sachs Group Inc.	MSFT	Microsoft Corp	DIS	Walt Disney Co

Fig. 17.1   DOW Components

S&P 500 (Standard and Poor 500)

It consists of a much larger number (500) of companies compared to DJIA that has only 30 companies. It also represents close to 70% of the US economy; hence a better representative of the overall health of the economy.

Wilshire 5000

It consists of almost all public companies (5000 of them) in the US. However, more people know about S&P than Wilshire 5000.

NASDAQ

NASDAQ is known for technology stocks though the index includes companies from other sectors as well. NASDAQ also includes many new tech companies.

Russel 2000

It consists of 2000 small companies in the US.

How do the indices move?

Many times, all the indices move up or down (the percentage change is not necessarily same) in sync representing the overall direction of the market. In such scenarios, most of the stocks gain while market goes up or most take a hit when the indices go down. However, sometimes, they move in opposite direction (typically NASDAQ and DOW/S&P), or there is no discernible pattern among the indices. In such cases, it is the individual stocks for that day that caused the price movement in a particular index without an overall direction for the economy.

How does buying index work?

Investors can buy ETF (Exchange Traded Fund) specific to a particular index. Refer to section 22.2 that describes how ETFs work. There are also index mutual funds. Some of the widely known index ETFs are SPY (SPDR S&P 500), VXX (S&P 500 VIX short-term Futures ETN), IWM (iShares Russel 2000 ETF), SDS (UltraShort S&P 500), and DIA (Dow Jones Industrial ETF). Some examples of index funds are FBCVX (a Fidelity blue chip value fund consisting of companies in S&P 500 and DOW), FBGRX (a Fidelity blue chip growth fund consisting of growth oriented companies from S&P500 and DOW).

Who should invest in Index?

As we have discussed elsewhere in the book, investing in index removes the risk of bad timing while it produces average return. It is an excellent choice for people who do not have a keen interest in knowing how stocks work or do not want to spend time analyzing stocks. It is also for people who are just starting out in the investment world and do not have a lot of experience and expertise yet. However, it is quite possible with experience and dedication to generate better returns by picking individual stocks rather than investing in indices.

17.10   Sell High Buy Lower (Shorting)

Selling high now and buying later is a strategy where you believe that the stock is overpriced now and going to go down in future. It is also called shorting. It is opposite of buying low selling high. Selling shorts has some inherent rewards and risks that we will discuss. Sometimes, a stock will skyrocket to dizzying height in a short span due to momentum buying which happens when everyone is after a hot stock. Then, it stalls, as there is no more positive news left to propel it higher. When it stops moving higher and coasts sideways, investors that are sitting with a huge profit will start selling and take profit. If you believe that the stock is at an idling point and does not have any ammunition left for further upward push, it can be a point to short the stock in anticipation that it is going to fall in future.

Another scenario is that the stock is simply overvalued and risky. The valuation is based on many assumptions that are not realistic. If your analysis and judgement convinces you that this is the case, it can be a point to short the stock. Another scenario is that a stock is overvalued by measures, such as very high P/E ratio and high market cap, and suddenly there is unfavorable news about the company. The stock price crashes, and one can short quickly hoping that negative sentiments and downward momentum will drive it further down. Next, let us discuss the mechanism of shorting.

In shorting a stock, you do not need to have the stock to sell it, which is different from going longs when you have to put the money upfront to buy the stocks. In shorting, you are selling a stock (in paper), and you are required to buy the stock within a certain period in future. If the stock price falls in future, you would realize the difference between selling and buying price minus the transaction costs as your profit. If it goes the other way, you have a net loss, and that amount of money will be deducted from your brokerage account. For shorting a stock, you do not need the full amount of money to sell and buy the stocks. You need to have enough money in your account for the broker to cover if there is a loss. It is considered as an advantage of shorting to be able to do larger transaction with relatively smaller amount of money. I consider it a form of risky leverage rather than an advantage. What are the risks of shorting a stock?

Risk of shorting

The main risk element is the time that is racing against you. If the share price goes up rather than going down, you need to cover your short position. It is also called a short squeeze. You have two options – you can cover the shorts with a loss, or you can rollover to a future date. But, rolling over to future, you are taking additional risk. The loss could be higher than the loss you have at this point. It is a difficult decision, and you lost money in either case. In going longs, you can wait as long as you want (when you are convinced that the stock is going to rebound eventually), and the loss is only a paper loss, as you have not sold it. However, in shorting a stock, you have to buy it back, and the loss is permanent. It is inherently very risky. It is quite possible that your analysis was correct, but the market is behaving opposite to your analysis and prediction, for whatever reason. You will be forced to cover your positions and take the loss.

Many hedge funds adopt a long and short strategy. They have the resources to do research and collect relevant information about a company to take short positions. In spite of all the research, they still have risk. Sometimes, even big hedge funds lose big on going shorts. I, personally, have not done shorting (it may change in future). I have nothing against it, but I feel it is risky for individual investors. My strategy has been going longs. In general, I believe that good companies with strong fundamentals will wither out the lean phase and eventually come out winner. I can wait out the lean phase and won't be forced to sell at a loss, which I cannot afford to do if my analysis proved to be wrong after I shorted a stock.

17.11   Diversify but Don't Overdo It

"Wide diversification is only required when investors do not understand what they are doing." – **Warren Buffett**

"Don't put all your eggs in one basket"

On one end of the diversification spectrum is putting all your investment into one stock; on the other extreme end is buying hundreds of companies. Putting all your eggs in one basket or putting all your investments in one stock is very risky, and there is no need to assume this risk. You may very well be convinced that this is the stock and nothing can go wrong with the company; you are in complete love with the company. You may be right, but do you really want to assume this huge risk? What if something bad happens (management impropriety, scandal, big accident, or simply you were wrong in your analysis)? It could prove to be financially disastrous. You can go overweight on a company from time to time but never put 100% into one stock. Besides, there are other stocks available with similar value propositions and prospects. Next question is, how much diversification is optimal?

Research shows that diversification after around 20 companies does not eliminate risk any further. It means holding stocks of one hundred companies provides similar risk protection as holding 20 companies in your portfolio. The gain will average out as you hold more and more stocks; they counterbalance one another and eliminate the highs and lows to produce average results. Also, it is practically not possible for an individual investor to perform quality research on so many companies and follow these companies well. Index (DOW, S&P, and NASDAQ etc.) is the ultimate form of diversification as it keeps a sample of all possible stocks in that field. Buying index funds may be the right strategy when someone is not interested about stock market operation or does not have the time. Also, it may be an OK strategy in the beginning part of investing career as you are learning on the job. As you gain more experience, expertise and feel more comfortable, you can gradually move away from index investing to take complete charge of your portfolio. When you have stocks in 20 companies rather than investing in index, you are ready to use your arbitrage advantage (experience, analytical skills, expertise) to make better gains than the indices - nothing wrong with that, and this is what many savvy investors do.

CHAPTER 17   The Game Plan

I, generally, keep 15 to 25 stocks in my portfolio. I have kept this number not because it was proven to be the optimum number by research but because I found it to be practical for me as an individual investor. I do a lot of research about the companies that I am interested in, consider all publicly available analysis and information before making my final decision. Fifteen to twenty-five is a practical number that I can digest while having a regular job. Another thing is that, it leaves me money to buy more shares at a lower price (averaging down good companies) when the portfolio is not too diverse. Next, we will discuss about diversification among sectors and asset class.

Look at you portfolio to see if you are diversified among sectors within your portfolio. There are different sectors, such as technology, internet companies, finance, commodities, and drug companies. Check if the portfolio is heavily tilted to one or two sectors. Let us say, you like certain sectors, or you are more knowledgeable about certain sectors. It makes sense to choose those sectors over the others that you are not familiar with or not comfortable with. You do not have to own stocks in all sectors. Within a sector, if you find two or three companies with very similar prospects and fundamentals, it is a good idea to spread the investment in that sector rather than buying one stock in that sector.

Then, there are national and international companies or investing in other countries. There is nothing right or wrong here. If you are not comfortable and knowledgeable about companies or laws of other countries, it is fine to focus in your own country. How about diversifying among small cap, medium cap, and large cap companies? Small cap stocks tend to be more volatile, meaning the gain/loss is much higher compared to large cap and med cap companies. Medium cap companies lie in the middle with medium risks and rewards. Large cap companies, in general, are more stable and do not have wide price swings. They tend to have smaller gains (15-25%) with a lower risk of losing a lot. It is typical to have 100% gain in a small company or 70-80% loss of capital in a small cap company. You are likely to get 15-25% gain from a large cap company but unlikely to suffer a 70-80% loss of capital.

I typically buy large cap and medium cap DOW, S&P, and NASDAQ companies. But, when I find a fundamentally strong but undervalued small cap company, I buy that too. Another observation I want to bring forth here is the relative performance among small, medium, and large companies during market peak and market trough. When overall market goes down from peaks, growth and small cap companies typically fall faster than large cap companies do. Similarly, when the market recovers, the small cap companies rise much faster than the large caps. So, if you are investing after a big downturn, you may want to shift weight to good small and medium cap companies. To summarize about diversification, the main takeaway is that you need to diversify but do not have to buy every sector, or stock from every countries. There are thousands of companies. You just need to buy 15 to 25 companies that you understand well to be successful.

Diversifying Among Different Asset Classes

There are many places to invest your money, such as stocks, bonds, mutual funds, savings accounts, gold, and real estate. Should one diversify in these asset classes or focus on one or two core areas of expertise? It depends. It depends on may factors, such as current market condition, interest rate, state of the economy, person's own experience in investing, willingness to take risk, and age. The interest rate has been very low for a while now, and it may not go up significantly any time soon. The rate of return on regular savings is close to zero, and even the yield on 10-yr Treasury note is less than 2% (April 2016). It is almost impossible to eke out any meaningful gain investing in savings account, CDs, or short-term bonds. Junk bonds or high-yield bonds provide higher returns (6 to 9%), but they are inherently risky. When no-risks investments, such as CDs, federal bonds provided 4-5% returns, it was a choice of investments for many risk-averse investors. So, where do we put our money in very low interest environment?

Before you do anything, build an emergency liquid fund (6 months of living expenses when both spouses are working and 9-12 months of living expenses when only one spouse is working). There is nothing scientific about these numbers, but it provides a reasonable buffer to get into a good job if you lose your job. Have this money available in the form of cash (saving account, or 3-6 month CD). The idle cash might be a non-performing asset, but this gives enough peace of mind so that you can focus on other important stuffs. After you have built an emergency buffer, you can focus on investing money to grow. If you are retired or close to retiring, it makes sense to invest some money in Treasury bonds and good corporate bonds (they generally provide a little better return than government bonds).   However, once retired, it does not automatically mean that you move everything away from stocks into CDs and bonds. If you have built a good net worth and money is not a problem, you should still consider stocks, as stocks would potentially generate better returns. Your children and grandchildren will be happy.

If you are young starting out your career, you have a lot of time in your favor but do not have any substantial experience in investing yet. You can invest some in index, mutual funds, and real estate. But, you should start investing in stocks and gain valuable experience in investing in stock. It is definitely required to read books and learn the fundamentals but nothing like real experience. When you are dealing with real money, the fear of loss might paralyze you, and it could be terrifying. But, as you gain more experience and live through market cycles, you will feel more confident. Investing is a feedback loop that constantly provides feedback to your investment decisions. As you gain these valuable experiences and build confidence, you can move more and more toward investing in stocks and managing it yourself. Done correctly and with high level of self-discipline, an individual investor can generate high returns in the stock market.

17.12   Opportunistic Play

To be a successful investor over the long run, you need to have a strategy (one from this chapter or have your own). How about tactical opportunities that you come across or something you should actively look for? Great players exploit tactical situations while they are executing a strategy to achieve great results. Let us try to quantify some of these in this section and see if these make sense.

Keeping an eye for possible merger and acquisition

When a small or mid-cap company is acquired by a larger company, the share price of the small company gets a big overnight boost. Merger of two large companies, generally, is not that interesting from the perspective of share price appreciation. It is the small and mid-size companies that provide the sudden windfall. To be able to anticipate that such an acquisition is likely to happen, you need to be an expert in that area and know the nerve of the industry. If a company has a very compelling product and the market cap is not very high yet, it may be an acquisition target. If the market cap is very high, even a large competitor won't be ready to put down such a large amount of cash unless the big company is in existential threat.

The other scenario is when a good company is struggling because of a particular sector is down, or the overall economy is down. The stock price is at a very depressed level for some time now. This is the time when a large company could acquire the small company mainly because it is affordable, and the small company brings value to the large company.

You can also look at other subtle signs that are available and try to connect the dots. When two companies are working as partners for some time now and the partnership is going good, there is some likelihood that the big one could acquire the smaller one. It is like dating before tying the knots. A fresh example is Altera and intel. Altera and intel had a close relationship were Altera used intel's leading-edge fabs to manufacture its chips. Intel acquired Altera subsequently. When you are trying to connect the dots, look at the acquisition or merger through the lens of antitrust issues. If there is a good possibility of limiting consumers' choice, the merger or acquisition may not go through. A recent example is Staples buying Office Depot. When SEC blocked the deal citing antitrust issues, Office Depot lost 40% of its value in a single day. There are other subtle indications as well. When a company is shedding non-core assets and adding core-assets through smaller acquisitions, it is an indication that it is preparing to put itself for acquisition. Keep your eyes and years open. There are clues out there in open public domain, and if you can connect the dots, it could be very profitable.

17.13   Dividends-based Investments

Dividend-based investment strategy aims to preserve capital while generating steady income through dividend payments. It can be an appropriate strategy for retired people who do not want to take large risk and needs steady cash flow to supplement their livings. However, there is never zero risk in stocks. For retirees, this strategy will work if they do not need to sell stocks to meet their living requirements. If they need to sell stocks to raise money regularly, investing in risk assets such as stocks could be financially risky for them. However, if they are well enough otherwise and just need regular cash flow, dividend-based stock investments could be a right strategy. It can also be an appropriate strategy for investors who are risk-averse while they want to generate steady returns compared to the very low returns offered by savings and federal bonds today.

The stocks that fit the profile of good dividend yields (3 to 5%) and low price volatility are large established companies, utility, and telecom companies. Some matured tech companies also offer respectable yields. Utilities and large established companies generate a steady profit, and they are not growing that much. They are left with the profit that they distribute as dividends to shareholders. These companies typically have a strong balance sheet, steady income, and positive cash flow. The dividend is financed through the profit but not from dipping into the balance sheet. Typically, the stock price neither appreciates nor depreciates by a wide percentage. The steady and good dividend yield acts as a support and prevents from falling too much. However, the lack of growth limits price appreciation to very modest numbers.

A Note of Caution

Do not buy a stock, just because the dividend yield looks so attractive. Analyze fundamentals and make sure that it is a good company irrespective of the dividends. Check if the yield has been steady or has gone up sharply recently due to big price drop. If the yield has gone up to 6-10%, it can be risky. It indicates that the company is most likely struggling. Look under the hood to see what is going on. A sudden big spike in yield is a precursor of dividend cut in not-so distant future. Having said that, do not get scared just because the yield is very high. Check if the company is good with strong and quality balance sheet (loan is low to moderate, good cash position, no short-term cash flow problem, assets are not obsolete, loss is expected to stabilize in near future, and the company starts making profit in next few quarters) and has the power to survive. This could be an opportunity to get a solid bargain. Even if the dividends are going to be cut, it could still yield at 3-4% after the cut. In some cases, the management may decide to eliminate the dividends completely, just to survive; which may be the right thing to do. Leaving dividends aside, the stock price could be very attractive at this point.

18 Give Me a Place, I will Move the Earth

> Give me a place to stand and with a lever, I will move the whole world.
> — Archimedes

> You only find out who is swimming naked, when the tide goes out.
> — Warren Buffett

> Opportunities come infrequently. When it rains gold, put out the bucket, not the thimble.
> — Warren Buffett

18.1 Using Leverage in Stocks

Caution: Leverage is a double-edge sword. Done right could be very profitable, and done the wrong way will be financially ruinous. Many lost their homes during 2008-09 housing crash, and many long-time financial institutions (Lehman brothers, Washington Mutual, Countrywide) became instantly extinct because of too much borrowing and too much leverage.

Leverage means borrowing money to invest and possibly make profit. To make a net profit, the gain from the investment must be higher than the interest you have to pay for borrowing the money. If you were to find a secured investment where the returns and the principal are guaranteed and it pays a higher return than the interest you have to pay, the decision would be simple. Borrow as much as you can and make a secured profit. Unfortunately, such a thing is not available.

You have to invest money in stocks or other assets that have inherent risks where the principal could lose value. Stocks provide the possibility of higher returns than the margin interest payment and the possibility of making profit.

The stocks could lose value where you would be required to not only pay back the original principal you borrowed but also the interest on the principal. The loss could magnify. The goal in this chapter is not to scare you or encourage you to leverage but discuss the possibility of making bigger profits with your investments. Two forms of leverage are the margin money and home equity line of credit.

18.2 Mechanics of Margin

Let us work through some examples to understand how margin could magnify your gain or magnify your loss.

Ex1: Gain is magnified

You bought 500 shares of a company at $20 per share. The total price you paid is $10,000. We are keeping the commission out of the calculations to make it simple. You also borrowed $4,000 from your margin account to buy additional 200 shares at $20 per share. You have to pay interest on the margin money at 6%. At the end of three months, the stock price has appreciated to $25 (price has gone up by 25%) when you decided to sell all 700 shares to book your profit. Let us calculate the profit and the return…

Sale price of 700 shares = 700x$25 = $17,500

The interest on three months would be I = P x R x T = $4,000x0.06x0.25 = $60.

Total gain = $17,500 - $10,000 - $4,000 - $60 =$3,440

Summary:
- Using margin, you made a profit of $3,440 by investing $10,000 of your money. Your gain: 34.4%
- If you did not use margin money, you would have made $2,500 with $10,000 investment. Your gain: 25%
- Margin provided additional 9.4% gain.

Ex2: Loss is magnified

Let us keep the same example, but the stock price has depreciated when you decided to sell. You bought 500 shares of a company at $20 per share. The total price you paid is $10,000. You also borrowed $4,000 from your margin account to buy additional 200 shares at $20 per share. You have to pay interest on the margin money at 6%. At the end of **six months**, the stock price has fallen to $15 (price has gone down by 25%). For whatever reason, you decided to sell all 700 shares. Let us calculate the loss…

Sale price of 700 shares = 700x$15 = $10,500
The interest on six months would be I = P x R x T = $4,000x0.06x0.50 = $120
Total loss = $10,500 - $10,000 - $4,000 - $120 = - $3,620

Summary:

- Using margin, you had a loss of $3,620 by investing $10,000 of your money. Your loss: 36.2%
- If you did not use margin money, you would have lost $2,500 with $10,000 investment. Your loss: 25%
- Due to margin, you had additional loss of 11.2%.

18.3 Using Margin - General Guidelines

Here are some general guidelines on using margin.

- Do not use margin for the first several years of your investment career until you get a good understanding of the market and live through some of your decisions.
- Do not use margin on risky bets that are highly volatile and speculative. The loss could be dramatic.
- Do not use margin at the peak or close to peak of a bull market. The chance of market going down is higher from a peak. Finding the exact peak is not always possible; you can judge it by looking at how the performance has been and if everybody else is treating it as the peak.
- Using margin at the bottom of a market is the safest and the most opportunistic position to make large gains. Even during down market, treat the margin money as your money. Always have a worst-case scenario and plan to deal with it. If the market were to go down even further and stay longer at that level, do you have the staying power without selling at big loss? Beaten-down Blue chip stocks with strong fundamentals are relatively safe even during a market crash. They also, in most cases, provide dividends that can offset some of the margin interest cost.
- Do not max out margin. Do not cross more than 50% to 60% of the money you have invested. If you have invested $100,000 in stocks, do not avail margin money more than $50,000 to $60,000.
- Always do fundamental analysis and look at margin of safety before buying stocks on margin.
- The margin interests are higher when the amount of margin loan is small, and rates come down gradually as amount of loan increases. You have to look at your individual position. When the margin rate is high, it

will require significant stock price appreciation to breakeven. It may not be cost-effective with small amount of margin loan. When your stakes in stock investment are higher with more money deployed, you will be at a level to avail larger margin money that is cost-effective.

- If you want to use margin money on specific stocks during market peak, be very careful in stock selection. It has to be a fundamentally solid stock where the price has gone down significantly and chance of going down further is less (look how it has stood up during previous market crashes). It should be paying a reasonable dividend. If you decide to use margin, total margin money should not be more than 25% to 40% of your investment money.

- In the beginning, use smaller amount of margin to get familiar and live through some of your decisions.

18.4 Home-equity Line of Credits (HELOC)

Home Equity Line of Credit is a type of loan that you can draw against, when you want and how much you want. Most people buy their primary home with some amount of down payment and rest as loan. The most popular loan is 30-yr fixed where you are going to pay off the loan in 30 years. Other loans, such as 15-yr fixed or adjustable rate loans are also available. Every month you have a home mortgage payment out of which, a part goes toward paying down principal and the rest toward the interest on the loan. In the beginning years, bigger part of the loan goes toward the interest payment, and smaller part goes toward the principal payment. As the years progress, more and more money goes toward the principal. Slowly and steadily, you build equity in your home. The equity also builds up when the price appreciates that typically happen in good areas.

When you have good equity in your home, can you and should you leverage it to invest in other assets? There are two types of loans - Home equity loan and home equity line of credits. Though both are based on the equity, there is a fundamental difference in flexibility in availing the money. Once home equity loan is granted, you have to take entire loan amount. If you have some specific purposes, such as children's education or buying investment properties, it may be a good idea. It is almost like another mortgage. You have to start paying interest on the loan for the entire amount from day one. On the contrary, with HELOC, you do not have to withdraw the entire amount. You can withdraw any amount within the limit and pay it back any time you want. There are no restrictions. You only pay interest on the outstanding balance for the period there is a balance. For example, if you balance is zero for 3 months, you do not pay any interest for these three months.

CHAPTER 18   Power of Leverage

HELOC provides this extraordinary flexibility. It provides a ready source of cash for emergency needs, or you can use it to invest in stocks when the time is right. When you have a good understanding of the market, know the risk-reward trade-off in the stock market, and are comfortable in taking risk to increase your returns, you may consider tapping the HELOC to invest in stocks. Granted it is your own money unlike the margin, which is borrowed money, but you still need to be an experienced investor to use it. I use the same guidelines of using margin money in using HELOC. Use it when the market is down, or a solid blue chip stock, that you want to buy, is down substantially.

What should you do if you have extra money after paying mortgage and other expenses? Should you invest them in stocks, or should you pay down the principal balance of the loan. Let us calculate the returns when you pay toward the principal. With the rate of 4.5% for a 30-yr fixed, you would save 4.5% by paying down the principal. You would get back approximately 1/3rd of that amount as tax deduction for mortgage interest. Therefore, the net savings is around 3%. This is guaranteed returns. What are the choices if you do not want to pay down the principal? If you invest in savings account or CD, you get 1% max. One third of that will go toward tax with a net gain of 0.7%. Paying down the principal is the clear winner. How about investing in stocks instead?

As we know, stock has its own risk and reward. Done right, stock investments can generate returns better than 4.5%. In the beginning phase, when you are in the process of understanding the stock market and gaining experience, it would be a good idea to split the savings into investing in stock and paying down mortgage principal. Paying down the principal helps in another way. When there is extra cash in hand, you are under pressure to generate reasonable returns on it. You do not want to sit idle on cash and generate very low returns from savings account or CDs. This pressure may lead you to buy stocks at the wrong time. Psychologically, it is just difficult to sit with idle cash. If you are paying down the principal, you are making guaranteed 2.3% net compared to savings account. On top of that, you can use it in the right time (during market downturn or when good stocks are down substantially). You are not under pressure to perform. Once the stock makes a reasonable gain, you can pay back the HELOC. Do not completely pay off the HELOC. Just keep a small balance so that it is open and available to you. To summarize, HELOC provides a very flexible source of funds that can generate sizable returns when deployed at the right time and on the right investment.

19 It is All in the Mind

19.1 Psychology and Personal Discipline

Investing, more than anything else, is a mind game. It requires a reasonable level of risk taking, personal discipline to resist the temptations for quick gain, mental fortitude to go against the crowd, confidence and patience to stay the course, humility and flexibility to admit a mistake, and a bit of luck.

19.2 Investing in Stocks Needs Risk Taking

To put it in a simple way, investing in stocks involves risks. No matter how smart one is or how prepared one is, there is always real chance of losing money. However, with preparation, dedicating time to understand how it works, and a game plan, there is a good possibility to make profits in the stock market. You have to play the game to win it. We all hate to lose money, but one has to overcome this mental barrier to take some risk and take the first step. Start with small, and analyze each buy or sell decision and learn from it.

19.3 Learn from Success as well as Failure

We are always happy when we win and make money in stocks. Try to understand why your decision was correct. The stock price constantly moves up or down based on new information. The stock price moves not just due to company specific information but moves in sync with economy and overall market. Check if the gain came because you had positioned yourself anticipating certain things would happen and it happened that way. Or, it happened completely due to something else you had not thought about. In such a case, be happy that you made money but consider such possibilities in your next decision.

After you constantly train your mind and gain experience, it will be your second nature to do these things effortlessly. Same thing goes when you lose money. Ouch, but you still need to learn what went wrong and you need to feed it back to make a better decision next time. Sometimes, even experienced players and experts go wrong, and you need to move on. To summarize, win or lose, use the experience and feed it back to the decision-making loop to make a better decision next time. In the beginning, I bought stocks by just looking at the price drop irrespective of fundamental analysis of the company, a case in point is Radio Shack. A lesson learned is that price itself is meaningless. First, it has to be a good company with a healthy margin of safety, and price comes next.

19.4 Stick to Your Game Plan

The great warriors and great investors always have a strategy they follow and stick to. As we have discussed, there are more than one strategy to be successful in stocks, but you need to stick to the one you understand and execute it without jumping all over the board. If your investment strategy is to buy only fundamentally strong and established companies when they are down 30-40%, stick to it. If they go down further after you take a position and fundamentals still look solid, do not sell them at a loss and move to another stock. You hold them or better yet, buy more at the lower price. If you desert it and sell it at a loss, the loss will become permanent. I am not sure what Warren Buffett meant by his famous quote, "Never sell at a loss," but I take it literally and always want to make money on a stock. I do not want to give in or give up easily before making a profit in a stock.

If your strategy is to invest in growth stocks, be the one to get in early when a new technology or trend is coming up and be prepared to lose money. If you jump in late, you may still make money, but chance of losing big also increases when things get clearer. Getting in early also has its risk, but the rewards are huge. If you have the knack to identify trend early and are good at picking the winners, the money you would make in a few successes will be much more than the loss you incur in others.

19.5 Think of Worst-case Scenario Beforehand

If you have thought about the worst case scenario and have a game plan for it, it will be much easier to sleep at night and make the right decision at the most difficult times. Otherwise, when market drops by 40-50%, it will be very agonizing, and you could very easily lose sleep over it. As an investor, you cannot go to cash 100% expecting that a crash is imminent. It may come tomorrow, or the market may continue to go up or move sideways for next several years. If you are sitting idle with all cash, you are going to lose returns for the next several years. Then after being away from the market and getting impatient as each day passes by, you would jump in big time, and then, the market crashes. On the contrary, if you are still invested and have some cash or margin money available, you know what to do when such a big crash happens. If your portfolio consists of good companies, they are more than likely to recover when the market recovers. You will not be tormented knowing that it is just paper loss and your portfolio will recover in due course. You are not going to sell these at a huge loss. You would be putting the cash and margin money to buy more stocks (same or new ones) and come out winning big when market recovers. Anticipating the worst-case scenario beforehand and being prepared for it, not only prevents from panicking but also helps to use the situation to your advantage.

19.6 Patience for the Right Moment

"I don't look to jump over seven-foot bars; I look around for one-foot bars that I can step over."   – Warren Buffett

"You don't have to swing at everything - you can wait for your pitch."

– Warren Buffett

Patience is a great virtue in the stock market. It has great relevance in both buy and sell decisions. One of the difficulties for investors is to sit with cash and not being invested in stocks. You have to have the patience for the one-foot bar to arrive rather than taking on the seven-foot bars. There are literally thousands of stocks, among which probably one hundred of them meet your investment criteria. But, they may not be available at the right price yet. If you have the patience, the stock market is going to offer you, may be, several of them at incredible price. With such bargains, you have already positioned yourself to win with lower risk.

It is better to wait a few months and buy at the right price than getting impatient and buying at higher price and seeing further drop in price. In the Baseball analogy, you do not have to swing at every ball – just wait for the right one. While making a sell decision, patience is required as well. Some companies need time to turnaround. If the fundamentals of a company continue to be good, it does not make sense to sell at a loss but to wait for the stock price to rebound.

19.7 Be Flexible when Required

Conviction and consistency are keys to success in the stock market. If you are convinced about your analysis and strategy, you would come out as a big winner when the market starts rewarding a stock its true worth. However, the conviction should not become stubbornness when things are just not going your way in spite of the best analysis. Humility and flexibility is the right antidote for such situations. Let me try to illustrate this with an example and describe the way I saw it. The oil price crashed to historic low level during 2015-2016, and it is still playing out. The stocks of many solid oil companies dropped by 30% to 50% from their all-time high. The usual reaction was that this is a temporary phenomenon and the OPEC and other big oil producing nations would cut production to bring price back up.

The prices of these stocks with such pristine balance sheets and lucrative dividends were becoming hard to ignore. Given good safety and possibility of big reward, I considered it a very reasonable decision to buy some oils stocks. However, as it turned out, the oil went further down. I added some more. Then, it went down even further. I decided to stop adding new positions even if it seemed very lucrative, as I did not want to allocate more money toward a particular sector. In the meantime, the market has come back a little, gone down a little, and come back a little. It has become highly volatile and continues to be so. Besides, as the market dropped by 10% in the beginning of 2016, there were other stocks available at attractive price points. I cannot tell for certainty whether my decision to not add more positions in oil sector after some point is right or wrong, but I felt that it was time to back off given the continued uncertainty and the volatility in the sector. I am just describing my personal experience to explain flexibility and not recommending for or against oil sector. My decision could change in future.

19.8 Analysis, Paralysis

Some people have a tendency to analyze things to death and are always waiting for the perfect and the safest condition. They would come close but will not pull the trigger for the buy order. Stock investment is not a perfect science and is never one hundred percent risk free. To be able to successful in stock market, you still need to analyze a lot before buying a stock, but at some point, you have to make a decision. Endless analysis without taking action not only wastes your time, but also could be very agonizing.

19.9 How to Avoid Big Losses

> Markets can remain irrational longer than you can remain solvent.
>
> -John Maynard Keynes

You may be doing fine with the rest of the portfolio, and one big loss brings down the net returns. It happens from time to time. I am not sure if there is a definite answer to this, but we can recognize certain patterns and behaviors that increase chance of big loss.

- **Jumping in too early with a big position**

    You have analyzed the stock thoroughly, and you are in love with the stock. The price looks very compelling, and you do not want to miss this gem before others discover its true value. You decide to put a significant portion of your investment in one transaction. It becomes risky as the market suddenly tanks, or the stock keeps going down for whatever reason. Now you do not have room to average it down, as it will make the stock overweight in your portfolio. When you enter a position, enter so that you have room to buy more when price drops further.

- **Using leverage heavily during market peaks**

    It can make you vulnerable when market suddenly crashes. Because of the over-leveraging at the wrong time, your loss will multiply quickly. You will be left with few good options. If the market stays low longer, you will have to sell some of your positions at the most unfavorable time with big losses. Also, if you decide to hold, you will continue to bleed money, as you still have to pay margin interest. The longer the downturn remains, the more difficult it will become for you to stay without selling at a huge loss. Now, the downturn, instead of being an opportunity, has become a big liability.

- **Betting big on speculative companies**

  Betting big on speculative companies that do not have the staying power or proven track record can result in permanent loss of capital. If you have to invest in speculative stocks, do not put a significant portion of your portfolio in such stocks. When such a stock crashes, it may not ever recover to the price you bought. These become indefensible positions (it becomes even riskier to average down), and the only way out is to sell the stocks at big losses and try to forget them.

19.10   Fear and Greed

Fear and greed are the two most powerful human emotions that are on frequent display in the stock market. During boom times, euphoria sets in, and everyone jumps in. The stock indices jump to sky-high levels, and P/E ratios reach much higher than the historical average of 16. People forget the concepts of safety and buy stocks at highly overvalued levels. Then, the market crashes as it inevitably happens after all bubbles. The NASDAQ, in 2000, is a good example where valuations reached sky high. When market crashed, many companies went out of business, and the stock price has not come back up to the 2000 level for many large established companies even after 15 years.

The other end of the spectrum is fear that engulfs people during big market crash. During the 2008-2009 huge economic downturn, the DOW plunged nearly 49% from its peak. There was fear everywhere, and it was very hard to escape. But, if you look back to the past 100 years of US stock market history, there are many boom-bust cycles. The market has always come back up (most of the times in 1-2 years, longer in other cases). People, who sold their stocks at the low with huge losses, lost it forever. Those who held on and did not let fear overtake them saw the market coming back in one and half years with a massive bull run that surpassed the previous peak and moved much higher.

19.11   Selling too Early

Another common mistake many investors commit is to sell it early and leave money on the table. Here is a typical scenario. An investor buys some stocks, and price went down by 20-25% in next several months. He or she is losing money (on paper and in mind). The stock stays there for quite some time (let us say 6 months to a year), and there is no sign of recovery. It is human nature to not sell at a loss, and in his or her mind, the investor is wishing if he or she could breakeven and get out. If the pick was based on fundamental strength, it is a good decision to hold on and not turn the paper loss into real loss. However, if the fundamentals have really deteriorated and there is very little chance of the stock coming back up, holding the stock forever and hoping it to rebound is also not right.

Whatever may be the case, he or she has decided to hold on and did not sell it. Now, after a year, the company turns around and is on to a sustained long-term recovery. The price starts coming back. Once it reaches the purchase price, he or she hits the sell button – cannot wait a minute longer. It is human nature to come out of an unpleasant situation at the earliest possible time without being harmed. However, at this point, it is no more an unpleasant situation. The stock has rebounded, and things are looking good. There is a great chance that it will move higher beyond the original purchase price. By selling at breakeven price as soon as the opportunity arrives, you are leaving money on the table. It is a common mistake that many investors do. When things start going right, do not get out too early.

20 Wise Adages in Investing

These are like pearls of wisdom. Some of these have come from long-term market observations, some from great investors, and some from common sense. Nothing is one hundred percent sure in stocks, but these can help as guidelines or quick "Dos and Don'ts" in your investment decisions. Just knowing and being aware of these will help you in making the right decisions and avoid costly mistakes.

20.1 Sell in May and Go Away

"Sell in May and go away, buy again on St Leger's Day." - Anonymous

Are there certain months or periods in a year better than others for stocks? The saying "Sell in May and go away, buy again on St Leger's Day" has been based on the observation that many investors and traders go on vacation in May and come back to stock market in September. There may be some statistical evidence that stock returns have been better in September-May period than May-September period. However, it may be risky to use this general guideline to base your investment decision, as there are many years when stock market has provided solid gains between May and September.

May to September Gain/Loss

Year	15th May	15th Sept	% gain/loss	Highest in between
2015	18,272	16,600	-9.2%	18,312
2014	16,446	17,031	+3.6%	17,137
2013	15,275	15,376	+0.7%	15,658
2012	12,632	13,593	+7.6%	13,593
2011	12,595	11,433	-9.2%	12,724
2010	10,620	10,572	-0.5%	10,698
2009	8,268	9,683	+17.1%	9,683
2008	12,992	10,917	-16%	12,992
2007	13,383	13,442	+0.4%	13,971
2006	11,428	11,560	+1.2%	11,560
2005	10,140	10,558	+4.1%	10,705
2004	10,012	10,231	+2.2%	10,479
2003	8,713	9,448	+8.4%	9,586
2002	10,243	8,312	-18.9%	10,353
2001	10,872	9,605	-11.7%	11,337

In the table above, for the last 15 years (2001-2015), we have the data for DOW on 15th of May and 15th of September each year. Out of 15 years, DOW went down for 6 years (total -65.5%), and DOW went up for 9 years (+45.3%). As we can see, number of loss-years and gain-years are somewhat even. The total loss is a little higher than the total gain, with a net loss of -20.2% in 15 years, with average yearly loss of -1.35%. I would not liquidate my portfolio every year in May and buyback in September.

September to May Gain/Loss

Year of sale	Buy 15th Sept Previous Yr.	Sell 15th May Current Yr.	% gain/loss	Highest in between
2015	17,031	18,272	+7.3%	18,312
2014	15,376	16,446	+7%	17,137
2013	13,593	15,275	+12.4%	15,658
2012	11,433	12,632	+10.5%	13,593
2011	10,572	12,595	+19.1%	12,724
2010	9,683	10,620	+9.7%	10,698
2009	10,917	8,268	-24.3%	9,683
2008	13,442	12,992	-3.4%	12,992
2007	11,560	13,383	+15.8%	13,971
2006	10,558	11,428	+8.2%	11,560
2005	10,231	10,140	-1%	10,705
2004	9,448	10,012	+6%	10,479
2003	8,312	8,713	+4.8%	9,586
2002	9,605	10,243	+6.7%	10,353
2001	10,927	10,872	-0.5%	11,337

If one bought in Sept 15, 2000 and sold in May 15, 2015, DOW would have gained from 10,927 to 18,272, with total gain of 67% in 15 years (4.5% yearly gain). On the other hand, if one bought every year on 15th of Sept and sold them 15th of May the next year, he would have made a total profit of 78% (5.22% yearly). The returns are slightly better (5.22% versus 4.5%) – not compelling enough. I would not liquidate my portfolio every year in May and buyback in September! I will be aware of this but won't make my investment decisions based on this.

20.2 Don't Catch a Falling Knife

There is a good chance that you would hurt yourself trying to catch a falling knife. The metaphor extends to stocks when a stock suddenly drops by a massive percentage – 25% to 40%, for example. Why would someone try to buy a stock that dropped so much? Because, it looks like a good bargain. The obvious thinking is that if the stock was selling at $40 yesterday, it must be cheap at $25 today.

There is a very good reason for the sudden big fall in the stock price. It could be a technology startup or any company that has gone up significantly based on projected future growth even if it does not have positive earnings yet. Then, suddenly the revenue stalls or does not grow as expected. You could see a big drop from the astronomical price. Or, there is scandal, management impropriety, accounting malpractices, or lawsuits involved that triggers a big drop in price. It could be due to a stock losing market share and becoming irrelevant.

Another thing is that it takes several sessions before the stock price stabilizes - it could fall for several trading days. Or, it could be the start of a long-term trend that will unfold in next several quarters or years where the stock would go much lower. Should you completely avoid buying the stock? There is no off-the-shelf answer. Buying the wrong company can result in massive loss, and buying the right company could be an opportunity to make good profit in the next several years. You have to evaluate the company on a fundamental basis. As Warren Buffett would say, you buy value not price. Would you consider buying the company based on the fundamentals - its management, balance sheet, earning, and cash flow irrespective of the price? If the answer is yes, consider taking new position or adding more. If it still maintains its competitive advantage, it is a solid company but going a rough patch, and the price has fallen to a level it looks very attractive, then this is an opportunity to make money.

Many successful investors recognize when it is falling knife to avoid and when it is a true buying opportunity to scoop up at a bargain price. Many solid companies get punished disproportionately by the Wall Street. I would give credit to analysts, as they are the ones who see the trend early. What is wrong, in my opinion, is that they amplify and extrapolate the good and the bad. Fortunately as an individual investor, if you learn how to evaluate a company based on its fundamentals, you can accumulate stocks of a solid company at a bargain price. There are many examples of solid companies that were punished severely only to come back strong in next several quarters. Apple was trading around $60 (post-split price) during June'13 and went up to $130 by Feb'15. Intel was trading around $20 during Nov'12 and went up to $35 by Aug'15. Chevron stock price had dropped to $70 in August of 2015 and went back to $98 by Nov 2015.

There are many more examples. In all these cases, these stocks were looking as solid buys - solid management, market leading products, pristine balance sheet, robust earnings, incredible cash flow, and very good dividend yield (Apple's dividends were a little less). Apple went up by 117% in two years, Intel gained 75% in three years, and Chevron went up by 40% in three months. You, most likely, would not be able to buy all the shares at the bottom and most likely would have started to buy before the bottom. However, the gain would be still impressive. You start accumulating at some point (it has fallen enough) and add more when it goes down further – only if it is a solid company, else just stay clear even if it is available at 20% of the price year ago. Radio shack is a perfect example of falling knife. The business was dying, but the dividends were great for some time. Eventually, the stock became worthless in a short few years.

Summary: Do not catch a falling knife but catch a falling angle.

20.3 Buy the Rumor Sell the News

"Buy the rumor sell the news" is a short-term trading strategy, not a long-term investment plan or a strategy based on fundamental analysis. It is based on some anticipated positive event that may or may not happen in future. There are instances when news came out about a company being bought out. The price would quickly move up in several days in anticipation of the event happening. One can make some good money if he can get out before it is late or the price starts declining. There are two main difficulties in this approach. First, it is risky - on the next day, the gain could get wiped out falling back to the original price. Second, because of this uncertainty, it is not wise to put substantial amount of money based on the rumor. If you put only a little money, it is not going to make a big difference in your overall portfolio gain.

The other case is when a company announces a new product or service that drives up the stock price until the actual product or service arrives. If the product does not turn out to be as good as originally thought, all the gains would get wiped out. Or, even if the product is as good as it was anticipated, the stock could still fall. This is because the product was already factored in to the price, and when the product arrived, people started taking profit as the news value has completed its course. The advice is, if you want to play "buy rumor sell news," to make some quick bucks, only put a little money, and sell it after it has gone up – it can be next day or before the news actually arrives. Do not wait until the actual news. You will make some money rather than the 50-50 possibility of not making any money or losing money. You got to be nimble!

20.4 Don't Fight the Fed

One of the common-sense investment guidelines is to not go against the Fed but to align your investments with the Fed's policy. As we know, the Fed, through its monetary policy, controls the short-term interest rate and money supply in the economy. It has huge influence on the economy and the stock market. Low interest and infusion of money into the economy help to buoy the stock market. When interest rate is low, the returns on checking account, savings account, money-market funds, and short-term CD are very low. This forces people to go for higher-yielding investments such as stocks. Also, when the Fed increases money supply and buys medium-term and long-term US treasury bonds through schemes, such as QE (Quantitative Easing), the treasury 10-yr bond yield goes down. This prods many people to go for stock rather than low-yielding investments such as US treasury bonds.

When the long-term borrowing cost goes down, many corporations borrow money at a cheap rate. They use the money to expand business, do acquisitions, and buy back shares. All these actions lead to stock price appreciation. So, it is clear that Fed policy has strong influence on stock market. In the recent past (last 5-10 years), not only the US but also other large world economies, such as Japan and Europe have adopted easy monetary policy. This has been reflected by huge gain in stock indices in many parts of the world. With such a huge tailwind on the stock market, it does not make sense to not invest in stock market during easy monetary policy. The opposite is true when interest rates and treasury yields are high. In such cases, look for individual solid companies that are undervalued and can grow by their own strength irrespective of monetary policy.

20.5 Stocks Take the Staircase When Go Up

Stocks take the staircase when go up and the elevator when go down. It is a fairly accurate statement that is true for the whole stock market as well as for individual stocks. The gain in a stock builds up incrementally over a period of time. If you look at a chart, it looks like a staircase or an upward slope. But, when it drops, it drops very quickly and precipitously. The typical bull market lasts for 6 years, and the typical bear market lasts for one and half year.

The amount of time it takes to drop to the bottom of a bear market from the top of bull market is much smaller compared to the time it takes to form the bull market. Most of the bull market tops are formed due to some forms of irrational exuberance with much higher P/E ratio compared to long-term average. Market in 2000 was highly overvalued with very high PE ratios. The market in 2008 coincided with the housing bubble. Nobody wants to get out when the momentum moves the market up and up. But, at some point, the market moves much ahead of the realities, and the forces that keep the market moving up are exhausted. Suddenly some bad news creates panic among everybody. Everyone runs for the exit door. People want to sell at any cost and want to get out as it might fall further if they wait longer. This creates a big downward pressure, and the market can drop dramatically over a few weeks to a few months.

The lesson to be learned for investor is that during market high or perceived high, you need to book some profit, keep some in cash, and leverage to the minimum. When it drops too much too soon, you may not get time to get out without a big loss. If you are not over-invested during market peak, you do not have to sell at a loss. You can hold and add more after the big drop.

20.6 Don't Put all Your Eggs in One Basket

It is about diversification to protect from catastrophic loss in a concentrated portfolio comprising of only a few stocks. If you have invested all your money in a few stocks and things go bad, you could have a huge loss. How many stocks is the right number for diversification? Is it 5, 10, 20, 50, or 100? Why just one or two is very risky? Things just happen, such as scandal, management impropriety, inept management, or losing competitiveness for good, even in very established rock-solid companies from time to time.

As a fundamental investor, I choose between 15 to 20 stocks in my portfolio. The number provides me protection from unforeseen catastrophic loss from a single company. The other reason of diversification is that sometimes companies go through lean phases where the money could be stuck for a long time. Unless I am diversified, I have to wait out longer that can reduce overall returns.

Beyond 15 to 20 stocks, it does not provide any more protection than one needs. If you want the full protection of diversification, index funds, such as DOW, NASDAQ, or S&P can be used. DOW comprises of 30 companies, NASDAQ consists of 3,100 companies, and S&P consists of 500 companies. History shows that you would get close to 10% returns from indices over a longer period. However, you want to do better or much better than the index funds, focusing on 15-20 stocks is enough.

Keeping it to 15-20 companies makes it easier and practical to research the companies, understand them well, and follow them in the market place. You cannot do the same level of due diligence on 50 companies. You should not choose all the stocks from one sector, such as technology, finance, oil, or consumers. Diversify your holdings into a few sectors and have the best 2-3 from each category. The next consideration is; should you allot money equally among all the stocks?

In general, keep the money allocation balanced among the components of your stock portfolio. However, it is not a hard and fast rule. There will be opportunities when one or two stocks or a new stock gets disproportionately punished. This provides big opportunities. As an informed investor and as you gain more experience, you should be willing to put more money into such solid but beaten down stocks. It is hard to quantify when you can do this, but your experience will tell you when it is the right time. And, do not be scared to take advantage of such opportunities.

Another thing to consider is not just your individual portfolio but also the 401K and IRA accounts. Over the years, these retirement accounts will grow and consider them into the portfolio allocation mix. If your retirement accounts already hold a good portion of a particular company or the company you are working for, then, you should not put a bigger chunk to that company in your individual holdings, unless it meets the criterion to make a short-term concentrated bet as we discussed previously.

20.7 Let Your Winners Run

It is the momentum that drives stock price to a very high level or brings down to a very low level. When a company turns around and performs well, it continues to do so for many quarters or several years. As more and more people know about the good news, they start buying the stocks that drives the stock price higher. On a quarterly window, this usually happens after a strong quarter. This stock price would continue to go up until the next quarterly earnings announcement. This happens almost always when the overall market is on an uptrend. However, when overall market is in a downtrend, individual stock performance is likely to stall.

Many people make mistake of selling it too early. They bought a stock that went down for several quarters. Now the stock has turned around, and long-term prospects look good. As soon as the stock price reaches their purchase price, they sell the stock only to see that stock kept its upward trajectory for next several months or quarters. People do not like losing money, and as soon as they are out of loss, they get out with a sigh of relief. However, do not be too greedy to hold on to winning stock too long to lose most of the gain. It is a difficult choice sometimes. If it is the last phase of a bull market that has been moving sideways for a few years now and you believe that the stock is now fairly priced, you should sell part of the positions to lock profit and redeploy the money into another fundamentally solid stock that is available at a cheaper price.

20.8 Never Lose Money

This is one of Warren Buffett's famous sayings, **"Rule No.1: Never lose money. Rule No. 2: Never forget rule No.1."** This looks so obvious and simple, and one would argue, why someone would want to lose money. It is simple on the surface but has profound meaning hidden.

The automatic inference from this is that if you can ensure that you never lose money, it automatically guarantees that you always make money. What it is saying that, do not get into speculative stocks or stocks without solid fundamentals and competitive advantages. If you have invested in one of the high-flying stocks or cheap stocks, you can make money. Also, you could lose money when the price crashes and the company never recovers. The loss would become permanent, and you would have to take a loss sooner or later. Such investments reduce your net returns as one or two of these can bring down your overall returns significantly.

On the contrary, if you have invested in market leaders and companies with strong fundamentals and have entered into positions when these were down, you can withstand temporary paper loss. Even if they go down after you bought them, you can wait it out or even add more but do not sell at a loss. Give several quarters, and these stocks would come back; you would not only eliminate the paper loss but also make money on these. Sometimes even the best stocks lose value along with the broad market. In such cases, do not panic sell and convert the paper loss to real loss. The market is very fickle and can come back up very quickly before you can buy them back! This wise adage is easy to remember but difficult to practice. If you can make it a long-term strategy, there is a high chance that you would be a successful investor.

20.9 The Best Time to Sell is Never

> The best time to sell is never – Warren Buffett

This is based on long-term investment strategy. The underlying message is that solid companies with good management keep doing better. They are always thinking how to grow the company, how to diversify, how to increase revenue, how to reduce cost by being efficient, and most importantly, how to retain their edge over the competitors. If your investment is meeting these goals, why do you want to sell a winner?

The other important thing is that these investments become cash cows. As these companies raise their dividends, the dividends you are getting on these investments become significant. It makes complete sense, and Warren probably wanted to accentuate it by using the word "never." We can follow the spirit but can break the rule once in a while to take advantage of the market inefficiency or irrational market behavior. If you can come across an equally solid company (may be you already hold some in your portfolio), that got unduly punished based on short-term expectations, it makes sense to sell some of the never-sell stocks and buy the unduly punished ones. It is, basically, a way to maximize your probability of appreciation while keeping the risk same. These opportunities do not come every day or every month, but they do come. Besides, you are not in hurry as you are sitting on a good portfolio.

20.10   Be Fearful When Others are Greedy

> Be fearful when others are greedy, and greedy when others are fearful.
> – Warren Buffett

This is another very famous contrarian quote from the oracle of Omaha. In principle, market is efficient and reflects the true value of stocks - when things change, stock price adjusts to that. However, the stock market does not always behave rationally. The dotcom boom of 2000 is not distant past when the stocks reached stratospherical levels based on future earnings projections. When the market reaches frenzied zones, it is the time to be fearful as everyone is talking about stocks and jumping on the bandwagon. The euphoria continues for some time, but eventually it crashes and does it very badly. The folks who join the party late suffer stunning losses that they would never recover. This is the time to resist temptation, as you would hear stories of friends making big gains.

The opposite is equally true and interesting. As the market goes up very high, the market also goes down very low when something big happens in the economy. The recent market crash of 2008-2009 is a perfect example. In matter of a little over a year, DOW went down from 14,000 in Oct'07 to 6,600 in Mar'09. There were many good companies available at bargain price. Everyone was scared and running away from stock as far as he or she could. This is the time to be greedy and buy good companies. For this, you have to have some cash available to use this to your advantage. This is also perfect time to maximize the use of home equity line of credits and margin account. If the bear market stays longer (usually it does not), you can select fundamentally strong companies that pay decent dividends. The dividends will offset the interest expenses from equity line of credit and margin account.

In practice, no one can guess the exact bottom, and you won't be able buy everything at the bottom. The best strategy is to start accumulating when things are sufficiently down and add when it goes down further. You have to have a strategy in place as to how much of your deployable cash you want to put depending on how much the market goes down. You do not have infinite cash lying around to deploy when market crashes.

20.11   High Tides Lift All Boats

This is true in a bull market. As high tide lift all boats, stocks get a lift from an overall up market. Everything remaining same without any company-specific news or sector-specific headwind, prices of individual companies gain when the DOW and S&P go up. It becomes easier to make money during the bull market phase. The opposite is more interesting. During a bear market or a market on a downtrend, it becomes difficult to make money. There are short-selling strategies to make money during downtrend market, but I personally do not adopt these strategies, as I am not willing to take short-term risk that I cannot defend if things do not go as I expected.

However, the best strategy during the height of a bull market or beginning of a bear market (not at the end of a bear market as smoke would have cleared up by then), is to focus on the micros – look at individual companies. There would be many good companies available at reasonable or bargain price. These companies have solid fundamentals but do not provide the usual high returns everyone is chasing. When the market takes a turn, the high-flying stocks suffer the most, and money flows to the not-so-interesting or boring stocks. These stocks do not suffer much during a downturn and provide reasonable gain when things start coming back.

20.12   **Bull Markets are Born on Pessimism**

> Bull markets are born on pessimism, grow on skepticism, mature on optimism, and die of euphoria."
>
> – John Templeton

These are the four phases of an investment cycle that repeats again and again throughout history. A bear market gives birth to the beginning of a bull market. When new sprouts of growth start to come out, a bull market starts to form. However, it is not clear at this time that a bull market is starting. This is the point when everyone is still pessimistic about the economy and stays away from the stock market. But, this provides the biggest opportunity for capital appreciation, and it is the time to invest and not back away. Stock market is unpredictable, but one thing predictable about stock market is the investment cycle – stock market does not stay at the bottom forever.

A bull market starts before many people realize it. As things are still tentative at this point, people are skeptical about the bull market. Then, as the market keeps climbing up steadily, more and more people are convinced that this is real and take part in the Bull run. The end phase is when people think that it can go up forever and throw caution to the wind; euphoria sets in. At this point, the stock market has reached a level where it cannot go up any further and eventually turns bearish, leading to big drop. And, the cycle continues!

Chapter

21

21 Story of an Individual Investor

We have discussed many strategies in this book where one can be successful in the stock market. As you become more knowledgeable and experienced in whatever strategy you are pursuing and learn from real experience, you would be on your way to become a successful investor. My goal in this chapter is to introduce my strategy, the thought process that goes into it, and how I do it. It does not guarantee that someone else will be successful or I, myself, will continue to be successful. However, I have been reasonably successful, and I am happy with it. I started investing in stocks in a meaningful way in 2011.

21.1 Why do I invest in Stocks?

Before deciding to invest in stocks, I ask, "What are the other alternatives?" Are there other alternatives that provide good returns with no risks? The answer has been NO for the last decade. Currently, risk-free assets earn very low returns (Savings account and CDs yield less than 1%, and 10-year note yields less than 2%). Some corporate AAA bonds could fetch 3%. High-yield junk bonds yield higher (6% - 9%), but these are risky, at least for me. Given this scenario, I believe investing in stocks provides much better returns, and it is a risk worth taking. If the situation is different in future, where CDs, government bonds, and corporate bonds pay 5%-6% returns, I could possibly look into these alternatives, at least to some extent.

When there are competing products that provide very reasonable returns with little risk, it puts a downward pressure on the stocks. Money flows from risk assets such as stocks to safe havens. In these environments, the stock price usually falls to a point where the dividend yields go up, and the stock price becomes attractive. The yield on the safe havens is directly linked to Fed interest rate. However, in a low-interest environment, stocks grab the limelight.

CHAPTER 21   An Investor's Story

21.2 My Stock Picking Process

Safety is my top priority. I pick a stock based on strong fundamental analysis so that it will be able to survive and come back. I do not want to permanently lose my investment in a pick. I invest in a company that most of the people would know (from DOW, S&P, and NASDAQ). I pick companies that are easy to understand and have products and offerings that most of the people use. It makes it easy to get a gut feel and have a reality check.

I look for companies from the DOW and S&P 500 that are currently down significantly from their recent top (last 1-2 years). This provides safety from further large fall. Another checkpoint is the P/E ratio. I rarely select stocks that have PEs higher than 15-16. My guideline for entry point for a stock is:

Large cap:	30%-35% down from recent top
Medium cap:	40%-50% down from recent top
Small cap:	55%-75% down from recent top

I periodically scan DOW and S&P to find out companies that meet this criterion. I also scan the losers of the day to see if anything is interesting to me. There are many esoteric companies that are 20-30% down almost every day, but I only look for market-leaders or companies that most of the households would know.

After a stock passes the entry-price test, it does not automatically qualify as a buy. I take it through a rigorous fundamental analysis (balance sheet, income statement, and cash flow study). I prefer stocks that have paid out steady dividends (2-5%). What is the payout ratio for the dividend? Do they have room to maintain dividends during tough times and increase dividends when things are good? A good dividend yield provides a floor and protects from dramatic price drop. I look for companies that have steadily reduced share counts via buybacks. I look at the management. Do they have strong record of turnarounds and history of success? Have they been conservative in their approach and haven't wasted a lot of cash in acquiring questionable companies?

Once a stock passes the entry price, P/E, and fundamental analysis, I go to the next phase, which is doing a thorough research about the company? What is going on in the company? Are the things really that bad, or is it something temporary that will be all right in due course? Is there still a feel-good factor or the company is losing it completely? I avoid a company where something dramatic or severe is going on or is about to happen. Established market leaders generally do not have these dire scenarios. I listen to earning conference calls and listen to CEO, CFO, and Q&A sessions to get a feel of it myself. If I believe it is a temporary situation and the reward outweighs the risk, I enter into a position.

When I enter a position, I always consider the possibility of further fall in price. When the price falls, I study the situation again and, in most cases, buy more. In some cases, I just hold if the portfolio is already heavy with a stock. I rarely sell at a loss. I hold them and wait for them to come back; and, in most cases, they come back in a few months or a year.

21.3 How Long Do I Hold a Stock?

Since I am a safe investor based on fundamental analysis and emphasis on value rather than explosive growth, most of my picks are not blockbusters or 10-baggers. When I looked back, what I found is that these stocks have gained only modestly in the last ten years, but there have been multiple 15%-30% ups and downs. In this scenario, long-term strategy does not work. From a tax perspective, short-term gains are taxed at a higher rate than long-term gains. However, if I wait for long-term gains for my picks, I would miss multiple ups and downs, and the net returns would not be good. I am willing to pay tax at a higher rate with a larger gain than at a lower rate with a smaller gain.

After I found evidence that holding for long-term gain is too long for the stocks I pick and too long in the current market condition (things have been moving sideways for last 2-3 years), it is the short term gains that I need to focus. **The more I can cycle through such gains, the higher my overall returns would be. It is similar to the capital turnover model**. The more number of times I can make 10-20% gains, or in some cases 5-10% gains in a year, the higher the overall returns would be. I do not have a fixed time period for holding. It can be a few days, a few weeks, or a few months. Generally, a beaten-down good stock appreciates 10-20% with relatively better news or results. Since the expectations are already low, it does not need a mega beat for the stock to appreciate 10%-20%. However, once they appreciate by 10-20%, they move higher at a slower pace from that point or fluctuate around that point. At this time, I either sell the stock (at least some of it) and rotate the money into another opportunity.

Sometimes, there would be quick appreciation, and, in some cases, the stock price would fall further. I generally average down in steps to the point they bounce back. When the turnaround or appreciation takes longer, I generally do not sell at a loss. I would hold it, sometimes more than a year, until it comes back up. In a nutshell, my thesis is to put money in stocks with the highest probability and possibility of appreciation and then move the money to another opportunity when the appreciation has completed. I believe, this strategy is working out well in a flat market where probability of these types of stocks hitting big is lower compared to the fluctuations they go through in a year. The strategy would be different if I am investing in a bear market when the stocks and indices are way down. When the stocks come back from a severe market downturn, they would keep appreciating for next 4-5 years, and it makes sense to hold long-term in such a scenario.

21.4 How about Transaction Cost?

Transaction costs eat into the profit margin. However, the cost of buying or selling has come down drastically in recent years - $6 to $9 per transaction. Transaction cost used to take a good bite out of the profit when it was $40-$50 per transaction. With the current low transaction cost, I believe, it is not going to be a deciding factor for most of the investors.

21.5 I Use Leverage

Using leverage (margin money) at the wrong time can be disastrous, but using it, sparingly and at right times, can be a very profitable proposition. I generally do not use margin money when the market is at its high or at the perceived high. No one can pinpoint a market high, but when many people are talking about a correction or the market is moving sideways for some time, treat it as real market high. You can incur significant loss using a lot of margin money at the peaks. In such scenarios, I have used margin money selectively with solid stocks that are significantly down at the moment, and the risk is low irrespective of the market high.

However, when the market goes down 10-15%, I start using margin. The recent example is when market went down 10-12% in the beginning of 2016. Since most of my picks pay decent to good dividends, the dividends offset some of the margin borrowing costs. If the market were to go down more, I would not bleed paying the margin interest. Also, since most of my picks are conservative good companies, the margin maintenance requirements are low. This means, I do not have to sell to meet margin calls, or I can avail more margin money for the same amount of net holdings.

21.6 Performance Comparison for 2011-2016

I am putting the data for DOW, S&P, and my portfolio returns for the years from 2011 to 2016.

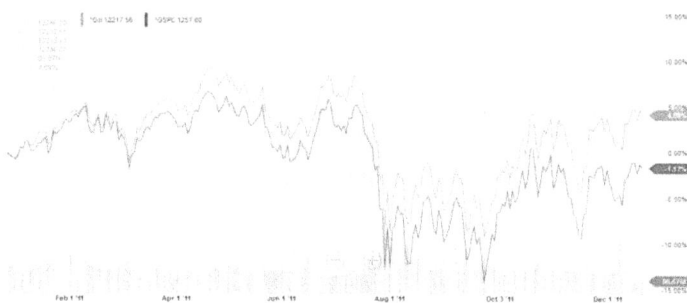

Fig. 21.1   **Dow, S&P- 2011** (Yahoo finance)

Fig. 21.2   **Dow, S&P- 2012** (Yahoo finance)

Fig. 21.3   **Dow, S&P- 2013** (Yahoo finance)

Fig. 21.4   **Dow, S&P- 2014** (Yahoo finance)

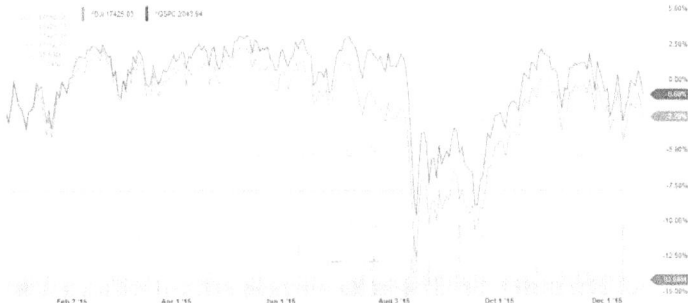

Fig. 21.5   **Dow, S&P- 2015** (Yahoo finance)

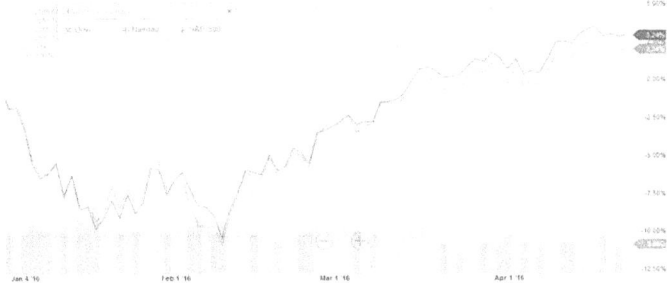

Fig. 21.6   **Dow, S&P- 2016 – As of 4/26/2016**

	DOW	S&P	Individual Investor
2011	4.69% + 2%	-1.12% +2%	28%
2012	5.7% + 2%	11.68% + 2%	5%
2013	23.59% + 2%	26.39% + 2%	25%
2014	8.4% + 2%	12.39% + 2%	20%
2015	-2.29% + 2%	-0.69% + 2%	10%
2016	3.24% + 1%	2.34% + 1%	19.6%
Total 2011-2016	**55.53%**	**62.99%**	**107.6%**

Notes:
- 2% average dividends yield is added to calculate total S&P and DOW returns
- I was lightly involved in the stock market in 2012
- Individual investor's (author's) gains include dividends
- Performance data for 2016 is as of 4/26/2016.

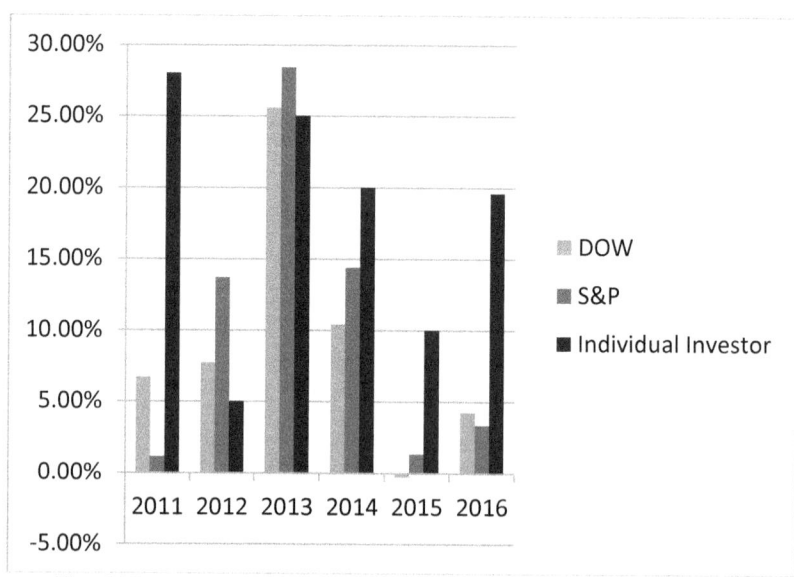

Fig. 21.7   Performance Comparison

21.7 Areas for Improvement

There is always room to improve, and I strongly believe in it. The stock market is always unpredictable, and every time, the situation, at hand, is unique. However, there are many things that tend to repeat under similar circumstances. I will discuss a few things that I believe I can improve upon based on my experience. The first one is **getting in too early with a big position.** It has happened a few times where I felt it was the perfect stock and wanted to get a lot of it. The stock selection was not wrong, but the size of the position was. When price goes down further and stays lower for a while, it becomes a very difficult decision to add more as the portfolio becomes more concentrated and increases risk. The other thing is that I had to wait longer for the stock to come back just to break even on that pick. This tied up a good amount of capital just waiting to breakeven without generating returns. This brings down the overall returns of the portfolio.

The other area I would like to improve is **vetting a company rigorously and be able to resist a seemingly good bargain.** This typically happens with smaller companies, companies without strong balance sheets, or tech companies where the technology is shifting quickly. When the price reaches a very low level compared to all time high, it looks very enticing and becomes hard to resist. The lure of making quick and big gain takes you to the deceptive goldmine that turns out to be landmine instead. Sometimes you make a good gain, but overall, it does not turn out good. In some cases, the stock price would lose another 40-50% and stay at a new low for a long time. If I sell it, I am incurring a big loss. If I add more, I am putting good money on a bad stock. In a few cases, I have lost a significant portion of the investment in these picks. Such cases bring down overall return of the portfolio. My goal is to be disciplined to avoid the big losers. **If I cannot defend a pick by adding more when it goes down, I should not have entered in to it in the first place.**

Section III

Mutual Funds and ETF
Options and Futures
Currencies
Real Estate

Chapter

22

22 Don't Want to Choose; will Buy All

Mutual funds and ETFs are ways to buy a broad category of stocks rather than picking individual stocks.

22.1 Mutual Funds

22.1.1   Introduction to Mutual Funds

Mutual funds are investment vehicles managed by professionals where a fund represents a group of stocks, bonds, or cash. Let us look at an example. In Fidelity web page on mutual funds, one of the mutual funds is Fidelity® Blue Chip Value Fund (FBCVX). The strategy of this fund is to invest in undervalued blue chip stocks. There are thousands of mutual funds, and each of these funds is created based on a strategy, such as large cap value, mid cap growth, or small cap growth etc.

Each mutual fund invests in multiple stocks in a particular category. Also, there are bond funds where the mutual fund invests in different types of bonds (government bonds, municipal bonds, and corporate bonds). The bond funds provide a steady source of dividends. As an investor, you can choose funds that meet your objective or investment goals. When you buy shares of a fund, you are the part owner of that fund and the part owner of the underlying stocks or bonds. When the stocks in the fund appreciate, the value of the fund goes up. Your share also appreciates accordingly. Next, we will discuss the pros and cons of investing in mutual funds.

22.1.2   Pros and Cons of Mutual Funds

Pros

- It is managed by professionals whose job is to invest in good stocks and make money for the investors. As an investor, you do not need to spend time to do research on buying and selling stocks. Of course, you still need to research the fund before putting money in it.
- Since it is diversified (a fund comprises multiple stocks), it reduces risk compared to investing in individual stocks.
- Historically, mutual funds, invested in stocks, have provided better returns than bonds, fixed deposits, or savings account.

Cons

- As you build your investment knowledge base, you can be a good individual investor. Over time, you will be better at it and can generate returns better than you would get from investing in mutual funds. You are letting someone else to manage your money.
- There are costs associated with managing the funds, which cuts into the profit generated by the fund. Expenses that are more than 1% of the asset values are on the higher side, and you should look for alternative funds with good returns but low fees.
- The fund manager sells and buys stocks within the fund to rebalance as needed. Sale of stocks generates capital gains. The net profit, at yearend, is distributed among fund holders even if he or she did not sell the shares in the mutual fund. The distribution is a taxable income to individual fund holders.
- The extreme form of diversification is dilution. Diversification reduces risk, but too much of it (dilution) reduces returns. MFs reduce risk due to diversification but usually provide lower returns than a seasoned individual investor can produce.
- The fund manager has less flexibility in buy/sell decision compared to an individual investor who manages his or her own stocks.

22.1.3   How is a Mutual Fund Created?

A mutual fund company (some examples: American, Blackrock, Franklin Templeton, Fidelity, Janus, John Hancock, JP Morgan, Oppenheimer, PIMCO, T. Rowe Price, and Vanguard) can start a fund by pooling resources together from a group of investors. A mutual fund has an objective or strategy where it buys stocks that fits the strategy. For example, a fund targeting large cap financials will buy stocks for larger financial companies. A fund targeting international mid-cap growth will buy stocks in medium-valued international companies that are growing.

The total value of the fund (assets minus liabilities) divided by the total number of outstanding shares is called the **NAV (Net Asset Value).** When a fund is launched, the total money raised divided by the total shares issued is the NAV. After the initial formation, the NAV is calculated at the end of each day, which can increase or decrease based on the price of the stocks in that fund.

22.1.4   Closed-end / Open-end Mutual Funds

There are three types of mutual funds: closed-end, open-end, and unit trusts.

Closed-end Funds

The total number of shares is fixed at initial offering, and no new shares are issued further. An investor cannot directly buy shares from this fund. The shares are traded in the secondary market similar to stocks. The price of each share can be more or less than the NAV. If there is more demand, the price in secondary market will be more than the NAV, or the price could be less when there is less demand. Closed-end funds are less popular compared to open-end funds and ETF. Actually when people talk about mutual funds, they refer to the open-end funds that we will discuss next.

Open-end Funds

Most of the mutual funds today are open-end funds. The mutual funds in our retirement accounts are generally open-end mutual funds. The funds are open to new investment money constantly. You cannot buy shares in secondary market. When you want to buy shares in an open-end fund, you provide money to be invested. At the end of the day after stock market closes, the NAV (Net Asset Value) is calculated, and you will receive as many shares (new shares) based on the amount you invested.

Example

The fund had total 10M shares with NAV $10. The total value of the fund is 10Mx$10 = $100M. You invested $10M with new money. You will be issued 1M shares for $10M you invested. Now, the total asset value for the fund is $100M + $10M = $110M, and the total number of shares becomes 11M.

Let us look at a case when someone sells (redeems) his shares. In this case, the total number of outstanding shares is reduced. If the fund has cash available, it will give it from the cash reserve. In worst case, it will sell some stocks to generate the cash to pay the seller. This is one of the downsides of open-ended funds where the fund manager has to produce large amount of cash when an owner or group of owners decide to sell shares. This is not the case with closed-end funds where the number of shares is fixed.

The fund generates revenue from dividends received from the stocks, interest earned from cash deposits, and capital gains from selling stocks. The net profit (after deducting expenses) is distributed to each investor based on number of shares he or she holds. The investor can take the distribution or invest them back by buying new shares. In either case, the investor has to pay income tax for the distribution.

Unit Trusts (UT)

Unit trusts are similar to open-end mutual funds that you can buy from the fund company or sell (redeem) to the fund company. However, there are many differences. UTs typically invest in a fewer number of stock and trade less often compared to open-end mutual funds. UTs offer a fixed number of shares during initial offering, whereas the share count in open-end mutual fund is variable. UTs do not have a group of professional advisors and managers as found in open-end funds that keep the operating cost of UT low. If you invest in a UT, you know which companies you own, whereas the stocks in a mutual fund could change from time to time, still within the objective and goal of the fund. Investing a percentage of your portfolio in UT can be a part of overall diversification strategy.

22.1.5   Analyzing a Mutual Fund – an Example

Let us look at Fidelity® Blue Chip Growth Fund **(FBGRX):** Data on 11/30/2015

Performance: As of 11/30/2015

YTD	1yr	3yr	5yr	10yr
7.00%	6.43%	19.47%	15.67%	9.46%

Details

Morningstar Category	Large Growth
Fund Inception	12/31/1987
NAV 11/30/2015	$69.63
Exp Ratio (Gross) 9/29/2015	0.89% ($8.90 per $1000)
Exp Ratio (Net) 9/29/2015	0.89% ($8.90 per $1000)
Minimum to Invest	$2,500.00
Turnover Rate 7/31/2015	51%
Portfolio Net Assets ($M) 11/30/2015	$20,994.02
Share Class Net Assets 11/30/2015	$15,479.12
12 Month Low-High 11/30/2015	$62.91 - $76.07

Expense Ratio is a measure of the cost to operate the funds. In this case, the cost of operation is $8.9 per thousand dollars of assets. Most of the time, the gross and net expense ratios are same. Many funds offer fee waivers and reimbursement to new customers. Net expense ratio includes all expenses as the gross expense ratio does, except the fee waivers and reimbursement.

Turnover Rate represents the percentage of fund's assets that have changed in a year. Turnover rate of 100% means all the stocks in the fund have changed.

Strategy for this fund (from Fidelity website)

> Normally investing at least 80% of assets in blue chip companies (companies whose stock is included in the S&P 500 or the Dow Jones Industrial Average, and companies with market capitalizations of at least $1 billion if not included in either index). Investing in companies that FMR believes have above-average growth potential (stocks of these companies are often called "growth" stocks). Normally investing primarily in common stocks of well-known and established companies.

Top 10 Holdings, 28.9% of Total Portfolio (AS OF 9/30/2015)

Apple, Google CL A, Amazon, Facebook, Google CL C,

Gilead Science, Home Depot, Salesforce, VISA CL A, Allergan

22.1.6   Categories of Mutual Funds

A mutual fund has an objective or a goal, such as growth, income, or combination of both. It can target small-cap, mid-cap, or large-cap companies. To get an idea about the varieties of fund available, let us look at Fidelity mutual fund offerings. Each broad category has further sub-categories within it. The list is not exhaustive but a sample to get the overall idea.

- Domestic Equity Funds
  - Large value, large blend, large growth
  - Mid value, mid blend, mid growth
- International Equity Funds
  - Core international
  - Regional and single country
  - Global
- Sectors Funds
  - Consumer discretionary
  - Consumer staples
  - Health care
  - Materials
  - Financials
  - Energy
  - Information Technology
- Fixed Income Funds
  - Short duration
  - Corporate
  - Municipal
  - Government
  - High yield
- Asset Allocation Funds
  - Target date
  - Target risk
- Index Funds
  - Nasdaq composite index
  - Spartan® 500 Index Fund
  - Spartan® Total Market Index Fund
- Money market Funds
  - Treasury and government money market
  - Retail Municipal
  - Retail Prime

22.1.7   How to Pick the Right Mutual Funds?

Choosing the right mutual funds can be a daunting task given the plethora of funds available. However, there are a few things that you need to be aware of. It will help to spot funds you should avoid and narrow down your choices to a manageable level.

- **Sales charge:** Do not choose funds that you have to pay sales charge to buy or sell. Some funds require a front-load fees (fees to buy the funds). Some need back-end charges (fees while selling the fund).

- **Expense ratio:** This is the ratio of administrative fees compared to the total assets. If the ratio is higher than 1%, it looks excessive. Avoid funds they have north of 1% expense ratio. Over the years, it will reduce the rate of returns.

- **Turnover:** Turnover defines how quickly the existing funds are sold and replaced by newly bought funds. One hundred percent turnover means all the funds will be replaced within a year. Excessive turnover increases admin fess, and the gain results in taxable income to the fund holders.

- **Track Record:** History is not a guarantor of future performance. Even if a fund has done well in the last 5 to 10 years, it cannot guarantee that it will perform well in future. However, look for consistent past history. Many funds that did relatively well during stock market crash, are likely do well during tough times.

- **Your Objective and Time Horizon:** Choose a fund that meets your objective (growth, value, longer time horizon for appreciation or current income). Also, consider your time horizon and your risk tolerance. If you are away from retirement, you would have time to recover from stock market crash, and it makes sense to be overweight in stocks to generate higher returns. On the other hand, if you are close to retirement or in retirement years, principal preservation, and current income is most likely is your primary objective.

- **Index funds:** If you are investing the money far into the future, you may consider an index fund.

22.2 ETF (Exchange Traded Funds)

22.2.1   Introduction to ETF

ETFs (Exchange Traded Funds) have been around for some time, but they gained popularity in last 5- 10 years. ETFs are similar to mutual funds, but they can be openly traded (bought and sold) in open market similar to stocks. You cannot buy mutual funds directly from the open market. You buy mutual funds from the mutual fund company at the end of the stock trading hours. So what are ETFs exactly? Let us look at some examples of ETF. **SPY** (SPDR S&P 500), **VXX** (S&P 500 VIX Short-Term Futures ETN), **EEM** (iShares MSCI Emerging Markets ETF), and **GDX** (Market Vectors TR Gold Miners) are some of the popular ETFs. SPY invests in the top 500 US companies (S&P 500) and tracks the S&P 500 index.

22.2.2   How do ETFs work – A Walkthrough

There are two parties involved in an ETF creation – ETF creator and Authorized Participant (AP). When an ETF company wants to create a new ETF, it puts the plan to the SEC for approval. If the plan is approved, the ETF creator asks the AP to buy the shares from open market. An ETF tracking S&P 500 index would ask AP to buy the stocks in the same proportion as the S&P represents. APs are well-capitalized large financial institutions (Fidelity, Vanguard, or Blackrock etc.) that have the financial strength to buy the stocks.

In exchange for the S&P company stocks that ETF creator got from the AP, it issues ETF shares to the AP. These shares are called the creation unit, usually in block size of 50,000 ETF shares. The AP then sells the ETF shares in open market that we can buy as individual investor. NAV (Net Asset Value) is the value of all underlying stocks in the ETF divided by the total ETF shares issued. As the real price of the underlying stocks would change every day, the NAV will also change every day.

Creation and redemption of ETF

The ETFs are bought and sold in open market similar to stocks. When you buy ETF shares, you buy it from someone who wants to sell. The price of the ETF can be higher or lower than the NAV depending on the demand for the ETF. When there is more demand, the ETF share price will be higher than the NAV. When this happens, the AP buys more underlying stocks from the market and delivers them to the ETF creator. In exchange, AP gets more ETF shares from ETF creator that it sells in the market. Since ETF is selling higher compared to NAV, AP makes a profit. More ETF shares also push down the ETF price bringing it close to the NAV.

When there is less demand, the ETF price falls below the NAV. The AP finds the ETF undervalued and buys them from open market. Then, it surrenders or redeems the ETF shares (blocks of 50,000) to the ETF creator and retrieves the underlying stocks that the AP can sell in the market and make a profit. As the ETF share count reduces, it brings back the ETF share price close to the NAV. The AP creation and redemption helps to keep the ETF share price close to the true value of the underlying assets (NAV).

As the ETF shares are exchanged for underlying stocks, there is no buying or selling of stocks. This eliminates capital gain tax and keeps the cost of operating ETF low. This is one big advantage of ETF compared to mutual funds where capital gain is taxed.

Who gets what benefits?

The AP makes money through arbitrage – by creating and redeeming ETF shares when the ETF share price diverges from the NAV. The ETF creator makes money by keeping part of ETF assets and profits as management fees. The individual investor makes money when the ETF price appreciates and through dividends from the underlying stocks. ETF provides the benefit of diversification of mutual funds without the cost. ETF also provides the flexibility of trading in open market similar to individual stocks.

22.2.3   Benefits of ETF

ETFs provide many benefits compared to mutual funds, and ETFs are becoming a part of investment portfolio of increasing number of investors. Some of the benefits are:

Trading Flexibility

You can trade (buy/sell) ETFs like stocks during regular trading hours. You can put limit order to buy or sell, and you know your price. To buy or sell mutual funds, you have to wait until end of trading hours, and the mutual fund price will be the NAV at the end of day. One day may not seem long for a longer time horizon, but during interesting times, a lot can happen in a day.

Lower Cost of Operation

ETFs involve less active management compared to mutual funds. This results in lower management fees and operating cost. Over a longer period, the difference in cost of operation between ETF and mutual funds can make measurable difference in returns.

Diversification

In this regard, both ETF and mutual funds provide better diversification compared to investing in individual stocks. It is not necessary that you are always better diversifying a lot. Too much diversification can reduce the overall returns. As an investor, as you gain more confidence and experience, you will be able to decide how much to diversify and when to diversify. There are many ETFs available - SPY tracking S&P 500 companies and many sector-specific ETFs, such as gold, oil, or semiconductor sector ETFs.

Tax Advantage

ETFs are structured differently from mutual funds. In ETFs, the ETF shares are exchanged with the underlying stocks; so, there is no capital gain. However, in mutual funds, there is capital gain when stocks are sold to take profit, rebalance the portfolio, or generate cash for shares redeemed. Every year, the capital gain tax is passed on to the investors of mutual funds.

However, the dividends from ETF may be taxed at a higher rate. ETFs have two types of dividends – qualified dividends and non-qualified dividends. If you have bought the ETF 60 days before the ex-dividend date of an underlying stock or sold it after 60 days of ex-dividend date, it will qualify for qualified dividend at a rate that is lower than tax rate on ordinary income. Dividends that do not meet the 60-day before and 60-day after window are non-qualified dividends and are taxed at higher rate as ordinary income.

Accountability

ETF creator publishes the list of assets daily. Mutual funds, on the other hand, publish list of assets less frequently, typically once in a quarter.

22.2.4   Selecting the Right ETFs

There are thousands of ETFs available, and how do you select the right ETF or decide which ones are right for you? There are ETFs focusing on index (S&P 500, Dow 30, and Russel 2000 etc.), sectors (semiconductors and finance), commodities (gold, silver, and oil), income (Fed bonds, municipal bonds, corporate bonds and high-yield bonds), and real estate. Before we answer this question, let us look at some of the ETFs with the highest trading volume.

From barchart.com Dec 4, 2015:

Top 10 ETF by Volume

Sym	Name	Last	Change	Percent	High	Low	Volume
SPY	SPDR S&P 500 ETF	209.62	+4.01	+1.95%	209.97	205.93	192,915,297
EEM	Emrg Mkts Index MSCI Ishares	33.88	+0.23	+0.68%	33.94	33.37	79,516,398
GDX	Gold Miners ETF Market Vectors	14.83	+0.75	+5.33%	14.86	14.23	76,943,203
VXX	VIX Short-Term Futures ETN Ipath	18.22	-1.80	-8.99%	19.61	18.19	75,078,797
XLF	Financial Select Sector SPDR	24.78	+0.64	+2.65%	24.82	24.22	42,686,801
USO	US Oil	12.46	-0.31	-2.43%	12.63	12.33	41,884,500
UWTI	3X Long Crude ETN Velocityshares	5.99	-0.48	-7.42%	6.26	5.82	41,088,797
QQQ	Powershares QQQ	115.14	+2.63	+2.34%	115.33	112.62	40,037,301
EWJ	Japan Index MSCI Ishares	12.42	+0.07	+0.57%	12.43	12.27	34,506,301
UVXY	Ultra VIX Short-Term Fut ETF Proshares	24.77	-5.43	-17.98%	29.00	24.75	33,759,699

SPY (SPDR S&P 500 ETF)

It tracks the S&P 500 companies. These companies in S&P 500 are good companies with good track records. SPY is targeted to mimic the performance of S&P index. If you invest in SPY ETF, you can expect to get good returns as the index has returned close to 10% over the long run. However, past performance is no guarantee for future returns.

Morningstar Style Box: Large Blend

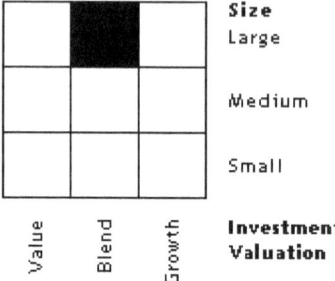

Fund Basics

Category:	Large Blend
Fund Family:	SPDR State Street Global Advisors
Total Assets:	180.51B
Legal Type:	Exchange Traded Fund

Performance & Risk

YTD Return: 3.02%

3y Avg Return: 15.99%

5y Avg Return: 14.29%

Beta (3y):   1.00

EEM (Emerging Market Index Ishares)

Morningstar Style Box: (Diversified Emerging Mkts)

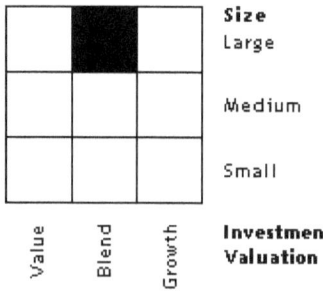

Fund Summary

The investment seeks to track the investment results of the MSCI Emerging Markets Index. The underlying index is composed of large and mid-capitalization emerging market equities. The fund generally invests at least 90% of its assets in the securities of its underlying index and in depositary receipts representing securities in its underlying index.

Fund Basics

Category:	Diversified Emerging Mkts
Fund Family:	iShares
Total Assets:	21.97B
Legal Type:	Exchange Traded Fund

Performance & Risk

YTD Return:	-12.84%
3y Avg Return:	-4.85%
5y Avg Return:	-3.51%
Beta (3y):	1.02

GDX (Market Vectors Gold Miners ETF)

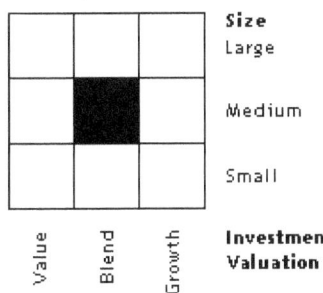

Fund Summary

The investment seeks to replicate as closely as possible, before fees and expenses, the price and yield performance of the NYSE Arca Gold Miners Index. The fund normally invests at least 80% of its total assets in securities that comprise the Gold Miners Index. The Gold Miners Index is a modified market-capitalization weighted index primarily comprised of publicly traded companies involved in the mining for gold and silver. The fund is non-diversified.

Fund Basics

Category:	Equity Precious Metals
Fund Family:	Market Vectors
Total Assets:	4.33B
Legal Type:	Exchange Traded Fund

Performance & Risk

YTD Return:	-25.14%
3y Avg Return:	-33.27%
5y Avg Return:	-24.85%
Beta (3y):	0.43

As we mentioned before, there are many ETFs available in the market targeted to different goals. Some are more stable than others are, and some are very volatile such as UVXY. The best way to treat an ETF is to ask the same questions you would ask before investing in a stock. ETFs provide the diversification in a sector or an index that you would not easily get by buying individual stocks. The best way is to go to a website such as yahoo finance and research about an ETF (its composition, investment objective, past performance, volatility) and then decide if it is right for you.

23 A Few More Options

23.1 Options, Futures, and Currencies

Beyond stocks, mutual funds, and ETF, there are other financial instruments, such as options, futures, and Forex (currencies) trading that provide high leverage within a short time period. These are more speculative in nature due to short time period involved and provide opportunities to attain much higher ROI. The other side of the coin is that you could incur bigger losses as well. These also require better understanding of the mechanics of carrying out the trades and constant monitoring of the market.

23.2 Options and LEAPS

23.2.1   Introduction to Options

When you expect that a particular stock price is going to go up in future, you buy call options. Option is another form of leveraged investing where gains can be much higher, but it also involves higher risk of losing money. To be successful in options trading, one needs to have a good understanding of the mechanics of option trading and have some forms of strategy in place. Unlike stocks, options have time component to them. You can hold on to a stock and do not have to sell at a loss - may choose to wait until the stock price recovers. However, in option, you have to take action by the **expiration date** – you make money or lose money. You cannot wait out if things are not favorable.

There are mainly two types of options – **call options** and **put options**. In each of these, you can either buy or sell options. If you are buying a call or a put, you are the **option buyer or holder**. If you are selling a call or a put, you are the **option seller or writer**. So, you can choose one of these four:

- Buy call options
- Buy put options
- Sell call options
- Sell put options

Option Buyer

The option buyer pays a **premium** to the option seller. By paying the premium, the buyer is reserving the **rights to buy or sell shares** at a contract price **(strike price).** After buying the option, he has several choices:

- He may **exercise the option**. Exercise means he actually buys from the option seller or sells the stock to the option seller. He can exercise it early or on the expiration date.
- He may close the option by selling the option to a third person. Here, he is not actually buying or selling the stock. Let us say, he had paid $2 premium for a $40 strike price to buy. Now after 10 days, the stock price is $42, and the current premium for $40 strike price is $3. The option has an intrinsic value and a time value. Here the intrinsic value is $2 ($42 -$40), and the time value is $1. The time value decreases as it moves toward the expiration date. He can close the option by selling the option for $3 and make a profit of $1 per stock.

Option Seller

The seller always keeps the premium. The seller also has the **obligation to sell the stock or buy the stock** from the option buyer, if the option buyer decides to exercise the option. When the buyer exercises the options, the seller will be assigned. What it means is that the option write (seller) will have to provide the stock (when sold call options) or buy the stocks (when sold put options). Assignment is not under the seller's control. It depends on the buyer exercising the option. The second course of action is to buy back the option he originally sold. This does not involve real buying or selling stocks as is the case in an exercise. The third option is to do nothing when the option expires worthless. This is what the option seller wants most of the time - option expires worthless, and he keeps the premium.

23.2.2   How Call Options Work

When you expect a particular stock price to go up in future, you buy call options. The best way to understand a concept is to go through an example.

Source:	Yahoo finance page
Stock:	Walmart
Closing Price:	$60.11 on Nov 20, 2015. The stock has dropped 33% in last one year.

Calls: Option Expiry Date: Dec 11, 2015

Strike Price	Last	Bid	Ask
57	3.35	3.05	3.45
57.50	2.77	2.62	2.87
58.00	**2.79**	**2.19**	**2.43**
......	......	......	......
60	0.99	0.79	0.87
60.50	0.66	0.56	0.64
61	0.41	0.38	0.46
......	......		......
63.50	0.16	0.04	0.10
64.00	**0.05**	**0.03**	**0.06**
65.50	0.10	0.01	0.04

Fig. 23.1   Call Option Example

Buying Call Options

You buy calls, when you expect the stock price to go up. You pay premium upfront to the seller of call option. You have the right to buy the stock at the strike price any time on or before the expiration of the option period. If the price goes up, you can sell at a higher price and make a profit.

Example: You bought 10 call options (1000 stocks, as each option is 100 stocks) for Dec 11 at strike price of $58.00. For each stock, the premium is $2.79. The total price of the contract you have to pay is 1000 x $2.79 = $2,790. Strike price of $58 means you have the right to buy each share at $58. You can think, your cost per each stock as $58 + $2.79 = $60.79. If the stock price goes up above $60.79 before the expiry period, you will make a profit. The breakeven price is $60.79. If price stays below breakeven level, you lose money.

Scenario1: Price went up above breakeven price.

The stock price went up to $66 before Dec 11 when you decided to close your position by selling the option. You made a profit of $66 - $58 = $8 per each stock. The total profit would be at least 1000 x $8 = $8000. We need to subtract the contract price ($2,790) from $8,000. Your net profit is $8,000 - $2,790 = $5,210.

You made a profit of $5,210 by investing only $2,790. Remember, you only needed $2,790 to buy options for 1000 stocks. Instead, if you wanted to buy 1000 Walmart stocks, you would have needed $60,110. As we can see, with much smaller investment, you can make a much bigger profit. However, what happens if the price went down to $57.00?

Scenario2: Price went down below strike price

Walmart stock was trading at $57.00 on the expiry date (DEC 11). In this case, you just let the options expire. You are not going to make money by buying it at $58 and selling at $57. You also lost the premium ($2,790) that you paid. The money is gone forever. If you buy stocks instead, you can hold it as long as you like, expecting price to come back.

To summarize, the plus and minus of options compared to holding stocks are:
+   With smaller money, you can make larger gain compared to investing the same amount of money in stocks.
-    You can lose the money permanently unlike stocks where you can hold it as long as you want.
-    Unlike stocks, you do not get dividends from options.

Let us look at a scenario where the stock price was between strike price and the breakeven price.

Scenario3: Price is above strike price but below the breakeven price

The stock was trading at $59 on expiry date. You exercise the option and buy it at $58. You are making $1 ($59 - $58) on each share, with a total of $1,000. However, you are still losing $1790 ($1,000 - $2,790).

In the money and Out of money Call Options

When the strike price is below the market price, it is called in the money call option. When it is above, it is called out of money call options. In the money means, you get some money by exercising the option. However, it should be sufficiently in the money (more than the premium) to be able to make a net profit.

Selling Call Options

The opposite of buying call options is selling call options. A person who sells call options is betting that the stock price is going to go down, and the buyer would not exercise the options. In such a case, the seller of call options would keep the premium.

If the seller owns the stock, it is called **covered calls**. In case the stock price went up very high, he has to sell the stocks to the buyer of the call options. He missed the big upside movement but at least, kept the premium.

If he does not own the stock, it is called **naked calls**. Naked calls could be very dangerous. If the price went up very high, he has to buy these stocks from the market at a high value. It can result in very large losses without any upper bound.

23.2.3   How Put Options Work

Puts work similar to call options, except you buy put options when you think the price is going to go down in future. Let us look at some examples.

Source: Yahoo finance page
Stock: Walmart
Closing Price: $60.11 on Nov 20, 2015.

Puts : Option Expiry Date: Dec 11, 2015

Strike Price	Last	Bid	Ask
57	0.25	0.24	0.28
57.50	0.19	0.31	0.35
58.00	0.41	0.40	0.46
.....	.....	......	.....
60	0.96	1.08	1.20
60.50	1.07	1.38	1.51
61.50	**1.53**	**2.10**	**2.24**
......	.....		.....
63.50	5.95	2.79	4.05
64.00	3.90	3.10	4.55
64.50	6.26	3.55	5.00

Fig. 23.2   **Put Option Example**

Buying Put Options

You buy put options, when you expect that the price is going to go down. You bought 10 put options (total 1000 stocks) at strike price of $61.50 per share. The premium you paid is 1000 x $1.53 = $1,530. On or before the expiry, you have the right to sell at $61.50.

Scenario1

A few days after buying the puts, the stock price is now $58. The premium for the put option is now $4 ($3.50 plus $0.50 time value). You can sell the put option and make a profit of $4 per stock, with a total gain of $4,000. Subtracting the premium ($1,530) you paid, the net gain is $4,000 - $1,530 = $2,470 – solid ROI for $1,530 investment. The other choice is to exercise the options early or on expiration date.

Scenario2

The lowest stock price at close or any day before expiry date is $62. Since the stock price ($62) is higher than the strike price ($61.50), you are not going to make money by selling at $61.50 and buying at $62 – you let the option expire. However, you lost the premium ($1,530).

Put options have the same plus and minus similar to call options. You get the leverage of getting higher ROI but have the possibility of losing money.

In the money and Out of money Put Options

When the strike price is above the market price, it is called in the money put option. When it is below, it is called out of money put option. In the money means, you will get some money by exercising the option. However, it should be sufficiently in the money that is more than the premium to be able to make a net profit.

Selling Put Options

You sell put options, when you expect that the price is going to go up. You have the obligation to buy the stock at the strike price if the buyer of put options wanted to sell it to you. If the price went up above the strike price, you can buy the stock at low price – good for you. On the other hand, if the price went down below the strike price, you will have to buy at a price higher than the current market price – a loss for you.

23.2.4   Options Diagram

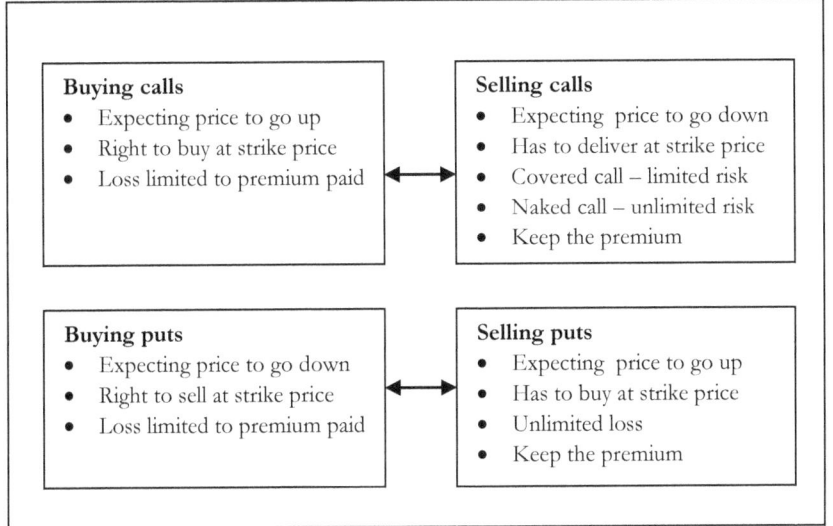

Buying calls
- Expecting price to go up
- Right to buy at strike price
- Loss limited to premium paid

Selling calls
- Expecting price to go down
- Has to deliver at strike price
- Covered call – limited risk
- Naked call – unlimited risk
- Keep the premium

Buying puts
- Expecting price to go down
- Right to sell at strike price
- Loss limited to premium paid

Selling puts
- Expecting price to go up
- Has to buy at strike price
- Unlimited loss
- Keep the premium

Fig. 23.3   Options Strategy

23.2.5   Bullish Options Strategy

You are expecting share price to go up. You can buy call options or sell put options.

Buying Call Options

You are expecting share price to go up during the option period. Three things could happen. For simplicity, we are omitting the commissions.

- Share price rises above the breakeven price (strike price + premium). You make net profit.
- Share price is above strike price and below breakeven price – You still exercise the option, but you will still have a net loss. Your net loss will be less than the premium.
- Share price is below strike price. You let the option expire. You net loss is equal to the premium you paid.

Selling Put Options

You have researched a stock, and the current price has come down where it looks reasonable and attractive to enter a long position. You expect that the price should go up from this point. However, you are not 100% sure, and you would buy it if the price went down further. If you wait, it may happen or may not happen. You can sell put options with strike price below the current price of the stock. If the price falls below strike price, you will be able to buy it cheaper and keep the premium. If the price stays between strike price and current price, you would still be able buy it cheaper than if you would have bought today. You keep the premium as well. If price stays above current price of today, you would miss the opportunity of buying it at today's price, but you still keep the premium. Let us look at Walmart example.

Walmart current price (11/21/15) is $60. You want to invest $11,400. You can sell put options at strike price of $57 that has a premium of $0.25 per share. If the stock price goes below $57 (let us say $56), you will have to buy at $57. You would have $11,400/$57 = 200 stocks or two put options. You would be rather happy as you were ready to buy at $60, but now you got it at $57.

What if the price went down to $54? In this case, you will have to buy it at $57, even if it is available at $54 in the market. This is fine as you were ready to buy it at $60 but got it at $57- not bad as you are temporarily losing less money than if you had bought it at $60. The person who bought the put options will make some good money. Both are happy. You also keep the premium equal to 200x0.25 = $50.

What if the stock price is between $57 and $60? You can still buy the stock from the market. This can be a cash generating strategy. However, if the stock goes above $60, you lost the opportunity to buy at $60. This strategy will work if you want to buy it only at a lower price and will generate some cash if that never happens. You do not want to use it as a cash generating strategy on a weak stock, as you have to buy it if the price falls below the strike price.

On the other side of the fence, why would someone (buying puts) throw away cash (premium)? He is betting to make a large gain from a small premium if price goes down. He is going in with a low probability and high ROI scenario. What is your trade off selling puts? You are trading off the certainty of buying it at today's price with generating some cash and possibility of buying it cheaper. If today was the bottom and the stock went up much higher, you missed a good opportunity.

To summarize:

- Sell puts for only those stocks that you wanted to buy in the first place if you were assigned.
- If you do not have money to buy the stocks assigned to you, do not sell puts. You are required by contract to buy if the share drops to the strike price.
- If you want to generate cash but really don't want to get possession of the stock, keep the strike price sufficiently below the current stock price where the probability of reaching the strike price is very low. However, the lower the strike price is, the lower the premiums you would get.
- If you are absolutely sure that you want to buy the stock, then buy the stock instead of selling puts.

23.2.6   Bearish Options Strategy

You are expecting share price to go down. You can buy put options or sell call options

Buying Put Options

You are expecting share price to go down during the option period. Three things could happen.

- Share price falls below the breakeven price (strike price - premium). You will buy at a lower price from the market and sell at a higher price to the seller of put options. You make a net profit.
- Share price is below strike price and above breakeven price – You still exercise the option, but you will still have a net loss. Your net loss will be less than the premium.
- Share price is above strike price. You let the option expire. Your net loss is equal to the premium you paid.

Selling Call Options (Covered Calls)

When you own a stock and do not want to sell it but want to collect premium, you can consider selling call options.

- You want to go for strike price that has low probability of happening so that you can still keep the stock and collect the premium. Go for strike price that is sufficiently higher yet provides reasonable premium.

- If the price stays below strike price, you keep the stock and keep the premium.
- If the price rises above strike price, you would have to sell the stocks at the strike price. With a strike price higher than the current price, you were able to sell at a higher price and keep the premium – not bad.
- How about if the price shot up way above the strike price? You missed a big upside. If you absolutely believe that stock price is going to get a pop and you do not want to sell the stock for a smaller profit or premium, you should not sell call options.
- Also, do not sell naked call options (you do not own the stocks). If the stock shot up very high, you are obliged to buy at high price and sell it at a lower price. Your loss is unlimited, and you do not want to be in such situations.

23.2.7   LEAPS

LEAPS (Long Term Equity AnticiPation Security) are types of option plans with longer durations. Durations of regular options range from a week to several months, whereas LEAPS are usually for a year or longer. LEAPS work the same way as regular options work. You can buy/sell LEAPS calls and buy/sell LAEPS puts.

The main advantage for having LEAPS is the longer duration. You have more than a year to make money or lose your premium. However, the premium for a strike price is usually higher than that of regular options, which means your potential gain will be lower than regular options. You are willing to take a lower profit while buying time to increase your chance of making some profit.

The best candidates for LEAPS are solid companies that have been beaten down recently due to poor performance or other reasons that could be temporary. If you believe that management is making the right calls to increase sales and reduce costs or taking other measures that will help the stock and increase EPS, there is a good chance that stock price would recover in a year or two. These kinds of companies will be good candidates for LEAPs where you can make large profit in a year or so. The wrong candidates would be the companies where the stock prices have gone down, the companies are losing market share quickly, and are expected to even go down in the long run. A drawback for LEAPS is that you do not get dividends as you would get from buying stocks. However, potential for gain is much higher for the amount of money invested, and lack of dividends does not become a major concern.

Let us look at an example for LEAPS and build the case if it makes sense to invest in LEAPS. We will look at Walmart.

Stock: Walmart			
Analysis Date: 11/21/2015			
Price	$60	Revenue last	2015 - $486B
52 Week high	$91	3 years	2014 - $476B
P/E	12.86		2013 - $469B
EPS	$4.67	Net Income	2015 - $16.4B
Dividend Yield	3.27%	last 3 years	2014 - $16B
Stock buyback Last 3 years	$17.6B		2013 - $17B
Market Cap	$193B	Cash flow	2015 - $28.6B
Tangible assets	$61B	last 3 years	2014 - $23.3B
			2013 - $25.6B

Fig. 23.4   LEAPS Example

The stock has lost almost 1/3rd (33%) of its value in the last year. Let us analyze the case if it is a good candidate for buying LEAPs.

CONs

- The revenue growth has slowed down
- Competitors (mainly Amazon) online sales are growing much faster than Walmart online sales. Amazon has an amazing online strategy and technology, and it is on a roll.
- Competitors' online growth is a big threat to Walmart business model as more customers want things to be delivered at home rather than shopping at physical stores.
- Employee wages and salaries are growing faster eating into profit margin with stagnant or declining EPS for next several years
- Walmart is spending almost a billion dollars a year on its online business. This will reduce EPS without any certainty that online strategy would work.
- Walmart is perceived as a provider of the best value (low price) but not the best buying experience.

As we can see, there are a plenty of things to worry about, and, it seems, the sky is falling for Walmart. Yes, these are difficult issues, but is the management working on these issues? Let us analyze what Walmart management is doing to tackle these issues. For any stock, nothing is black and white, and this makes investing in stock difficult and interesting. However, with experience and good analysis, one can find which issues are real, which ones are temporary, and if it is a good bargain. Identifying a solid bargain maximizes gain while minimizing risk of losing a large sum of money.

PROs

- Walmart is serious about its online strategy. It is investing large sum of money on its online business. This is a temporary hit on the EPS, but it will result in overall revenue growth. It will reverse the trend and stabilize the revenue it is losing to competitors on online sales.
- The revenue from physical stores is still growing, though at a slower pace. As Walmart has large number of physical stores, it is working on an online plus physical stores strategy where it can provide options to deliver at home or pick up from stores. As long as it can provide customers the convenience and low price, it will be successful.
- It is anticipating that higher wage will make employees motivated to work and take care of the stores and customers.
- Walmart is revamping store layouts to make it cleaner, good-looking, and navigation-friendly. All these will lead to better customer experience and higher revenue.
- It has started to bring more number of smaller stores into city areas so that it does not lose out business where customers just buy a few things several times a week.
- Walmart has a solid balance sheet with $61B in tangible assets.
- It is a blue chip DOW stock with low P/E (3 to 4 points lower than the average)
- It has always been profitable with $16B profit last year.
- It has maintained a steady upward dividend payment with a good yield of 3.27%.
- It has spent money on buybacks to reduce available stock count. Over the long run, this is good for shareholders as their share of profit increases. This is good for the company as they have to pay less on dividends. To look it in a different way, they can increase the dividend for existing shareholders without spending extra on dividends.
- Walmart has been a successful company with a long track record.
- There could be other stuffs that we do not know. A good management is always thinking to increase revenue. They may add more stores in the US and international markets. They may acquire companies. These are not facts, but management in good companies is always thinking how to increase shareholder value. They are working for the shareholders.

Looking at the pros and cons and having previous experience on similar cases, I would feel comfortable buying LEAPs expiring on Jan19, 2018. Between Nov'15 and Jan'18, it is more than two years. Two years gives a sufficiently long window where I can expect the price to appreciate 20-25% from the current low price of $60. It has to reach $72-$75 within the next two years for yearly gain of 10-12.5%.

If I buy the stock, my overall ROI will be 10-12.5% plus dividends of 3.3%, with total yearly gain of 13.3% to 15.8%. Let us say, I want to take calculated risk by buying LEAPS for $5,000. Remember, I might lose the whole $5,000 if stock price does not turnout the way my analysis suggests within next two years. The amount of $5,000 is a hypothetical figure here, and everyone needs to evaluate what percentage this represents with respect to his or her portfolio. This is risk money, and one needs to be aware of that.

Stock: Walmart
Closing Price: $60.11 on Nov 20, 2015.
Investment amount $5,000

Calls: LEAPS Expiry Date: **Jan 18th, 2018**

Strike Price	Premium	Break even Price	# of stocks	Exercised at				
				$66	$71	$76	$81	$86
				Net Profit				
$45	$15.71	$60.71	318 (3 lots)	$1682	$3272	$4862	$6452	$8042
$50	$11.65	$61.65	429	$1866	$4011	$6156	$8301	$10446
$55	$8.60	$63.60	581	$1394	$4299	$7204	$10109	$13014
$60	$6.00	$66.00	833	$0	$4165	$8330	$12495	$16660
$70	$3.00	$73.00	1666	-$5000	-$3334	$4998	$13328	$21658
$75	$1.93	$76.93	2590	-$5000	-$5000	-$3334	$10541	$23491
$80	$1.36	$81.36	3676	-$5000	-$5000	-$5000	-$5000	$17056

Fig. 23.5   LEAPS Analysis Case Study

We computed the gains for different strike price and different exercise price, as shown in the table above. Among the various exercise prices, the highest probability of making any profit is $66. Let us analyze if we are going to make enough profit. The best strike price would be $50 with $11.65 premium. For $5000 investment, the net profit would be $1,866, which gives 18.66% yearly return – not bad. If we bought stocks instead for $5,000, we would have made a profit of $490 in two years. Including dividend yield of 3.3%, the yearly return would have been 8.2%.

The other thing to look at is that the gain is higher for higher strike price and higher exercise price. The best strategy for LEAPS would be to look for a reasonable ROI (15-20%) and then choose the least breakeven price (usually low strike price). If you are looking for high ROI, the strike price and the breakeven price would be much higher which reduces the probability of the stock reaching the high exercise price. In which case, you may not make any money or may lose the investment ($5,000 in this case) completely.

Lesson

Even if there is possibility of high ROI, do not go for those investments where the probability is low. You may be lucky occasionally, but it will not work out well over the long run. **On the contrary, even if the ROI is low to medium, go for investments where the probability is higher.** As a conservative investor, I go for high-probability, low/medium ROI choices rather than low-probability high-ROI investments. You can build slow but steady wealth over the long run.

CHAPTER 23   Options and Futures

23.3 Futures

Future is a form of highly leveraged financial instrument where the gain and loss can be high. It is a contract between two persons, where one is agreeing to buy a commodity (corn, oil, or gold for example), and the other one is agreeing to sell the commodity at a price agreed by both parties. It is called future as the exchange of commodity is going to happen in future, on a target date, and at an agreed price. It is a binding contract that both parties need to honor.

23.3.1   History of Futures – No Pun Intended

Before futures market came into existence, the farmers in US Midwest produced their crops and brought to Chicago, which was the commodity center, to sell their crops; sometimes they would get a good price, and other times there were not many buyers. In these cases, they had to sell at a very low price, or things would just go waste. The future market started around 1850s in Chicago where buyers and sellers would agree on a price and a place where the crops would be delivered on a future date. This helped both the buyers and the sellers. The producer now has a sure buyer and a known price - he can accordingly plan on raising crops. The uncertainty was removed. The buyer also has certainty now. He is sure to have access to the crops at a known price on a future date. He can plan better to manufacture finished goods.

Fast forward to today's futures markets, the same principle of futures applies today. The buyer and seller sign a contract where the seller delivers a commodity at an agreed price on a future date. The traders who are interested in real physical exchanges of commodities are called **hedgers**. They are hedging to protect themselves from future price fluctuation. However, today, there are more players who do not sell or buy physical commodities. The future trader is betting that a price would increase or decrease in future. If the bet goes right, he makes money; else, he loses money. The groups that are betting to make money but not interested in real physical exchange of goods are called **speculators.** Today's future market deals not only with agricultural commodities but also with many more things – gold, silver, oil, DOW index, and S&P index.

23.3.2   Future Trading Walkthrough

To trade in futures, you need to open a future account with a broker (most of the brokers who deal with stocks also deal with future trading). Let us work through an example on future trading. You want to buy gold future. Each gold future contract is for 100 troy ounce of gold. On this date (Nov 25, 2015), gold future for Feb 2016 (GCG16) is trading at $1072.5 per troy ounce. Source www.barchart.com

You are expecting gold price to go up in future. You would buy one gold future contract for Feb 2016 (GCG16). The total value of the contract is 100x$1072.5 = $107,250. You do not need the full money ($107,250) to buy one future contract. You need only a fraction (typically 4.5%) of the contract value called the **margin money**. In this case, you need $4826 to buy one gold contact.

If you really wanted to buy 100 oz. of real gold and take possession of physical gold, you do not need to worry about what happens between Nov 25, 2015 and Feb 2016. You will pay ($107,250) to receive 100 oz. of real gold. However, like most future traders, you are not interested in buying the real gold; you are interested in making money if the price of gold increases. You are not going to hold the future contract until the delivery date. You are going to close the contract before the delivery date. If you bought a contract, you will sell it at some point to close the contract and take the profit or loss. Let us see what happens after you bought the future.

After one day of buying the future, gold price has moved up to $1074.5 per troy oz. The contract is now valued at 100x$1074.6 = $107,460. You made a profit of $210. Your account will show your balance as $5,036 ($4,826 + $210).

At end of day2: Gold price is $1073.6. You lost $100. Your trade balance will be $4,936.

The trade balance is calculated on a daily basis and reflected in your account. The minimum amount, the value of gold can change, is $0.1 or 10 cents, which is equal to $10 per contract. The minimum amount any contract can change is called the **tick**.

Let us say, after 25 days, the price of gold is $1,125.2. Now you have a paper profit of $5,270. At this point, you decided to take the profit. You closed (sold) the contract and took the profit of $5,270. That is a huge ROI for the investment in less than a month. As you can see, in futures trading, you are controlling a large amount with a much smaller amount of your money. It uses a very high leverage. With initial margin money of only $4826, you are controlling $107,250 worth of gold. Because of high leverage, you can make great profit. The opposite is also true. If the gold price drops after you bought, you would incur a big loss as well. You could lose your entire margin money of $4826. You could even lose more if you did not put a stop order.

If you believe that the gold price is going to go down, you would sell a future contract instead of buying it. How do you know which way the price would go? It depends on your analysis of market conditions, experience, historical data, and geo-political factors. Always close your future contract before the delivery date; else, you would have to take possession of the commodity if you bought the future. You need to have the money to buy the commodity. If you sold the future contract, you have to provide the commodity at the delivery date as per the contract terms. Imagine you bought a future contract for livestock and forgot to close. Now you are the proud owner of all these wonderful creatures!

23.4 Forex Trading

Forex or Foreign Exchange trading is buying or selling one currency versus another. For example, if you believe that Euro is going to appreciate against the Dollar in next several months, you would sell your dollars and buy Euros now. In next two months, Euro appreciated against dollar as you expected. Since Euro has appreciated against dollar, you would get more dollars for the Euros you are holding. Now you have more dollars at your hand than you started two months back – you made a profit.

However, if things did not turn out the way you expected, you would lose money - when you convert the Euro to Dollar, you would have less than what you started with. This is, basically, how Forex or currency trading works. You are speculating (hopefully not completely wildly but based on your analysis of international economics, trades, politics, and what not) that one currency in a currency pair will move in certain direction. If things turn out right, you make money; else, you lose money. The legendary investor George Soros is known as the person who broke the bank of England. He shorted British Pound against Dollar predicting that Pound would fall with respect to Dollar. The Pound fell, and he made a profit of $1B.

23.4.1   Forex Market

- Forex (short hand FX) market is highly liquid, trades 24 hrs. a day, and 5 days a week.
- FX market got started in 1971 when international trade transitioned from fixed to floating exchange rate.
- There is no commission in forex trading, but the dealers make their money through the spreads (we will talk about spreads in next section)
- The main participants are central banks, commercial banks and financial institutions, hedge funds, and individual investors.
- Currency trading is done for different pairs of currencies, such as, Dollar/Pound, Euro/Dollar, Dollar/Yen, Euro/Yen, Pound/Yen, and US Dollar/Canadian Dollar etc.
- Individual investors can use high leverage ratio (200:1) and control large amount of money with a small investment.
- Because of very high leverage, the gain or loss could be very high.
- Forex is a self-regulated market without any central regulating agency.

CHAPTER 23   Options and Futures

23.4.2   Forex Trading Walkthrough

First, we have to understand how to read the currency pair quote. Let us look at Euro and Dollar quote.

EUR/USD quote on 11/25/2015

Base/Quoted	Bid (sell)	Ask (buy)
EUR/USD	1.0605	1.0610

- The quote has two prices - the bid and the ask prices.
- The difference between the two is **spread**. The first currency in the pair is called the **Base currency**, and the second one is called the **quoted currency**. In the example above, EUR is the base currency, and USD is the quoted currency.
- When you buy a currency pair (going long on the base currency), you are buying the base currency and selling the quoted currency
    - If you are long on Euro, you would buy Euro and sell Dollar. For every Euro, you would pay 1.0610 dollars.
- When you sell a currency pair (going short on the base currency), you are selling the base currency and buying the quoted currency
    - If you are short on Euro, you would sell Euro and buy Dollar. For every Euro you sell, you would get 1.0605 dollars
- The spread in this case is $(1.0610 - 1.0605) = 0.0005$

Having established the currency pair, ask/bid price, and spread, let us take up some real examples. You want to sell one lot of EUR/USD expecting that Euro will depreciate against Dollar in future. One lot of Euro would be €100,000, which is roughly equal to $94,251. Do you have to have $94,251 or €100,000 to start trading? You need a much smaller amount to trade (buy or sell) one lot. With a ratio of 200:1, you would need to put roughly $530 to carry out a trade for one lot. However, the institutions would require initial deposit $5,000 to $10,000 to open a forex account.

Day1   Quote on 11/25/2015

Base/Quoted	Bid (sell)	Ask (buy)
EUR/USD	1.0605	1.0610

- You are expecting Euro to depreciate against Dollar. You would sell one lot of EUR/USD. You are selling Euro and buying Dollar. For selling €100,000, you would get 100,000x1.0605 = $106,050 (at the sell rate of $1.0605 for each Euro).

- With a margin of 200:1, you need $530 to carry out the transaction.

Day10
     Quote on 12/05/2015

Base/Quoted	Bid (sell)	Ask (buy)
EUR/USD	1.0405	1.0410

- Now Dollar has appreciated against the Euro as per your expectation.
- You decided to sell the dollar and buy Euro. For $106,050 you are holding, you would get ($106,050/1.0410) = €101873. You are getting one Euro for every 1.0410 dollars.
- When you sold Euro on day1, you got the bid (sell) rate, which is lower than the Ask (buy) rate. When you bought Euro on day5, you paid a higher rate on it. The FX broker makes the money from the spread.
- For you to make money, gain from the appreciation of the currency must be more than the spread hit you would take.
- On day10, you are holding €101873. You started with €100,000 for the transaction. You made a profit of €1,873, which is equivalent to $1,770.
- Since you are on margin, you have to deduct the margin interest from your profit. You needed $106,050 for the transaction, but you put only $530. At 6% annual interest rate, you need to pay $174 toward margin interest. Your get gain is $1,770 - $174 = $1,596 – tremendous returns on $530 investment in 5 days!

Things to be aware of in futures
- Due to high leverage, the gain and loss are greatly magnified.
- The currency you are betting to appreciate or depreciate has to overcome the bid/ask spread to make any profit.
- The longer you hold the transaction, the more you would have to pay for margin interest

Chapter
24

24 The Real Deal

24.1 Real Estate

Real estate is one of the relatively safer investment choices, and many people have done it successfully. One thing is certain that the usable land is fixed, and the population is going up. There is plenty of land available in remote areas, but few people want to go there. The lands where people want to live are fixed, and the long-term expectation is that real estate price would go up in these areas. In most cases, real estate prices have gone up in the long run. It does not mean that you cannot lose money in real estate. Generally, real estate moves in cycles. It would go up for several years and then stall or go down for few years. There are cases, where home prices have not recovered back to the price even after 10 years. We will analyze the real estate Dos and Don'ts so that it will help you to minimize risk and maximize potential for success.

24.2 Location, Location, and Location

As they say, the top three requirements for real estate are location, location, and location. The price of real estate in good locations is high compared to other locations, but they provide better protection during downturns and better appreciation during good times. The areas with good school districts attract more buyers and appreciate better compared to other areas.

Look for areas that are going to have population increase due to natural growth and influx. You need more demands for houses to maintain price or price to appreciate. Real estate is a function of demand and supply. Areas with good climate generally attract more people in the long turn. Look for areas with steady job growths and companies that have long-term prospects to stay in the areas. Look for areas with multiple companies and not just one or two big companies.

CHAPTER 24   Investing in Real Estate

A city or town with one company as the major source of employment could be risky during economic downturns. If the company decides to downsize, it could have a big impact on the house prices for a long time.

Areas with large natural bodies of water do well in real estate. As the saying goes, you cannot lose money in real estate in places that have plenty of water. Water is the most basic ingredient of life. All the old civilizations formed around big rivers. Modern technology can somewhat neutralize this by forming water grids and transporting water to places that do not have water nearby. However, areas with large sources of water, such as rivers, lakes, and oceans have the natural advantages and have the highest population densities.

24.3 Cost of Ownership

If you are planning to stay in the house and not sell it within 3-4 years of buying, it makes sense to consider buying. Even if you leave the area, you can still own the house and rent it out. In a hot housing market, the house could appreciate significantly even in just 3-4 years. We will go through an example to see how much it costs to own compared to renting. What we find is that buying a house is financially better than renting, unless you are absolutely sure of selling the house within several years of buying. The main reason is that it typically costs 5-6% of the sale price as commission that the seller pays. If you sell within a few years of buying, you could lose money.

The total cost of owning a house is not an absolute value, as you still have to pay rent to live somewhere - it is the difference between the cost of owning a house and the cost of renting. The question is whether you can bear the differential. In fact, it may come out cheaper in some areas to own than to rent. Let us go through an example.

You bought a house for $500,000 with $100,000 down payment. You financed the rest ($400,000) through a 30-yr fixed loan at 4% interest. Let us calculate the monthly cost of owning the house.

- Monthly interest payment toward the loan would be: $400,000x0.04x(1/12) =$1,333
- You have to pay property tax at around 1.2% annually: $500,000x0.012 = $6,000 per year or $500 per month.
- Add $1000 for insurance and around $3,200 for yearly maintenance. It comes out be $4,200 yearly, or $350 per month.

- In some cases, there are other charges, such as PMI (mortgage insurance) and homeowner's association fees. That could be another $200/month.
- Opportunity Cost: If you did not buy the house and invested $100,000 at 8% returns in the stock market, you would be getting $667 per month. After deducing approximately $1/3^{rd}$ of it as tax that you have to pay, the opportunity you are losing out every month is: $667x(2/3) = $445
- In fact, you would get back roughly $1/3^{rd}$ of the interest payment and property tax as itemized deduction in your tax return. You would get back $1/3$ ($1,333 + $500) = $611.

Real cost (monthly) of owning a house is =

Mortgage interest payment
+ Property tax
+ Home insurance + house maintenance
+ PMI + HOA
+ Opportunity cost of down payment
− Tax savings due itemized deduction

= $1,333 + $500 + $350 +$200 + $445 - $611
= $2,217.

In most cases, the monthly rent would be around $2,217 or a few hundred dollars less. In some hot markets, it could even cost more to rent. What are the advantages of owning a house? Apart from the intangible benefits of owning your privacy in the house, memories associated with it, and other things, there could be huge financial benefits when the price of the house appreciates. We will see the power of leverage here. We assume that the monthly cost of owning the house is same as the monthly rent for renting a similar house or apartment.

24.4 Building Wealth – Power of Leverage

Let us assume the house price appreciates 3.5% per year for next 30 years. With a very reasonable rate of 3.5% compound growth for 30 years, the $500,000 house will be worth $1.4M. The gain is $900,000. Here is the beauty! The gain is not on the basis of $500,000. It is based on how much you paid initially which is $100,000. So, the net gain is $900,000 on investment of $100,000. This is a whooping annual average return of 30%. The other beauty is that, for married couple, up to $500,000 profit from your primary residence is tax free.

24.5 Cash Flow

Real estate is all about positive cash flow. We established that buying a house with 20% down payment could generate annualized return of 30% for the next 30 years. The down payment could be less than 20% in many cases making the returns even better. If it were a business, the returns are fantastic, and the stock price would sky rocket. So what is the catch?   It is the cash flow.

Many people may not realize, but they are using leverage while buying their homes. With any leverage or any business, cash flow is very important to stay alive and avoid bankruptcy. If you cannot meet the monthly obligations, you would be forced sell the house or rental property. Let us tee off the calculation we made in the last section to calculate the cash flow requirements for owning the house.

Cash Flow Requirement for Primary Residence =

> Mortgage interest payment
> + Property tax
> + Home insurance + house maintenance
> + PMI + HOA
> − Tax savings due itemized deduction
> + Payment toward principal.

In the cash flow calculation above, we included everything except the opportunity cost of down payment, as this is the benefit you are forfeiting, but you do not have to pay this. You also need to pay some amount toward principal (let us keep this $500). The cash flow requirement comes out to be: $1,333 + $500 + $350 +$200 -$611 + $500 = $2,272.

In fact, this is no bad; you would have to pay similar amount if you rented instead. For this very reason, many people decide to buy a house instead of renting. How about buying a second house or condominium as rental property? We will discuss it next, with the focus on the cash flow issues for rental properties.

24.6 Rental Property as Investment

The cost structure for a rental property is similar to a primary residence. You need to put down some money as down payment and finance the rest from loan. You need to pay interest on the loan, property tax, property insurance, rental property maintenance, PMI, HOA, payment toward principal. The interest is generally a little higher for a rental property compared to a primary residence.

It is advisable to form a limited liability company (LLC) in your name to hold the house instead of holding it directly under your name. In most cases, you are only liable up to the value of the rental property. It protects your other assets, such as primary residence or other rental properties from claims on this rental property. It will cost some money toward the LLC yearly dues. Also, it is advisable to buy larger amount of insurance against claim. If there were a claim, the money would first go from the insurance rather than directly from the rental property. It would cost a little more for the insurance compared to insurance on your primary residence.

Also, you need to take care of the maintenance needs of the rental property. If it is within 30-40 miles of your home and you do not mind taking care of it yourself, you can manage the property yourself. Managing does not mean you are going to fix it yourself but calling the plumber, electrician, or whoever and taking care of the problem. However, if the property is farther or you do not want to manage, you can hire a property management company to take care of the properties. They will take care of all maintenance needs including finding tenants, vetting the tenants, and collecting rents. You still have to pay the cost of maintenance that the property management company usually deducts from the rent it collects. Managing the property through a property management company eliminates most of the hassles. In fact, you most likely won't even see the tenant. However, they charge around 6-8% of the monthly rent as their fees.

Cash Flow Requirement for Rental Property:

> Mortgage interest payment ($1,400): rate is higher for rental prop.
> + Property tax ($500)
> + Insurance and rental property maintenance ($350)
> + PMI and HOA ($200)
> + Payment toward principal ($500)
> + LLC fees ($100)
> + Insurance premium to cover claims ($150)
> + Property management fees ($192, round it to $200)
>
> = $3,400

CHAPTER 24   Investing in Real Estate

This is how much you have to spend every month. Most of it will be covered from the rent you would get. If the property fetches monthly rent of $2,400, it would cover most of the cash flow requirements. You still have to pay $1,000 every month out of pocket. Actually, the real cost is $500 every month as $500 payment toward principal reduction is still your money. Given the historical appreciation over a period of 30 years, you would still make a lot of money. However, here is the catch.

For rental property, you need $3,400 every month even if you do not find a tenant. It produces a tremendous cash-flow burden. Another case is, if you are laid off and do not have the financial wherewithal to pay $1,000 that is not covered by the rent, it will be really problematic. One difference between stocks and real estate during a downturn is that, it is a paper loss for stocks. It is not a real loss until you sell it. If you had done the due diligence and bought solid dividend-paying companies, you just need to hold and wait until the stock market comes back. In fact, you would continue to receive dividends during downturn. This is not the case with real estate. You still need to pay the mortgage interest and everything else whether you have a tenant or not. The other difference is that stock market downturns are much shorter than real estate downturns. Most of the cases, the stock market recovers from a bear market within two years, whereas it may take several years to 5-10 years for real estate market to come back. The third major difference is the locality. The stock market depends on the whole US economy whereas real estate markets are highly local. Some parts may recover, and some may not or may take much longer.

It is very critical in real estate that you solve the cash flow problems in difficult times. Many bought houses and investment rental properties leading up to the 2007-2008 crisis with subprime loans. The cash flow requirement went up after the initial low teaser rates expired. Many lost their jobs, and many houses could not be rented out, lying vacant for months and in some cases, for years. This became a tremendous cash flow problem. Many houses were foreclosed, and the housing market collapsed. The critical lesson is that you know your financials well and make sure you could absorb the shock if a downturn happens. The other critical lesson is that invest in areas where it is easy to get tenants. Even if the rents would go down during a downturn, you will still get some amount of rent instead of not getting any. It will help a lot to absorb the cash flow shock. If you can survive the downturns, you would come out winner in the long run.

Section IV

Personal Development
Personal Finance

25 Meet the Most Important Person

The most important person in the world who can help you is you. Let us spend some time to understand you and make the best of you. We will talk about life skills that will help you throughout your life.

25.1 Health – The Biggest Asset of All

At first, I thought, "does this topic belong in this book?" But, when I looked deep, realized that the biggest asset is you and your health. Everything else is dependent on sound health, positive feelings, and getting excited about life.

25.1.1   Healthy Habits

Incorporate many good habits into your life, and you are bound to see positive results. Once something becomes a habit (good or bad), it becomes an integral part of life and works on autopilot mode. Getting rid of a bad habit is not easy. While you focus on acquiring good habits, do not invite bad ones to your life. Here are some good habits. Most of these are obvious, but we often forget them to carry out for one reason or the other.

- **Eat healthy:** Cut down on fat, sugar, and salt, the three major contributors of health issues down the road. Excess fat and cholesterol can cause heart problem, excess sugar can cause diabetes, and salt increases blood pressure.

  Eat plenty of fruits and vegetables. The benefits are huge as they provide vitamins and minerals that our body dearly needs.

- **Exercise:** Do some physical exercise, three to five times a week. Sign up for an inexpensive gym and use it to keep healthy and in shape. Walk for 15 to 30 mins every day at work. If your job is sedentary, just take a 5 min break (depending on the job) every hour to stretch and take a mini walk down the aisle.

  Another routine you can include is Yoga. Yoga is a form of mind and body exercise that works on various parts of your body, externally and internally. A part of Yoga is about breathing exercises that bring life and energy to the body and mind. Originally practiced by the ancient sages in India, Yoga is now popular in many parts of the world.

- **Get enough sleep:** Our body needs certain amount of sleep to function at the highest level. With internet readily available, it is easy to spend hours on internet at night. With a good night sleep, you will easily experience high productivity or the opposite without it.

- **Drink plenty of water:** Water keeps our body hydrated. It keeps the energy level and mood up. It reduces blood pressure, reduces blood sugar, helps kidney function, keep skin healthy, and improves many other things in our body.

- **Laugh heartily:** Laughter is the best medicine for your health and mood. When appropriate, do not shy away from a hearty laugh and infecting others.

25.1.2   Vitamins and Natural Sources

Vitamin A
- Good for vision and healthy eyes
- Helps in immunity and reproductive behavior
- Found in carrot, sweet potato, and spinach

Vitamin B
- Vitamin B is a group of vitamins, prominent ones are B6 and B12
  - **B1 (Thiamin)**
    - Helps convert carbohydrates to energy
    - Helps proper functioning of brain and nervous systems
    - Found in pine nuts and soybeans
  - **B2 (Riboflavin)**
    - An antioxidant and helps body in fighting disease
    - Found in beef liver and fortified cereals

- o   **B3 (Niacin)**
  - Converts food to energy
  - Found in peanuts, chicken, and beef
- o   **B6**
  - Helps to digest food, helps to form Hemoglobin in the blood, stabilizes blood sugar, and make antibodies
  - Found in chickpeas, fish, and beef liver
- o   **B7 (Biotin)**
  - Necessary for cell growth
  - Helpful in maintaining steady blood sugar
  - Help strengthen hair and nails
  - Found in peanuts and leafy green vegetables
- o   **B9 (Folic acid)**
  - Helps prevent birth defect for pregnant women
  - Found in leafy green vegetables, fruit nuts, and spinach
- o   **B12**
  - Critical for healthy nervous system and formation of red blood cells
  - Found in animal products (beef liver, salmon, tuna)

Vitamin C
- It fights common cold. It is an important antioxidant.
- Found in citrus fruits (oranges, lemons) and red peppers

Vitamin D
- Helps Calcium absorption and bone growth
- Helps develop immunity and fights inflammation
- Sunlight helps our body to create vitamin D
- Cod liver oil, sword fish, and salmon are good sources

Vitamin E
- An important antioxidant and protects cells
- Important for immunity and helps blood clot formation
- Found in sunflower seed and almonds

Vitamin K
- Critical for blood to clot when you get a cut
- Green and leafy vegetables (collard greens)

25.1.3   Minerals and Natural Sources

Calcium
- Body needs for strong bones, teeth, and muscle function
- Found in milk, eggs, yogurts, and leafy greens

Iron
- Body needs this to form hemoglobin in blood
- Protein needs iron to carry oxygen to cells
- Found in red meat, fish, chicken, lentils, and beans

Lycopene
- Has antioxidant properties and protects from heart disease and cancer
- Found in tomato and watermelon

Lysine
- A type of Amino acid that helps body absorb calcium
- Helps for strong bones and strong connective tissue
- Helps regulate cholesterol levels in body
- Proteins (red meat, legumes, nuts, and soybeans) are good source

Magnesium
- Keeps heart beat steady and bones strong
- Helps in correct nerve function and muscle function
- Found in multi-grain unrefined breads, almonds, cashews, and spinach

Omega-3 fatty acid
- Helps in good brain health and reduces inflammation
- Found in vegetable oil, green vegetables, nuts and seeds, and tuna fish

Potassium
- Controls electrical activity of heart
- Builds muscles and breakdowns carbohydrates to energy
- Found in sweet potato, red meat, chicken, and fish

Selenium
- Prevents chronic disease, helps regulate thyroid function
- Found in brazil nut and tuna fish

Zinc
- Plays important role in immune system
- Found in Oysters, chickens, and Alaskan crabs

25.1.4   Herbs and Benefits

Basil (Tulsi)	Has anti-bacterial and anti-inflammatory properties. Source of beta-carotene and anti-oxidant agents, good source for minerals
Cayenne Pepper	It contains capsaicin that helps reduce appetite. Believed to have anti-cancer properties
Celery	Used to reduce blood pressure
Cilantro	Lowers bad cholesterol, a good source of minerals and anti-oxidants
Cinnamon	Lowers blood sugar and has anti-diabetic effect
Cumin seed	Keeps blood sugar in check. Helps prevent stomach ulcers
Fenugreek	improves blood sugar control
Garlic	Helps fight cold. Reduces blood pressure
Ginger	Has anti-inflammatory properties and helps fight nausea
Ginseng	American Ginseng is known to fight blood sugar level. Chinese Ginseng is known to boost immunity
Mint	Relieves IBS (Irritable Bowel Syndrome) pain and may help fight nausea
Oregano	Has antibacterial and antifungal properties
Rosemary	Higher levels in blood enhance brain cognitive function
Sage	Improves brain function and memory
Schizandra	Known for its anti-aging properties
Thyme	Full of anti-oxidants. Improves health and fights cancer and aging
Turmeric	Strong anti-inflammatory effect

CHAPTER 25 The Most Important Person

25.2 Personality and Attitude

25.2.1 Habits to be Effective and Happy

- **Manage time properly.** There are only 24 hours in a day, and you need to use it properly. Someone wisely said, "Time is money." As you would not want to waste money, so you should not waste time. Often, lack of time results from inadequate prioritization and inability or unwillingness to say no. As you learn to prioritize, important things will get done, and you will have quality time to think and do fun stuffs.

- **Be results or goals oriented:** Once you have a goal or goals (doing well at work, loving your kids, treating others nice, saving money, learning about investments, help out others, do workout, or whatever), it puts the spotlight at the end result and brings you slowly toward that. Just by having a goal, you are halfway through, and chances of achieving the goal are quite high. Without an end goal, you may be spending time, but it could be just activities.

- **Look at the big picture:** The best way to not get stressed and be happy is to look at the big picture. Imagine what would be the driving experience if you looked only ten ft. in front of you – you would be constantly adjusting the steering to keep the vehicle within the lines. When you keep your view one hundred feet ahead, you are hardly making any steering adjustment, and driving is fun. This is also true in investing. When you have researched a company well and have understood it well, you will stay the course and not capitulate when things do not go in your favor.

- **If you could have only one thing in life, choose fun:** Fun makes life meaningful and worth living. It makes everything go smooth and easy. Whatever is your goal or whatever you are trying to achieve, never lose sight of fun.

- **Listen carefully:** In a meeting or a conversation, listen carefully and show your sincerity. It will help in getting support and getting your work done.

- **Learn to appreciate:** Happy people are always appreciative. Thank and compliment people. You will be happy and make others happy. Negativity will be out, and positivity will be in.

25.3 Managing Your Career and Workplace

Your career is one of the most important things in your life. A person is likely to have a working career spanning 35 years (25 to 60). It is our primary source of income, and one has to manage it carefully and smartly. Here are some of the things that one needs to be aware and make the most of it.

- **Choose career wisely:** It is important that you choose a career that you are going to enjoy and that pays well as well – both are important. If you enjoy what you are doing, things will be easy on the job, and you are more likely to perform well. Also, it is a fact that certain jobs pay better than others do. If you have a choice, choose one that offers both.

- **Understand what ownership means:** To grow in the company, think what you would do if you were the owner of the company – do not think about the benefits but the responsibilities. Before you get a promotion to a higher position, demonstrate the ability, and behave as if you are already there.

- **Identify your natural frequency:** Politics at work is shortsighted; it is going to come out sooner or later. Identify your personality type. Are you more comfortable being content expert in certain areas, or are you a people person who genuinely like to work with others and get things done by delegating rather than doing yourself? Many companies have both of the paths where one can grow and be successful. If you try to be what you are not, you are going to hate it. However, you still need to learn the things that are not natural to you; one cannot completely isolate oneself and have a successful career or be a good manger without a basic understanding of how things work.

- **Effective Communication:** In meetings, speak concisely and to the point. Do not give roundabout answers or show evasiveness and ambiguity. If speaking in front of others is not natural to you, make conscious effort to make it better. Same thing holds good for writing emails. Do not write very long emails. If it requires a long email, first summarize in a couple of sentences what you want to communicate and give details later.

- **Assertiveness and persuasiveness:** Be nice to others but be assertive. You do not have to please everyone at the expense of losing your ground easily. If you believe that you have a good idea or something worth pursuing, talk to key people in one-on-one sessions to explain them and get their buy-in.

- **Humorously Serious:** Take business seriously with a coating of humor. We got the job to contribute to company's success and be useful for the company. That is job number 1. But, keeping a sense of humor goes a long way and creates an environment where everyone is working as a team and enjoying the work.

- **Make it known:** Do not complain but communicate your needs. You do not have to brag your accomplishments but communicate what you accomplished in email and one-on-one meeting with your boss. Share with team how you solved a problem or found a way that will help the company and other employees. Out of sight, out of mind! Communicate to your boss that because of such and such contributions, corresponding raise (salary, stock options, or other benefits) would be appropriate. If you have done a good job and communicated well, the rewards will be better than keeping silent.

- **Networking:** At work and outside work, have a strategic network, which you can tap when needed. In big companies, good opportunities open up that can give an instant boost to your career. Similarly, keeping a network outside will help you when you are looking for a job, or you will come to someone's mind when opportunities come up.

- **Keep yourself employable:** As the nature of jobs is changing often due to rapid changes in technology and internationalization of jobs, keep yourself employable by takings courses, training, and doing self-study from time to time.

25.4 Negotiations 101

Whether aware or not, we negotiate regularly – negotiate our salary and benefits in a new job, negotiate for a good price when buying a car, or ask for good behavior or good results from kids in exchange for some rewards or special things they want. Negotiation involves two or more parties (usually two) where each side is trying to maximize what it gets out of the deal. Both sides may not get everything they want, but if they are satisfied with what they get, it is a win-win deal. How can you maximize your gains or be able to strike deals? Knowing and learning negotiation skills will help you to get the best out of it.

Preparation Phase

- **Do your homework**

  The most important thing in negotiation is doing the homework – arm yourself with information and relevant details. If you are buying certain car, know the price of same car sold in your locality and get information from internet as much as possible. When negotiating salary, know the salary range and benefits companies are paying for similar positions. Without information, you may end up getting less, or the deal may not go through.

- **Have a clear idea when you can say yes**

  Have a clear idea about the approximate range or minimum you would agree before you go to a negotiation. This will prevent you from making bad on-the-spot decisions. Have a second alternative. If you are ready to walk out when your reasonable demands are not met, you would be in much better position to negotiate, and you would get your demands. It is always good to negotiate from a position of strength and clarity than weakness and lack of a plan.

Negotiation Phase

- **Sell yourself**

  Even if you have put your achievements in resume, express in own words your expertize and how you are going to do the best job. Instead of saying in vague terms, corroborate your case with anecdotal accomplishments from previous jobs. If you look more believable and likeable, you stand to gain more.

- **Ask relevant questions and listen carefully**

  By asking questions, you will know what the company is looking for and what their urgency is. This will help you to judge how far you can press.

- **Don't say yes to the first set of choices**

  There are many components to a deal. A job compensation package, for example, comprises of basic pay, benefits, bonus, stock options, and RSUs (Restricted Stock Units). You may rearrange the various components of the package to maximize your overall compensation. However, keep in mind that base salary is the most important component, as many other benefits are based on that. Do not give up too much ground on the base pay.

  Employers are most likely to keep some room for negotiation; so do not feel shy about asking more. You may not get everything you asked, but the final offer is likely to be more than the first offer you got. Do not put minor or smaller demands in the beginning phase of negotiation. Once both sides agree on the major points, smaller points can be accommodated relatively easily. Do not bring any new major demand or condition after both sides have verbally agreed on a framework. It can easily piss off the other side, and deal may not go through.

- **Willing to take additional responsibility**

  When asking for a big raise, be willing to take up additional responsibilities or come up with suggestions on how you can contribute more to the company. Each manger has a budget, and he is trying to match the responsibilities with compensation. When it is not clear to your boss how your contributions are going to be visibly better, it would be difficult to get a big raise.

26 Hello Mr./Mrs. CFO

Call yourself the co-CFO (Chief Financial Officer) of the family and give a pat on your back – your spouse is the other co-CFO. It is a very important job, and you will make many critical financial decisions – setting priorities, allocating capital for diverse family needs, coming up with a budget for spending and savings, and making investment decisions. You will deal with balance sheet (net worth), income statement (salary and other sources of revenue and expenses), and cash flow (managing loans and credit cards wisely). Among other roles, you are definitely the co-CFO of your family.

26.1 Personal Finance

As we discussed in the beginning of the book, building wealth has many components to it, and one need to be smart in each of the areas. Just reiterating here:

- Earning – a steady source of predictable income from job or business
- Spending – spend wisely so that there is money left for investments
- Leveraging – using reasonable amount of leverage that you can digest
- Investing – invest in stocks and other assets to grow wealth

Formula for building wealth = $(E - S + L) * I$

- Maximize E (Earnings)
- Minimize S (Spending)
- Reasonable Leverage (L) that you can digest
- Maximize I (Investment growth), must be greater than 1

26.2 Savings and its Importance

26.2.1　Saving Comes before Spending

Even in the dictionary, saving comes before spending. Make it your goal in real life as well. As Warren Buffett said, "Do not save what is left after spending, but spend what is left after savings." Another apt quote is from Robert Kiyosaki, author of Rich Dad Poor Dad, "It's not how much money you make, but how much money you keep, how hard it works for you, and how many generations you keep it for."

It is a fact that you need to save money to be able to invest and build up your net worth. It is not necessary that only high-earners can save money. Everyone can and should. In the beginning of your career, the earnings are less, and so are the expenses. As you advance in your career and grow older, the earnings will grow, and so will be the expenses (children, home, medical, and other expenses). In every stage of life, make a budget and make it a goal to save money. Remember, everything you save is from post-tax dollars. At 33% tax rate (Federal + state), if you saved $100, it is equivalent to $150 of pretax income. In other words, you would have to earn $150 to keep $100 after paying federal and state tax.

One way to force saving is to directly deposit 15%-20% of the take-home pay into a separate account. Then, you can use the money in this special account to invest in stocks, bonds, CDs, or Real Estate. One can question this as tricking the mind and unnecessary. I understand that we, as human beings, are rational people and can do without it. If you are a determined person, I am very happy for you. However, if something automates the saving process, go for it. Whatever works.

26.2.2　Why People Find it Difficult to Save?

It is the present versus the future. The benefit or the gratification of the present takes the front seat pushing the real benefit of savings to the back. The benefits of savings and investing are not readily apparent or visible at the current moment. How much is it going to buy me if I save $250 every month? I am not going to be rich; so, why bother, or what is the urgency? I can wait and start saving later. Time passes by, and we are in the same place 5 yrs., 10 yrs., or 15 yrs. later.

The real benefit comes from the accumulation and the compounding effect. The compounding has magic! Think how much money you would accumulate if you start saving $500 every month at the age of 25, for the next 35 years. Assuming 8% return, you would have more than a million dollars (approximately $1.117 million). At first look, it is not at all visible that a $500 per month can create over a million dollars when you are about to retire.

When I look at saving money, I see two broad categories – first one is paying less for the same services or benefit, and second one is making conscious decision to forego or downshift some services, goods, or amenities to save money. There should not be any excuse to pay more for the same benefit. Most of us waste money due to lack of information, not paying close attention, or simply being lazy. The second category is also important but very personal. It depends on how motivated you are and how far you want to go. However, keep it practical and realistic – do not make savings a religion that it starts to take the fun out of life. Also, do not let it go out of hand - living large where spending is excessive and disproportionate to the earnings. Rich people spend money on many things that may look unnecessary or excessive, but on a percentage basis of their income and net worth, this may not be material. They are living within their means.

26.3 Budgeting and Expense Worksheet

There are two ways you can manage expenditures:
- Spend as it happens and as required (ad hoc)
- Make a budget and spend as per the budget

The first one is an ad-hoc way of managing expenses that most of us adopt, but it has many drawbacks. It is difficult to prioritize spending as everything could look important, and it does not leave much room for maneuverability. The second method of managing spending through a budgeting process is better one as it easily puts everything in the right perspective and helps in planning and prioritizing. However, it needs a little bit of effort - the rewards, in the long run, could be huge. The first step in the budgeting process is to identify the various monthly expenses. Instead of having to do everything in the head every time, we will make the process easier. We are going to introduce the Expense Worksheet that lists all the major expenses. Not everything will be relevant to everyone, but the expenses are standard expenses that most of us incur on a regular basis.

The reader has the permission to take printouts of the Expense Worksheet or type it into an excel file in his or her computer. Once you log all the expenses applicable to you, it will help you in two ways. First, you will immediately know how much you are saving every month that you can start investing. Second, it will give a good idea where your money is going. Out of the various expenses, some are mandatory where you do not have much leeway. However, there are some expenses that you can consider reducing, eliminating, or doing differently to save more. Now, you have everything in one place that you can see and work on.

Monthly Expenses	$ Amount
House	
Mortgage Payment (interest + principal)	
Property Tax*	
PMI*	
Home Hazard Insurance*	
Earthquake Insurance*	
Flood insurance*	
HOA (Homeowners Association) Fees*	
Cooking Gas	
Electricity, water, and sewerage disposal	
Home Warranty	
Home repair and maintenance*	
Alarm and Security	
Safe deposit box	
Renting	
Rent	
Renter's Insurance*	
Living Expenses	
Grocery	
Dining out	
Dining out at work	
Coffee and beverage outside	
Movies and shows	
Dress and apparels	
Haircut and parlors	
Jewelry and cosmetics	
Health club or other associations	
Children – Karate, Swimming, Games…	
Children – Kumon, Dance, Music …	
Automobiles	
Auto loan – vehicle1	
Auto insurance – vehicle1*	
Auto servicing and repair – vehicle1*	
Gas – vehicle1	

Auto loan – vehicle2	
Auto insurance – vehicle2*	
Auto servicing and repair – vehicle2*	
Gas – vehicle2	

Monthly Expenses	$ Amount
Medical	
Out-of-pocket medical expenses*	
Out-of-pocket dental expenses*	
Out-of-pocket vision expenses*	
Education	
Tuition	
School expenses (books, dues, donations etc.)	
Boarding and Dining	
Phone	
Cell phone	
Landline	
Vonage or internet phone	
Cable and Internet	
Cable or DISH	
Internet Connection	
Pet	
Pet supplies (Food and other things)	
Pt Medicine (Vet and other)	
Charity and Donations	
Charity contributions*	
Gift and Events	
Birthdays, Anniversaries, Graduation etc.*	
Travel and Vacation	
Travel and vacation expenses*	
Total	$

Note: Items that have * marks are generally not monthly expenses. These could be every three months, six months, once a year, or as required. Based on the yearly expenses, calculate the monthly expenses and enter the monthly amount. For example, you would probably pay property taxes twice a year and HOA four times a year.

26.4 Twenty Smart Ways to Save Money

26.4.1   Shop Around to Get the Best Deal

You should always look at multiple places for your auto, home, and life insurance to get the best deal, and possibly have them from one agent to get even a better discount. Most people, after they have an agent, do not change agent for many years. Before you lock in, do the due diligence, else you will be paying more for many years. While buying big-ticket items, such as cars, TVs, computers, or home appliances, check out a few places. There is always room for a 5-10% discount and do not shy away from asking for it. Over a period of 25-30 years, it will add up and boost your net worth.

26.4.2   Use Online Bill Auto-payment

It has many small benefits that can add up to be big.

- It will save time and postage
- You can have your cash for longer. If you send by mail, you have to send at least 10-15 days in advance. On the other hand, if you set it up for autopay, the money will be deducted from your account just a couple days before - which means you keep your cash 10 days longer. Add this up for all your bills and think for 50 years.
- You will avoid late-payment and finance charges. Remember the moments and the frustrations you have to go through when you had to pay late fees and finance charges on top of that! We are all humans, and who has not gone through this?
- Even if things are automatic, check the bills to make sure that there are no incorrect charges, unnecessary charges, or charges you do not recognize. Report immediately and get the credits or dispute charges that are not yours.

26.4.3　Postpone Big Expenses

If you can postpone any big-ticket item for may be, six months, you will get it at a cheaper price, especially electronic items, such as TVs, phones, computers, and laptops. Or, you get a newer model with more features for the same price you have budgeted. If you are planning to replace a big-ticket item, see if you can manage with the current one for another six months to a year and get a little more value out of it. In general, you want to accelerate your income and slowdown expenses as humanly and as safely as possible.

26.4.4　Control Impulse Buying

Think if you really need it, or you want to buy just to have it. Convert the pleasure of pursuit to the satisfaction of saving. It may not look big at a time, but things add up.

26.4.5　Buy Things in Bulk

Things that you need round the year (paper towels, soaps, tissue papers, detergents, tooth paste, and many others), buy them in bulk from stores, such as Sam's club or Costco. The per-unit price is much less when you buy in bulk or larger quantities. Have a second refrigerator in the garage where you can store food items you buy in bulk. Buying in bulk also saves you time and gas. Most of the goods or merchandize have per-unit price (price for ounce or price for lb.) listing that you can use to compare quickly two or more items to see where you are getting the best value.

26.4.6　Buy Things on Sale

Look at the items that are on sale. If you find what you are looking for, you will save a lot of money. Sale does not automatically mean bad quality or things not trendy. Many times, things are on sale to move things faster and increase sale. In some cases, you probably have to wait a bit until it is available on sale.

26.4.7　Generic Medicine

Generic medicines cost much less than branded medicines. If you are using some medicines regularly such as allergy medicine, generic can save you a lot. The ingredients are same as branded medicine. Also, you can save by buying store-brand items rather than buying more expensive branded items. As one advertisement says, "If you cannot see the difference, why pay the difference." However, talk to your doctor before using generic medicine.

26.4.8   Pay off Credit Card Debts

Credit cards usually have very high interest rate, around 20%. If you have credit card balance, pay it off before investing money elsewhere. Where can you get a guaranteed return of 20%? Another critical thing, many people may not be aware, is that you accrue this 20% interest charges for all your new purchases when you have an outstanding balance. There is no grace period as we usually get when we pay off the balance every month.

If you have an outstanding balance, you are paying 20% interest charge! Save aggressively and pay off credit card debt. Better yet, avoid getting into such a situation, unless there is an emergency financial situation that you need to address. Use the credit card as a convenience card, not a source for credit where you have to pay high interest.

26.4.9   Contribute to 401K and FSA Accounts

Contributions to 401K or retirements accounts reduce your current tax and grow tax deferred. The employer also contributes to the retirement account. You can use the pre-tax contribution to FSA account for medical expenses rather than using post-tax money.

26.4.10   Promotions and Discounts

Whether it is your cable, TV, Wi-Fi, cell phone, or home security, all the providers are competing to win your business. They provide special promotions and discounts from time to time. You can avail these when you switch or ask for promotions that they can offer while you continue to be a valued subscriber.

26.4.11   Refinance Home Loan

If interest rate drops, refinance your home loan for a lower rate. Check to make sure that refinance charges are not tacked on to the loan balance. It may take years before the savings from newer lower interest match the extra finance charge. Ask if they can still lower the interest rate and monthly payment without adding to the loan balance. Ask for zero-cost, zero-fees, no increase to loan balance, and a cut in the interest rate.

26.4.12   Not Having to Pay PMI

If your equity in the house is below 20%, you have to pay PMI (Private Mortgage Insurance), mandated by the lender. Save aggressively so that the equity builds up to go beyond PMI requirement, and you do not have to pay PMI any more.

26.4.13   Improve Your Credit Score

A good credit score is important when applying for loans, be it auto, home, home equity, or equity line of credits – you can get interest rate quarter to half percentage points lower. Over a period of years, the savings would add up to big amount.

Make sure that you pay your bills on time, as late payments adversely affect credit score. Accounts, in collections, bankruptcies, foreclosures, and liens, adversely affect credit score. Something called **open credit card utilization** is a factor in determining credit score. It is the amount of credits you are using compared to the total credits available to you. Utilization of 35% or less is desirable. Closing credit cards, that you are not using, reduces the total available credit line and increases credit card utilization ratio - not good for your credit score. However, if you are paying yearly fees without equal benefits, it may be beneficial to close it and not pay yearly fees year after year. Too many credit inquiries in a short span of time can reduce your credit score. Co-signing a credit card with someone else could hurt your credit score, if he or she misses payment or sends payment late.

Credit Bureaus and FICO Score

There are mainly three credit-reporting agencies - Equifax, Experian, and TransUnion. Most lenders report financial transactions to these three agencies. These agencies use different credit scoring formulas to find a person's credit score. The most commonly used credit score the FICO score that we all are familiar with. FICO scoring formula was developed by **Fair Isaac Co**, and that is how FICO came about. FICO scoring ranges from 300 to 850. As per Experian, here is what a FICO credit score means:

800 and above:	Exceptional - Score is well above average
740-799:	Very good – Score is above average
670-739:	Good – Median credit score
580-669:	Fair – Credit score is below average
579 and lower:	Poor

26.4.14   Pay Insurance Semi-annually/Annually

Pay your auto insurance semi-annually instead every quarter. Pay life insurance premium once a year rather than every month. This will reduce your fees and payments.

26.4.15   Say No to Extended Warranties

Extended warranties, in general, are expensive and not a good value for your money. Decline when asked to buy. Refer to Warranty section for details.

26.4.16   Increase Your Deductible

The insurance premium goes down when the deductible goes up. Make sure it is not too high either. Check the deductible versus premium for a few slots and find the best or the sweet spot. The relationship between deductible and premium is not linear. If the deductible is going up faster than the premium is dropping, stop there. You do not want to a go for a higher deductible without a corresponding savings in premium.

26.4.17   15-yr Rather than a 30-yr Mortgage

The monthly payment for 15-yr mortgage is higher than a 30-yr mortgage, but interest rate is usually lower (quarter to half percentage) for 15-yr mortgage. If you can afford the higher monthly payment, go for 15-yr mortgage. You will build equity in your home faster with a 15-yr mortgage. If you want to be aggressive, you can go for 5/1 ARM or 7/10 ARM that provides even lower interest rate.

26.4.18   Utilities are Ongoing Expenses

Utilities are ongoing expenses that you have to pay every month for the rest of life. Any savings, small or big, will have a big compounding effect over a period of 35-40 years. First, do not waste water or electricity. Second, use energy-efficient lighting and appliances. Energy efficient lights may cost more, but they last longer and consume less wattage. You can get solar panels installed on rooftop that will save money on electricity bill. If you have a lawn that needs watering, see how many days the sprinkler needs to be turned on. You do not need to water every day. Adjust for summer and winter.

26.4.19   Optimize Driving

Optimize your grocery, shopping, and errands so that you are not moving across the town back and forth like a bee. If you plan it out, you can get all things done with fewer trips and save gas. Carpool wherever it is convenient and keep it 50-50, not one-sided. It is fair that away, and that will keep it going.

26.4.20   Use Credit Card, not Debit Card

First, do not use credit card as an ATM machine. However, for something that you have to buy anyway, use credit card instead of debit card, check, or cash. When you use credit card, you have to pay it roughly a month later. If you use debit card or check instead, the money is debited from your account immediately. Why not use free money even for a month on a regular basis? The other benefit is that you accrue reward points with credit cards that will grow to decent to good cash value at the end of a year. You can use the points for restaurant cards, airlines mileage, and many other things. Credits cards also give protection for disputed charges. It also builds your credit score when you pay credit card dues in time.

26.5 Big Decisions

26.5.1   House – Buying Versus Renting

The house prices have appreciated handsomely over the long run. Please refer to section 24.4, where we have shown that if you buy a house with 20% or less down and the house price appreciates at an average rate of 3.5% for the next 30 years, you would make an average yearly gain of 30% for 30 years. This is hard to beat by any other investment. The over-sized appreciation is possible due to leverage. The house price appreciation is based on the total purchase price, but your initial investment is only 20% or less. The other big deal is that gain on primary residence is tax free up to $500,000 for married couple.

At least, buying one house as primary residence makes a lot of sense. You get tax benefit as you can itemize the interests on the mortgage and the property tax. The other thing is that you still need to pay rent if you decide to rent and not buy a home. The rent will come close to the mortgage interest and property tax payment after accounting for the itemized tax gain you would get. This is true for most people and most of the cases. There are exceptions, and in some cases, buying a house may not be a good decision. If you are going to move out in a year or so and do not want to keep the house as rental property after you move out, you could lose money. You need to pay approximately 6% of sale price as commission, and the house may not have appreciated that much. However, once you decide to call a place your hometown and plan to stay there longer, it makes good sense to buy your home.

Buying a second house as an investment rental property has its pluses and minuses. Cash flow is very critical for owning rental properties. When it is easy to find tenants, the rent will cover most, if not all, expenses, such as interest payment, property tax, and other expenses for the rental property. If you run into cash-flow situation, you would be forced to sell the property at an unfavorable time and may be at a loss. If you are financially stable and can manage short-term cash-flow problems, it could be a good idea to buy a rental property.

26.5.2   To Pay off or not to Pay off

If you have taken 30-yr fixed loan (the most popular) at 4.0%, you would get back roughly 1/3rd of the interest payment and property tax as tax savings. The net cost for having the mortgage loan is around 2.7%. This figure will be different when the 30-yr loan interest rate is different. Out of the monthly mortgage payment, part of it goes toward the interest, and a part goes toward the principal reduction. But, the question is, should you pay down principal more than you are required as per the original loan agreement? Should you send extra payment toward principal from time to time? If you decide to invest the extra money instead of paying down the principal, you have to earn 4.0% return on the investment to breakeven with the interest payment on the loan.

So, where can you get 4.0% guaranteed returns? Hardly is there any place that has guaranteed 4.0% return! CDs pay around 1%, and 10-yr Treasury bond pays less than 2%. Stocks, over the long run, have provided around 10% annual gain. In fact, if you spend time and become a good investor, you could even earn better than the index average. However, there is no guaranteed return over a shorter horizon. Some prefer to pay down the principal, as they want to secure 4.0% return without taking any risk. Some invest the money in the stock market or on an additional rental property. Some are in the middle – they invest some of the savings in stocks, mutual funds, and use part of the savings toward principal reduction. I prefer the middle ground when you are starting out your career and are in the process of gaining experience in the stock market, for three reasons. The first one is that you do not have a lot of experience in other investments and are getting 4.0% return without any risk. The second reason is that having a good equity in your house gives you strength and a sense of financial stability. The third thing is that as you build equity in your house, you can open a Home Equity Line of Credit (HELOC). You can tap into the line of credits from time to time when markets are down significantly or when fundamentally strong individual stocks are significantly down. You can make large gains if you invest after big drops.

26.5.3   Buying Your Car

While buying a car, consider the total cost of ownership, not just the purchase price. Everything from insurance premium to tire replacements cost more for sports cars and performance cars. The costs other than purchase price are:

- **Fuel cost:** The higher the mileage, the lower the fuel cost
- **Maintenance and repair cost:** Sports car, performance cars, and luxury cars have higher maintenance and repair cost.
- **Insurance cost:** Sports car, performance cars, and luxury cars cost more to insure.
- **Depreciation cost:** Certain cars depreciate faster than other cars. In other words, certain cars retain value better than others do.
- **Vehicle Tax:** The higher is the purchase price of your car, the higher the vehicle tax you have to pay.

26.6 Insurance and Warranty

Insurance protects you from big expenses that can otherwise cause havoc in financial life. The cost of it is the premium you have to pay that takes a bite out of your income. When you add all the insurance premiums, it becomes a sizable amount, and you should give some thoughts to get the best coverage without paying too much.

The insurance needs and the risk you are willing to take will change as you advance in your life and career. The insurance needs of a couple starting their careers are different from the needs of couple who are in their fifties or retired. We will go through various insurance needs, such as home insurance, auto insurance, medical insurance, and life insurance. The following points apply to all types of insurance needs.

- **Shop around** to compare price and coverage
- Ask for applicable **discounts** before you sign up
- Ask for savings when you **bundle** home, life, and auto from one company
- Choose the right **deductible**. Higher deductible brings down premium.

26.6.1　　Medical Insurance

Most companies offer medical, vision, and dental insurance. Medical costs without insurance are very high, and one needs to have coverage either through the employer or by purchasing on his/her own. A sudden, unexpected large medical expense without insurance can derail your life.

26.6.2　　Home Insurance

- **Coverage:** Understand what it covers and what it does not. Home insurance does not cover earthquakes. If you are in earthquake prone area, you may consider buying earthquake insurance. However, there is usually a big deductible (15% replacement cost) for earthquake insurance. Home insurance policy typically does not cover flood damage. If you are under a flood zone, you may consider buying flood insurance.

- **Replacement cost versus Market value:** Replacement cost is the money required to replace the house. It does not include the cost of the land. Market value is the money required to buy the house in the market. If your house is in a metropolitan area, the replacement cost would be less than the market value due to high value of the land itself. In such cases, the premium would be much less for replacement policy, and you would be better off taking a policy for replacement cost rather than the market value.

In other cases (rural area or older homes), the replacement cost could be more than market value. In such cases, you may opt for a policy for market value or go for replacement cost at a higher premium so that you can rebuild the house without much out-of-pocket expenses.

- **Alarm System, Smoke Detectors:** Such protective measures not only protect your house from burglars and fire but also reduces the insurance premium.

- **Deductible:** Analyze the trade-off between deductible and premium. The higher the deductible, the lower the premium is. However, at some point, the premium will not go down as much when you increase the deductible. Find out the sweet spot and choose the right deductible.

26.6.3   Auto Insurance

- **Shop around** for the best deal – AAA, Allstate, Farmers, Geico, Nationwide, Progressive, and State Farm etc. It varies from one agent to another agent as well.

- Ask for various **discounts**; grab as many as you qualify for.
    o Good-driver, professional, good student, and driver education discount
    o Airbag, anti-theft system, ABS (Anti-lock Brake System) discount
    o Customer loyalty discount and multi-car discount.
    o Discount for Home and Auto policies combined

- Evaluate **deductibles versus premiums**. When you are starting out and do not have a lot of driving experience, do not keep your deductible too high. As you gain more experience in driving and can afford to handle bigger repair cost, you can increase the deductible and keep the premium low.

- **Collision, Comprehensive, and Liability coverage**: Collison and Comprehensive parts of the insurance cover the cost of damage to your car, whereas liability covers the cost of damage to the other car. Collision covers the cost when your car is involved in a collision with another car or object. Comprehensive covers the damage to your car other than collision, such as theft, vandalism, fire damage, or flooding.

You should always take liability coverage. Taking collision and comprehensive coverage depends on market value of your car. If it is old or has been 7-10 years since you purchased coverage, the value of your car may be much less now. Even if you are covered with collision or comprehensive insurance, insurance company will pay only the present market value not the purchase price. You may opt not to have collision or comprehensive coverage.

If you have an auto loan, the bank may require you to take collision and comprehensive insurance. In any case, if you want to keep collision and comprehensive coverage, or you are required to have both, renegotiate the premiums based on lower present value of your automobile.

- **Types of Cars:** The insurance premium depends on the type of car; luxury cars and sports car cost more to insure. If you love certain car, you should buy it but be aware of the fact that the premium varies.

26.6.4　　Life Insurance

- **Why Life Insurance?** When the family depends on your income, it is wise to have a life insurance.

- **Life Insurance from Employer:** Many companies provide basic life insurance at minimal or no cost. Beyond that, you can buy extra insurance from the company.

- **Term Life versus Cash Value Insurance**: Beyond the life insurance from your employer, you can buy life insurance from outside. There are two types of insurance, term life and cash value – Term life is for certain number of years (20, 25, 30 yrs.) and pays the insured amount upon death.

Cash value insurance is for life. Whole life, variable life, and universal life are types of cash value life insurance. In addition to paying insured amount upon death, it accumulates cash value that grows tax deferred. The insurer can draw from the accumulated value later in life or pass on to heirs.

However, the premiums for cash value life insurance are much higher than term-life insurance. It is also difficult to evaluate the investment part of the cash value insurance. The best option, in most cases, is to go for just the term life insurance and use the extra money to invest in 401K, IRA, or other retirement plans.

- **When to buy?** The best time to buy life insurance from outside is around when you are 35-40. Buy a term life for 25-30years that will cover you up to retirement when your children won't be dependent on you as the main earner in the family. Buying around age 35 will help you to lock in for 30 years with a very low premium. The main reason is that you may not have to undergo medical examination, or you most likely will be disease free at this age. This keeps premium very low. If you buy your policy later and have some medical conditions, the premiums will be quite high.

- Another reason to get a life insurance from the market apart from the policy from employer is that many of us are likely be without coverage when laid off or start our own businesses.

26.6.5   Umbrella Policy

The auto policy or home policy covers us from liability up to certain amount. However, as we grow older, our assets and investment value goes up, and these policies won't cover the assets. An umbrella policy provides coverage beyond the auto and home policy, and it can be purchased up to a million dollars or more depending on your net worth. The umbrella premiums, generally, are low.

26.6.6   Extended Warranty

Are extended warranties warranted? It is a good trade off to decline warranty on TVs. TVs, once mounted on a wall or put on a stand, do not move, and there is very little chance that it would go bad. In addition, the price drops rapidly – A TV worth $1000 today, probably will be worth several hundred dollars in five years. Also, it will be a good tradeoff to decline warranty on desktops. It will be reasonable to buy warranty on laptops, especially for children, for 3 years but not more. The laptop, in five years, will have no value left. Same thing goes for cell phones. But, check how much the warranty costs. If it is large (20% or above), it is not a good trade off to go for warranty. If you decline extended warranty, the seller is likely to come back with an offer that is much less – it happens quite often.

26.7 Retirement Savings Plans

The money you would receive from social security would not be enough to meet your financial requirements in retirement years. You need to save money in your working years. Savings for retirements has three main benefits. First, it will force you save money during your working years. Second, you get upfront tax benefits by putting money in retirement accounts. The employers also add money to the account depending on the plan. Finally, the money in retirement accounts grows tax deferred. You pay the tax in retirement years at a lower tax bracket, as income, during retirement years, would be less for majority of the people.

26.7.1   401(k)

401(k) Plan

401(k) is a retirement savings plan offered at work by the employer. It is a good idea to put money in 401(k) retirement accounts as it provides tax savings now, and the money grows tax deferred. The other major benefit is that many employers match up to certain percentage (3% for example) of the employee contribution. Let us look at some examples with a salary of $100,000, and the company policy is to match up to 3%.

Example1   You decided to contribute $18,000 to your 401(k) account. The employer will add 3% of $100,000, which is $3000. The total money will be $21,000 – the best strategy depending on how much you can stash away without impacting your current cash flow needs.

Example2   You decided to contribute $3,000 to your 401(k) account. The employer will add 3% of $100,000, which is $3000. The total money will be 6,000 – not bad as you are saving some and still getting the free money from the company.

Example3   You decided not to contribute any money to your 401(k) account. The employer will NOT put any money. It is not a good financial decision as you are leaving free money on the table, not saving for retirements, and paying more on tax now.

401(k) Contribution Limits

The amount of money one can contribute to 401(k) account is adjusted to inflation. It was $17,500 in 2014 and $18,000 in 2015. For 2016, it is same as the 2015 limit ($18,000). People approaching retirement (age 50 and above) can contribute an extra $6,000 to their 401(k) account – it is called the catch-up contribution.

26.7.2   Small Business - Simple IRA, SEP IRA

SIMPLE IRA

Simple (Savings Incentive Match Plan for Employees) IRA is similar to 4101(k) account but is for companies with fewer than 100 employees. It has much less administrative cost and requirements compared to 410(k) plans.

Under this plan, it is mandatory for employer to contribute to each employee, which is different from 401(k) plan where it is optional for employer to contribute. Employers need to contribute 2 percent for everyone making over $5,000 or match the first 3 percent put by the employee. For 2015, the contribution limit was $12,500 ($15,500 for employee, 50 or older).

SEP Plan

Unlike 401(k) plan, SEP (Simplified Employee Pension) is a retirement plan for self-employed people or small business owners. In 2015, SEP contribution limit was 25% of income or $53,000, whichever is less.

It is one of the best ways for successful entrepreneurs to contribute a large sum each year toward retirement plan and save a bunch on current federal and state tax.

Individual or solo 401(k) Plan

This is meant for self-employed people without any full-time employee excluding business partners and spouse. In 2015, the contribution limit was 25% of income or $53,000, whichever is less.

Also as an employee (you are both owner and employee), you can contribute $18,000 for 2015 ($24,000 for 50 or older). The total contribution as employer and employee is limited to $53,000 ($59,000 for 50 or older).

26.7.3   Traditional IRA or Just IRA

All the retirement accounts (401(k), SEP, SIMLE IRA), we have discussed so far, are based on pre-tax income. Any contributions to these accounts reduce your taxable income. IRA (Individual Retirement Account) provides opportunities to save for retirements with your post-tax* dollars from earned income. The amount you contribute to IRA is not tax deductible, but the money grows tax deferred. If you start withdrawing at 59.5 or later, there is no 10% penalty for early withdrawal. The yearly IRA contribution limit in 2015 was $5,500 (or $6,500 if you are 50 or older). There is no income limit to contribute.

*If your employer does not provide any retirement plan, your IRA contribution is tax deductible.

Spousal IRA   If one of the spouses has earned income, the other spouse is eligible to contribute to his/her IRA account. That means, total family contributions can be up to $11,000($13,000 if both are 50 or older).

Strategy   The contributions can be tax-deductible, or it will still grow tax deferred even if it is not tax deductible. Make this a part of your investment strategy. You will still be able to buy individual stocks or invest in mutual funds in your IRA account, as you are able to do if you invested outside IRA.

26.7.4   Roth IRA

If you have earned income, you can contribute to Roth IRA. However, eligibility to contribute starts phasing out when income reaches certain amount. For married couple filing jointly, phase out starts at MAGI of $184,000 and becomes ineligible at $194,000 – 2016 figure.

You do not get upfront tax savings when you contribute to Roth IRA, but the money grows tax-free. You also do not need to pay tax when you withdraw from Roth IRA. The contribution limits are same as traditional IRA ($5,500 for less than 50 and $6,500 if you are 50 or older).

Strategy   If your income is within the limit and you have already maxed out on 401(k) or traditional IRA, it makes sense to invest through Roth IRA than investing it outside. When you invest it outside, you have to pay tax on your gain, but Roth grows tax-free, and you do not pay tax when you withdraw.

26.7.5   Overall Strategy for Retirement Accounts

- Consider both spouses as to how much you can contribute together
- Max out on upfront tax-deductible and tax-deferred growth plans
  - 401(k)
  - Traditional IRA when it is tax deductible
  - FSA (Flexible Spending Account) up to anticipated medical cost
- Then, max out on tax-free growth and tax-free withdrawal plans
  - If you can save further and are eligible, max out on Roth IRA
- Then, max out on tax-deferred growth plan
  - If you can save further, max out on traditional IRA
- You can consider investing some money in to tax-deferred annuity.
- If you have more money, invest in non-retirement accounts - stock, real estate, or whatever is your specialty.

26.8 Annuities

Annuities are investment vehicles for generating income during retirement years. The money you invest does not provide pre-tax benefit (does not reduce your tax) but grows tax-deferred. The money you would receive from annuity during retirement years will be taxed as regular income. You can start drawing money after reaching 59.5 years without having to pay 10% early withdrawal penalty. There are two types of annuities, deferred annuities and income annuities.

26.8.1   Deferred Annuities

Deferred annuities, when appropriate, are started long before retirement so that money grows tax deferred. These have the same profiles as investing post-tax dollars in stocks and mutual funds but grow tax-deferred.

Deferred Fixed Annuities

- You can put a lump sum or contribute periodically (every month or year) in to the account
- It provides a fixed rate of return (usually not high) like a CD, and the money grows tax deferred
- You have to take a close look – do you want the low tax-deferred returns from these types of equities or would you be better off by investing in stocks?
- Annuities are not FDIC insured

Deferred Variable Annuities

- You can put a lump sum or contribute periodically (every month or year) in to the account
- The money provides variable growth (could be higher than the fixed annuities). However, it has similar risk profile as investing in stocks and mutual funds.

26.8.2   Income or Immediate Annuities

You pay a lump sum money shortly before retirement, and you would get steady source of income during retirement years. The goal here is to preserve money without taking risk, as there is not much time to play and recover from big loss that could happen investing in stocks. However, it depends on your goal and risk appetite. Moreover, these do not provide any tax-deferred advantage. You could rather invest the money in stocks, mutual funds, or CDs.

Immediate Variable Income Annuities

- It provides immediate income for rest of the retirement years.
- The income payment is variable as it depends on performance of the annuity investments – it may be more or less.

Immediate Fixed Income Annuities

- It provides immediate income throughout for rest of the retirement years or for a fixed number of years.
- The payment is fixed, and it does not depend on annuity performance.
- The returns and payment are less than that could be possible under the variable income plan. You are basically, trading in higher returns for certainty.

Deferred Income Annuities

- You have to wait for certain number of years before you start receiving payment.
- Since you forgo payment for certain number of years, the payment would be usually more than the payment under the fixed income annuities plan.

26.8.3   Annuities? If Yes, Which One?

For retirement savings, you should first max out 410(k) accounts as these provide pre-tax as well as tax-deferred growth. Then, you should consider contributing to IRA and Roth IRA. Once you have maxed out 401(k) and IRA, you can consider savings through tax-deferred (fixed or variable) annuity for retirement as annuity grows tax-deferred.

The Income annuities provide steady income but are hard to evaluate in terms of the rate of return. Moreover, there are usually high fees and commissions for these annuities. Since income annuities are signed during retirement years, you really need to consider if you can manage money on your own rather than buying these annuities. You may get a better return by investing in stocks or mutual funds. You have to take a close look.

26.9 College Prep and Financing

One of the major events in life for a student and the parents is the student graduating from high school and going to his or her dream college. However, the cost of 4-year college education has skyrocketed, and it plays a major part of financial planning. In this section, we will go through the college preparation/application process and look at different options to fund college education.

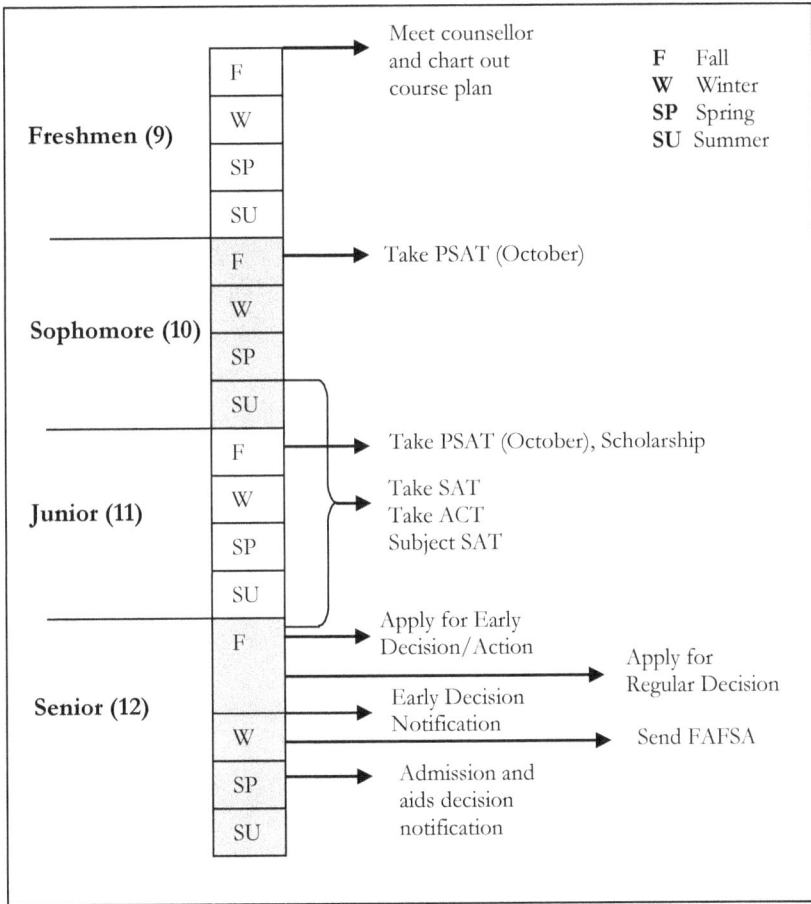

Fig. 26.1   College Prep Timeline Graph

26.9.1   College Admission Tests (SAT, ACT)

PSAT (Preliminary SAT)

- You can take the PSAT only once a year. The test is administered in fall (October) every year. Students can take the PSAT in the sophomore and Junior years. Fees are paid by school.

- PSAT has two major benefits. First, it prepares the student for SAT and gives an idea how he or she is going to perform in SAT. Second, PSAT score from junior year is used for National Merit Scholarship Program.

- Total score 1520
    - Evidence based Reading and Writing – 760
    - Math – 760
- Test duration: 2hrs 45 mins
- No guessing penalty

SAT (Scholastic Aptitude Test)

- Offered seven times a year - October, November, December, January, March/April, May, and June.
- Total score 1600
    - Evidence based Reading and Writing – 800
    - Math – 800
    - Essay – optional
- Test duration: 3hrs, plus 50 min for optional essay
- No guessing penalty
- Available in print or on computer

ACT (American College Testing)

- Offered 4-6 times a year
- Total score 36 – average of 4 tests
    - English
    - Math
    - Reading
    - Science Reasoning
    - Essay – optional
- Test duration: 2hrs 55 mins, plus 45 mins for optional essay
- No guessing penalty
- Writing is optional

Subject SAT

- Subject tests are hour-long, content based tests
- It allows student to show strength and preparedness in certain areas
- There are 20 subject tests in five areas (English, Math, History, Science, and Language)
- Each Subject SAT score out of 800

26.9.2   Early Decision/Early Action

Early Decision (ED) Process
- Can apply to only one ED college
- Can apply to other colleges under regular admission plan
- Apply early (November) and get admission decision by December
- ED is binding – if accepted, you must attend the college and withdraw from other colleges.

Early Action (EA) Process
- Apply early (November) and get decision early (Jan/Feb)
- Can apply to other colleges under regular admission plan
- EA is non-binding – it is not mandatory to attend the EA college. Accept/decline admission by May 1.

26.9.3   Regular Admission

- Apply typically in early January
- Can apply to multiple colleges
- Admission decisions generally sent late March/Early April
- Accept/decline admission by May 1.

26.9.4   Cost of Financing College Education

College education is expensive. As per collegeboard.org, the average tuition fees for college education in 2015-2016 is:

Type of College	Average Yearly Tuition and Fees
Public Two-Year College (in-district students)	$3,347
Public Four-Year College (in-state students)	$9,139
Public Four-Year College (out-of-state students)	$22,958
Private Four-Year College	$31,231

Then, you have to add cost for boarding, food, books, and other things amounting to $10K-$15K. It is a big financial consideration for parents as well as children. For parents, it could be a conflict between savings money for retirements and paying for children's education. For students, they can get the money from parents, or avail loan to finance college. If they avail a big loan, it could be a big burden for children graduating from college and starting their own financial lives.

There are no easy answers, but it is critical that each student get the best college they can get into. It may be a short-term burden, but it will pay more than the cost in the long run. **College education is an investment for the future.** There are many ways college education can be funded – scholarship, financial aids, student loan, and parents' contributions.

26.9.5   FAFSA

FAFSA (**F**ree **A**pplication For **F**ederal **S**tudents **A**id) is the application for federal grants, loans, and work-study funds for college education. It is administered by the U.S. Department of education that gives out around $150 billion as student aid every year. The eligibility for receiving grants or loans depends on the student's financial need, based on the information provided in FAFSA. In addition to Federal aid, many states and colleges use FAFSA information to determine eligibility for state and school aid. Some private financial aid providers may use FAFSA information to determine whether you qualify for financial aid.

26.9.6   Federal Grants

Federal grants are free money that you do not have to pay back.

FSEOG (Federal Supplemental Educational Opportunity Grant).

- It is a grant for undergraduate students with exceptional financial need.
- The amount of the grant varies from $100 to $4000 per year.
- Does not need to be paid back
- Students who receive Pell grants get priority for FSEOG grants.

Federal Pell Grant

- Awarded to Undergraduate students only
- Does not need to be paid back
- The maximum award is $5,815 for the 2016–17 award year. The amount you get depends on your need and cost of education.

26.9.7   Federal Loans

The federal loans are money loaned for college education that you need to pay back with interest. Federal loans, generally, have lower interest rates and have better repayment options than private loans. There are two types of federal loans - Federal Direct Loan (Direct Loan) Program and the Federal Perkins Loan Program

Federal Direct Loan Program

- It is the largest federal loan program
- USDE (US Department of Education) is the lender
- Different types of direct loans. Direct subsidized and direct unsubsidized loans are also known as Federal Stafford Loans.
    - *Direct Subsidized Loans*
        - Loans made to Undergraduate students based on financial needs.
        - $3,500 - $5,500 per year
        - 4.29% interest in 2016

- Interest accumulation does not start until you graduate
    - *Direct Unsubsidized Loans*
        - Loans made to undergraduate, graduate, and professional students. It does not depend on financial needs.
        - $5,500 to $20,500 per year
        - 4.29% interest for undergraduate and 5.84% for graduate students in 2016
        - Interest accumulation starts immediately
    - *Direct PLUS Loans*
        - Loans made to parents of undergraduate and graduate students
        - Does not depend on financial needs
        - Maximum amount is cost of attendance minus any other eligible aid
        - 6.84% interest in 2016
        - Interest accumulation starts immediately

Federal Perking Loan Program

- Loans made to Undergraduate students based on financial needs and availability of college funds
- College is the lender, not USDE
- Up to $5,500 per year for undergraduate and Up to $8,000 per year for graduate students
- 5% interest in 2016
- Interest accumulation starts after a grace period of 9 months after graduation

26.9.8   Non-govt Scholarship and Aids

There are many other sources of scholarship and aids available besides the federal grants and aids. These can be from private institutions or the school itself. You have to apply them separately besides applying FAFSA. Start researching and applying for scholarships in the summer after the junior year.

26.9.9   Interest is Tax Deductible

The students can deduct the interest up to $2,500 on the student loan as an adjustment on his or her tax returns when MAGI is less than $80,000 for single tax payer and $160,000 for joint return. The parents, who took loans for funding his or her children's college education, are also eligible for taking this adjustment subject to MAGI limit.

26.9.10   College Savings 529 Plans

You can put after-tax money in 529-college savings account for your children. The money does not provide pre-tax advantage as the 401K plan does, but the gain from the 529 account is tax free, and the investment grows tax-free. You can withdraw the money tax free for your children's college education. However, if you do not use it on eligible college expenses, you generally will be subject to income tax and an additional 10% federal tax penalty on the earnings.

Unfortunately, the assets in a 529 plan will be treated as parental assets in calculating family contribution for college cost and can reduce the aid you would get. It can reduce the need-based aid by a maximum of 5.64 percent of 529-plan asset value. Let us say you have $30,000 in your 529 plan. The financial aid will be reduced by $1,692. However, the tax-deferred growth and tax-free withdrawal can provide better appreciation than loss of financial aid by having a 529 plan. Each college is different in deciding how much weightage to put on the 529 plan assets for calculating the need-based aid. The other thing is that if a grandparent has a 529-plan account, the money withdrawn is counted as income for the student in next year. Grandparents should delay withdrawals from 529 plans until after January 1 of college junior year.

27 Personal Tax, Estate, Soc Security

27.1 Personal Tax and Tax Planning

Note: The exact tax rates and tax laws change from time to time, and you need to consult a tax software or other relevant sources to get the latest information. However, the goal in this chapter is to explain the tax structures in a simple way.

27.1.1 Tax Flow Diagram

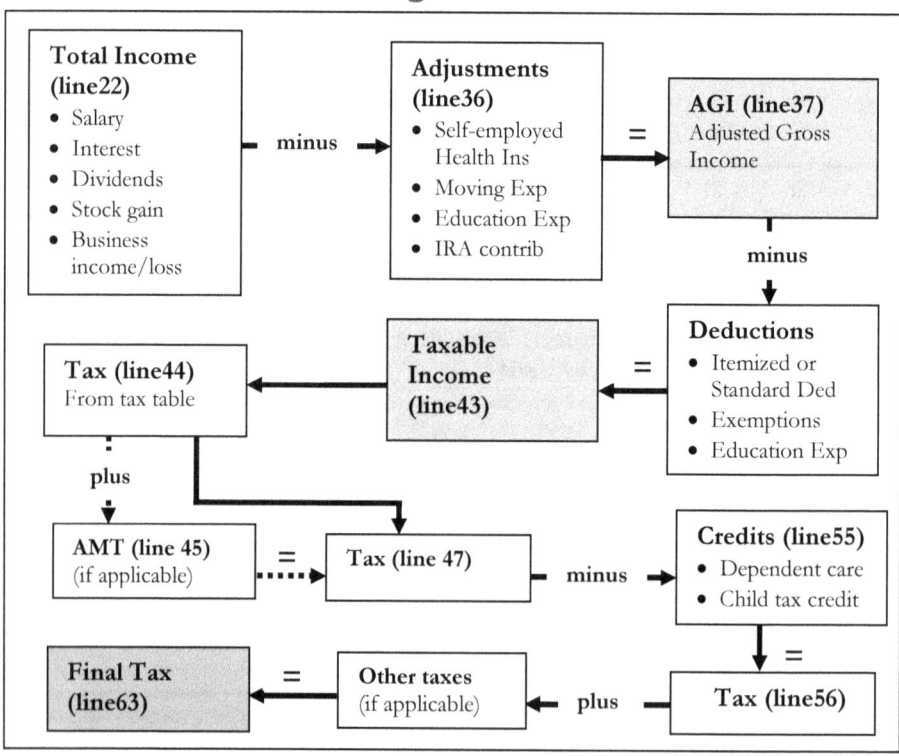

Fig. 27.1   Tax Architecture

CHAPTER 27   Tax and Tax Planning

Many people are not interested in understanding the tax structure or how it works. They rely on tax software or an accountant who files for them. You do not have to remember all the codes or the nitty-gritty details, but you need to have a good understanding of different types of taxes and the broad components of the tax structure. There is a saying, "Penny wise, Pound foolish" which may be relevant here. You may be pinching pennies, which is a smart thing by itself, but you do not want to miss out on the big things. It will help you to take measures so that you can minimize tax and maximize your wealth. The major tax components are:

- Total Income - line 22
- Adjustments - line 36
- Adjusted Gross Income (AGI) – line 37
- Deductions
    - Itemized deduction
    - Standard deduction
- Personal Exemptions
- Taxable Income – line 43
- Alternative Minimum Tax (AMT) – line 45
- Tax Credits – line 55
- Final Tax – line 63

It starts with the total income, which is sum of all incomes. After you take out the applicable adjustments from the income, you get the most important figure, the AGI (Adjusted Gross Income). It is the figure on the last line (37) of the first page of federal tax form. As we will see later, AGI is a very important figure as many itemized deductions phase out over certain AGI figure.

From AGI, you are allowed to deduct either sum of many itemized deductions or standard deduction whichever gives you a larger deduction amount. Also, you deduct personal exemptions from AGI. The figure that remains after you subtract the deductions and exemptions is your **taxable income (line 43).**

From the tax table, you figure out your tax (line 44) based on your taxable income (line 43). So far, we have discussed the standard way of figuring out the tax. You also need to calculate your tax in another way (AMT). We will discuss AMT in details later. The main difference is that in AMT method, when AGI crosses certain threshold, some of the deductions are not allowed, which could result in larger tax compared to standard way of figuring out tax. If tax calculated based on AMT is higher, you add the extra amount to line 44 to get tax at line 47.

From the figure at line 47, you can further reduce your tax burden by taking applicable credits, such as dependent care credit. This brings you to line 56 of the tax form. We are almost there. If you have some other types of tax, such as self-employment tax and household employment (not typical), you add that to line 56 to arrive at your final tax figure **(line 63)** – your federal tax liability.

Tax Strategy in a Nutshell

- Understand how to lower your total income for tax purpose without lowering your real income – contributions to retirement accounts (401K) reduces your income for tax calculation without reducing your real income.
- Understand how to increase adjustments and deductions to keep your taxable income low.
- If you fall under AMT, figure out AMT strategy to reduce tax.
- Finally understand and plan for credits that may be applicable to you.

27.1.2   Total Income

> The only thing that hurts more than paying an income tax is not having to pay an income tax – *Thomas Dewar*

The only way you can build wealth is to generate income. Total income includes all types of income and forms the starting point of tax calculation. The various forms of income are salary (W-2 forms), interest, dividends, capital gains (loss), business income (loss), rental income, royalties, and farm income etc.

Your goal is to reduce your total income (for tax purpose) without reducing your real income. Here are some strategies, mainly based on tax deferral, to reduce your income subject to tax but not the real income.

- Go for a retirement plan. You can contribute up to $18,000 (year 2015) toward your 401K plan. If you had $100K salary, taxable portion of your salary would be $82,000. You did not lose $18K (still growing in your retirement account), but your tax will be less. 401K has also other benefit where employer contributes some money. If you are 50 or older, you can contribute up to $24,000 per year toward 401K – the extra is called the catch-up provision to help quicken retirement savings for people getting closer toward retirement.

- You have a big realized capital gain from stocks, meaning you made profit by selling some stocks. You also have an unrealized loss by end of the year (you have a paper loss, but you have not sold the stocks yet). Should you sell the losing stocks to reduce your capital gain?

Just because it will reduce your taxable capital gain, you should not sell the losing stocks. You will lose more money by selling at a loss than you will save by paying less in tax. In this way, you are never going to make money. However, if you can find another stock in the similar category which is in same type of business, has been equally affected, and expected appreciation in future is comparable, then you can sell the losing position and buy the new stock on the same day. This will not result in a wash sale. You need to analyze it very carefully though.

How about selling the losing stock and buying it back after the wash sale window (30 days) is over? It could be very risky. In thirty days, when you want to buy it back, the stock might have shot up, and your loss will become permanent.

27.1.3　Adjustments

Adjustments and deductions both reduce your taxable income, but adjustments generally do not have any limitations whereas deductions can phase out based on AGI.

- Adjustments (usually called pre-AGI or above-line) always reduce your AGI and taxable income.
- Adjustments reduce your AGI that affects deductions. If your AGI is high, you may not avail some of the itemized deductions such as medical expenses.
- Adjustments also reduce your AMT tax liability
- Adjustments include:
    - educator expenses,
    - certain business expenses,
    - health savings account deductions,
    - moving expenses,
    - self-employed SEP, SIMPLE plans,
    - self-employed insurance deduction,
    - alimony paid to spouse,
    - Traditional IRA : You can put pre-tax dollar to IRA account along with 401K account. You can put up to $5,500 or $6,500 (if you are 50 or older). IRA deduction can phase out beyond certain AGI number.
    - Student loan interest deduction. This can phase out beyond certain AGI number.

   o   College tuition and fees for yourself, your spouse, and children. This can phase out beyond certain AGI number.

Strategy: If your AGI is becoming large enough to disallow some itemized deductions (medical expense, child dependent care expenses), think how you can reduce your AGI by increasing adjustments. Enroll for a health–savings account at your company, contribute money to IRA, take some classes to improve your skills, and claim tuition and fees as adjustments.

What is MAGI?

MAGI (**M**odified **A**djusted **G**ross **I**ncome) is the amount after adding back certain deductions to the AGI number. Some of the deductions that get added back are:

- Student loan interest
- Qualified tuition expenses
- One-half of self-employment tax
- Rental losses
- IRA contributions
- MAGI is important, as it affects your eligibility for certain tax credits or deductions (IRA contribution, child adoption credits etc.)

27.1.4   Deductions

Deductions can be categorized into two types - itemized deduction and standard deduction. You calculate the total applicable itemized deduction and standard deduction independently and take the larger one so that your taxable income is reduced. Itemized deductions are subject to income limit and phase out beyond certain AGI. Here are the most commonly used itemized deductions:

Itemized Deductions
- State and local income tax that you paid
- Property tax you pay for your home
- Out of pocket medical and health expenses
- Casualty and theft losses
- Charitable contributions
- Tax filing fees, bank locker fees, and other miscellaneous expenses.

Standard Deductions

- Standard deduction is not subject to income limit and does not phase out beyond certain AGI. However, standard deduction is usually less than the itemized deductions for most people.
- Standard deduction is upward adjusted for inflation every year, and for 2016 it is:
  - Single or Married but filling separately   - $6,300
  - Head of household   - $9,300
  - Married filing jointly   - $12,600

Exemptions

- You can claim exemptions for yourself, your spouse, and your dependents (children).
- In 2016, each exemption is $4,050. A married couple, with two children, can take four exemptions amounting to $16,200.
- However, exemptions are subject to phase out when AGI is over certain threshold.

27.1.5   Tax Credits

Tax credits are meant to encourage people toward certain behaviors such as energy credits to encourage use of solar energy or helping out certain sections of the society such as earn income credits for people whose annual income is low. Some of these credits come and go, and new credits get introduced from time to time. We will discuss some of the available credits, and you can use these, when applicable to your circumstances, to reduce tax burden.

One big difference between credits and deductions is that credits reduce your tax liability dollar-for-dollar whereas deductions reduce your tax burden, may be 20% to 30% depending on your tax bracket. Study shows that people sometimes forego credits they are eligible or do not take advantage of credits, which could reduce their tax bill. For details on each of the credits, please refer to https://www.irs.gov/Credits-&-Deductions.

Child and Dependent Care Credit

You can claim credit when you spend money for childcare or dependent care while you and your spouse work or are looking for work. You can get credit up to $3,000 for each child or dependent that is between 20% and 35% of total qualifying child and dependent care expenses. The credit is subject to phase out depending on your AGI.

Adoption Credit

You can claim credit for expenses paid to adopt a child. The credit may be taken for adopting child with special needs even if there are no expenses. The credit phases out when MAGI is above $201,920 and becomes zero when MAGI reaches $241,920 (2016 figure).

Education Credit

Education credits helps in reducing tax for higher education expenses. This credit allows you to get a refund when the credit is more than the tax you owe. There are two forms of educations tax credit available – American Opportunity Tax credit and lifetime learning credit. You can get this credit for pursuing higher education by yourself, your spouse, and children. The credit is subject to phase out based on AGI.

Earned Income Credit

Earned Income Credit (EIC) is targeted to help people with low to medium income. When eligible, a taxpayer can claim credit to reduce the tax bill or get back money when the credit is larger than the tax he or she owes.

Retirement savings contribution Credit (Saver's Credit)

It is aimed at encouraging people with low to medium earnings to contribute to their retirement savings. When eligible, taxpayers contribute toward retirement savings account, and they can get back certain percentage of their contributions as tax credit.

27.1.6   Strategy for Reducing Tax Bill

> "I am proud to be paying taxes in the United States. The only thing is I could be just as proud for half of the money."–*Arthur Godfrey*

You cannot eliminate your tax (we all need to pay some tax for efficient functioning of government), but we can plan it properly so that we do not have to pay more than we need to. Actually, it is just not us; the rules and laws are designed to encourage certain actions such as saving for retirements that is good for us and the government.

- **Contribute to Retirement Accounts:** You can defer tax by putting aside pre-tax money in retirement savings accounts, such as 401K, IRA. The money will grow tax-deferred for many years until you reach retirement. Since, income usually becomes less during retirement years, the effective tax rate will be less, and you will pay less in tax during retirement years than paying tax now. You can go for both 401K and IRA.

- **Use Health Savings Account (HSA).** Take advantage of Health Savings Account set up by your company. You put certain dollars in to this account and spend it for medical expenses throughout the year. The contribution is pre-tax, meaning you take care of medical expenses with pre-tax dollar rather than using after-tax dollar. However, there is one caveat – any unused amount in a year will be forfeited.

  Look at previous years and find out how much, on average, you are spending on out-of-pocket medical expenses. Keep the amount at 75% of that. You are not likely to lose any unused dollar. Also, adjust the amount accordingly if you or your family members are going to have dental works (crown, bridges, and braces). These expensive dental works are typically not covered by dental plans. Get the card from your employer and start debiting directly from the card rather than reimbursing later by submitting receipts.

- **Reduce your AGI:** Another important thing is that contributions toward 401K, IRA, and HSA reduce your AGI. AGI decides whether you will be eligible for certain adjustments, deductions, and credits. When AGI reaches certain figure, you could lose out some of these tax benefits. Keep AGI low by putting money into these accounts – it is a double play.

  Do not pay off low-interest Mortgage Loan: When mortgage interest rate is low (30-year at 3 to 4%), you could be better off by not repaying the loan but investing the money in stock market for the long term. As we know, investment in stocks, over a longer period, can provide the best ROI. However, you need to be disciplined as investing in stocks involves risk of losing money. You can get back roughly 1/4th to 1/3rd of the mortgage interest payment as itemized deduction. This makes the effective interest rate for the loan even lower (2% to 3%). **Another advantage of home mortgage loan is that the interest payment reduces AMT tax.**

  On the contrary, there is a strong case for paying off mortgage and using home equity line of credits instead (refer to section18.4 for detailed discussion on this).

- **Offset Capital gain with Capital Loss:** As we discussed before, you can sell losing stocks to offset gains you have made from winning stocks. Do this only when it makes sense overall.

- **Smart way to make Charitable Contributions:** You can donate stocks rather than donating money after you sell the stocks. First, make your decision as to how much you want to contribute toward charitable causes that you care and want to help. Then, donate stocks that have appreciated. If you sell the stocks, you have to pay tax. However, when you donate, you do not pay tax, and the charity that receives the stocks does not pay tax either. For certain amount of after-tax dollar that you wanted to donate, you can make a bigger contribution by donating stocks, or you can reach the goal by donating fewer number of stocks.

- **College Savings Account:** You can put money in 529-college savings account for your children. The money you put is after-tax money and does not provide pre-tax advantage as 401K. However, the gain from the 529 account is tax free, and the investment grows tax-free.

- **Roth IRA:** You can put money in Roth IRA account. Here also you put after-tax money, but the gain grows tax-free until you start withdrawing money tax-free during retirement years.

27.1.7   AMT (Alternative Minimum Tax)

So far, we have discussed the tax liability and the strategy based on standard way of determining the tax liability. However, there is an alternate way of determining tax liability, called the AMT. AMT was originally meant for high earners so that they pay minimum tax. However, over the years, more and more people are being subject to AMT tax payments.

- Many itemized deductions, such as state and local taxes, property tax, and personal exemptions are not allowed under AMT

- However, mortgage interest, charitable contributions are still allowed under AMT.

- If the tax, calculated under AMT, is more than the standard tax, an extra amount is added to the standard tax. This becomes the final tax liability. If tax, based on AMT is less, then, there is no addition to standard tax.

- It is quite possible that many couples (when both are working) will come under AMT and have to pay extra tax due to AMT.

27.1.8   Ways to Reduce AMT Tax

- **HSA Account:** Sign for Medical expense account with your employer as the money spent is pre-tax dollar and reduces your AGI and AMT tax liability

- **IRA Contribution:** Contribute pre-tax dollar to IRA account, as this will reduce AGI and AMT tax.

- **Home Mortgage Interest:** Mortgage interest, that you pay, reduces the AMT tax liability. So consider this aspect if you are planning to pay off mortgage loan. Instead, you might consider keeping low-interest mortgage longer and invest the money in the stock market.

- **Real Estate Tax Payment Timing:** Since you do not get tax benefit for paying real estate tax and pre-payment of estimated state tax in the year falling under AMT, push these tax payments to next year (January) rather than paying in the AMT year (December).

- **State Tax Refund:** If you have a state tax refund in current year and had to pay AMT previous year, then some or most of the state tax refund won't be counted as income this year. This is because, last year, you had to pay AMT, and you did not get the benefit of state tax itemized deduction.

- **Incentive Stock Options:** Another thing that catches people by surprise is exercise of incentive stock options (ISOs). When you exercised stock options but did not sell the stock, the gain is paper gain. Under normal tax calculation, this paper gain is not taxable but taxable under AMT. Many cases of people getting hit by large AMT bill were abound during dotcom boom in 2000.

  Be careful of exercising ISO. If the stock falls later on, you still need to pay large AMT tax for the paper gain you had when you exercised the ISO stocks.

27.1.9   Federal Tax Rate and Tax Table

2016 Tax Rate: source bankrate.com

Tax rate	Single filers	Married filing jointly or qualifying widow/widower	Married filing separately	Head of household
10%	Up to $9,275	Up to $18,550	Up to $9,275	Up to $13,250
15%	$9,276 to $37,650	$18,551 to $75,300	$9,276 to $37,650	$13,251 to $50,400
25%	$37,651 to $91,150	$75,301 to $151,900	$37,651 to $75,950	$50,401 to $130,150
28%	$91,151 to $190,150	$151,901 to $231,450	$75,951 to $115,725	$130,151 to $210,800
33%	$190,151 to $413,350	$231,451 to $413,350	$115,726 to $206,675	$210,801 to $413,350
35%	$413,351 to $415,050	$413,351 to $466,950	$206,676 to $233,475	$413,351 to $441,000
39.6%	$415,051 or more	$466,951 or more	$233,476 or more	$441,001 or more

The tax system is a graded system where the rates are low for lower income. The rate goes up in notches as the income goes up, with the top rate at 39.6%.

27.1.10   Capital Gain Tax and Dividend Tax

Long-term capital gain/loss   When the asset (stock, for example) is held for 1 year or more, it results in long-term gain or loss.

Short-term capital gain/loss   When the asset is held for less than a year, it results in short-term gain or loss.

Qualified Dividends   Qualified dividends are dividends from stocks that you hold for a minimum holding period. On form 1099-DIV, qualified dividends are reported in box 1b.

Long-term capital gains and qualified dividends are taxed differently than ordinary income - usually at a lower rate. Short-term capital gain does not get better tax treatment; it is taxed at the same rate as ordinary income.

Tax Rates on Long-term Capital gain and Qualified Dividends

Tax Rate	Single Filer	Joint Filing
0%	up to $37,450	up to $74,900
15%	$37,450 to $413,200	$74,900 to $464,850
20%	above $413,200	above $464,850

Example1

> Married couple filing jointly had total taxable income of $70,000 ($65,000 ordinary income and $5,000 long-term capital gain).
>
> $65,000 ordinary income will be taxed based on the tax table, but $5,000 long-term capital gain will not be taxed at all (0% rate).

Example2

> A Single filer had total taxable income of $70,000 ($50,000 ordinary income and $20,000 long-term capital gain).
>
> $50,000 ordinary income will be taxed based on the tax table, and $20,000 long-term capital gain will be taxed at 15%.

Example3

> Married couple filing jointly had total taxable income of $490,000 ($400,000 ordinary income and $90,000 long-term capital gain).
>
> $64,850 of the capital gain will be taxed at 15%, and rest ($25,150) long-term capital gain will be taxed at 20%.

Capital Loss

> When there is net capital loss (sum of short-term and long-term), you can take up to $3,000 loss to reduce your taxable income. If loss is more than $3,000, you can carry over the loss (over $3,000) to the next year or years.

Net Investment Income Tax (NIIT)

> Net Investment Income Tax is an extra tax of 3.8% for investment income. Some of the common net investment incomes are interest, dividends, capital gains, rental, and royalty income. NIIT takes effect for joint return AGI over $250,000 and single filer AGI over $200,000.

27.2 Estate Planning

It is important to work with an attorney and a tax advisor on your estate plan. The law could change, and you will need more details than what is provided here. However, the goal of this section is to provide information so that you are aware of the various options available and develop a basic understanding to navigate further for a detailed engagement.

27.2.1   What is an Estate

Estate is the collection of all your assets (house, stocks, bank balance, cars, and life insurance proceeds) that will be distributed among your beneficiaries upon your death.

Why does one need estate planning?

When someone dies, not the entire estate or the assets are passed to the surviving family members. Federal and state estate tax will be deducted (paid to government). Probate court fees and attorney fees would be deducted if it goes through probate process. The remaining estate value is passed to the survivors. Proper and prior estate planning can reduce the bites and maximize what goes to your beneficiaries.

27.2.2   What is Probate?

The probate is a court process that occurs after someone's death to distribute the estate among the beneficiaries. The steps are:
- Identifying estate properties and estate value
- Payment made from the estate
  - Any tax, dues owed by the estate
  - Payment of federal and state estate tax when above exemption limit
  - Paying attorney fees and court fees. Having a trust or a living trust avoids the lengthy probate process and expensive attorney and court fees.
- Distributing the remains among the beneficiaries
  - If there is a Will, it will be distributed as per the Will, or the state will decide it in the absence of a Will.

27.2.3   Federal Estate Tax

Here are the basics, but the law could change. A surviving spouse won't have to pay estate tax. When the estate is passed to surviving children or relatives (other than spouse), the exemption limit is 5.45M per spouse or $10.9M for both spouses. The estate tax rate is 40% of the estate value over the exemption limit.

27.2.4   What is a Will?

A Will is a legal document that describes who gets how much of your estate after your death. Without this, the state will decide the distribution among your beneficiaries, and this may not be what you would have wanted.

A Will usually includes the following:
- Beneficiaries – who will inherit the assets
- Designation of the executor, who carries out the Will
- Mode of distribution of the assets – How and how often
- Guardians of minor children

27.2.5   What is a Trust?

A trust is a fiduciary arrangement that allows a trustee to hold assets on behalf of the beneficiaries. One of the main advantages of a trust is the provision of distributing the assets from an estate without going through the lengthy and costly probate process. There are many types of trusts, but trusts are broadly classified as irrevocable trusts and revocable trusts. Once the assets are passed to an irrevocable trust, you do not have control over the assets. If you change your mind later, you cannot change the terms and conditions of the trust. It also has a few benefits. You are not liable to pay taxes on the income generated from the trust assets. Also, the trust assets are protected from any judgement against you. Revocable trust is also known Living Trust.

27.2.6   What is a Living Trust?

A Living trust is a revocable trust that helps to transfer assets without going through probate while keeping control over the trust. The terms can be changed, or trust can be dissolved any time. Upon death, the terms of the living trust becomes binding. You can name yourself as the trustee or co-trustee. You can also assign someone else as the successor trustee in the event of your death or incapacity.

27.3 Social Security

It is a hot-button topic whether the government will have enough money to pay social security benefits at the current rate and as per the current age eligibility. In future, the age limit may be increased, the benefits may have to be reduced, or government will have enough revenues to keep it at the current structure. There are many possibilities, and nobody knows for sure, how things would be in next 10 or 20 years. Our goal is to discuss how things work today and get an idea how much you can expect from social security payments at the current structure. Then, plan other savings accordingly to have enough money in retirement.

27.3.1   How does Social Security Work?

It is a system where the working people pay to the social security fund in their working years and collect benefits during the retirement years. There are two types of taxes withheld from the paycheck – FICA (Federal Insurance Contributions Act) tax and Medicare tax.

One needs a minimum of 40 credits to be eligible for receiving social security benefits. You earn one credit for every $1,260 you earn and can accumulate up to maximum of four credits in a year. You do not have to earn credits every year or four credits every year; the total cumulative credits need to be forty.

27.3.2   Age Eligibility for Soc Sec Benefits

- You are eligible to receive social security benefits at the age of 62
- You can start collecting social security at 62 or defer it to later. However, you cannot defer it beyond 70, when you must start collecting social security benefits.

- Full retirement age is the age when you can get the maximum benefits. If you start taking benefits before the full retirement age, the benefits will be reduced. The full retirement age and the reduction of benefits depend on when you were born and when you start collecting benefits. The following table provides the details:
  https://www.ssa.gov/planners/retire/agereduction.html

- For example, if you were born in 1960 or later:

  o   The full retirement age is 67. If you start receiving benefits at 62, the benefits will be 70%.

- o For each month you delay in collecting benefits, the benefits go up a little and reach full benefits at age 67.
- o If you start collecting at 65, you would get 86.7%.
- o Refer to: https://www.ssa.gov/planners/retire/1960.html

- When you collect earlier than full retirement age, you collect less every month, but you would collect for more number of years. When you delay it, you will be receiving a larger monthly payment but for fewer number of years. The idea is that the total lifetime payment is expected to be the same irrespective of when you start collecting benefits.

  It is an involved decision, and it is not an isolated decision. It depends on your overall health, life expectancy, financial condition, your income, your spousal income, and tax situation. You have to think through it carefully and determine what the best course of action is, or you should consult with a social security benefits planner.

- What is the breakeven year when both benefits are same? – Start collecting at 62 versus start collecting at 67. Let us call it x years.

  1 (x) = 0.7 (5 + x) solving for x, x= 12 years. If you live up to 67 + 12 = 79 years, you get same amount in both options. If you live beyond 79, the benefits would be more if you had started collecting at 67.

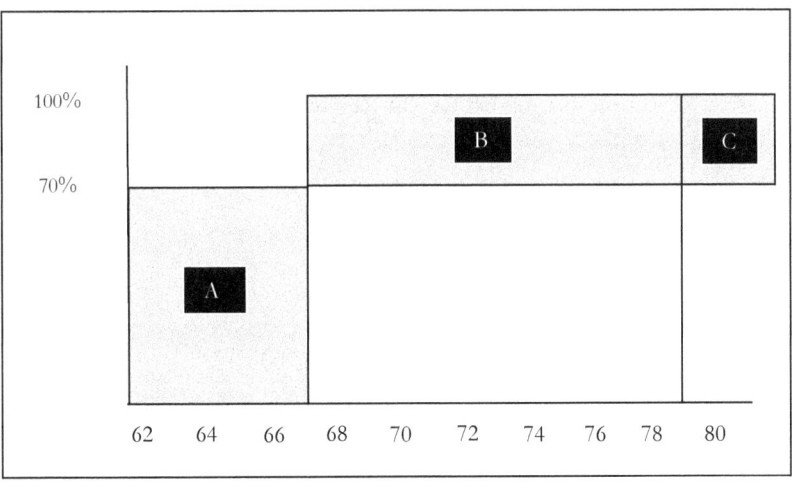

Fig. 27.2   Social Security Breakeven Plot

In the diagram above, 'A' represents the amount you would have received by age 67 when you start collecting at 62. The area noted by B represents the extra amount you would receive at the full payment if you start collecting at 67. When you reach 79, the area of B is same as the area of A – it is the breakeven year (the total benefits are same in both options). For age beyond 79, delaying benefits to 67 would fetch more compared to starting at 62, as represented by area C. C will keep growing as the years pass by beyond 79.

27.3.3   How Much Payment can you Expect?

The amount of social security, you would receive, depends on how much you have earned over lifetime and when you start collecting benefits. The amount of your benefit is based on your 35 highest-earning years. For benefit calculation, the maximum earning considered in a year is limited to the maximum social security wages (for 2016, it was $118,500). For example, if you had earing of $160,000 in a year, only $118,500 is considered for benefit calculation.

If you do not have 35 years of earning, the years without earnings will be counted as zero contribution, which can decrease your monthly payout. You can address this by working longer and retiring later. Once the highest 35 earnings years are figured out, the earnings are adjusted for inflation, and then, an average monthly social security earning number is calculated. Based on this monthly average number, social security payout is calculated as follows:

- 90% of the first $856 in average monthly earnings
- 32% of the amount between $856 and $5,157
- 15% of the amount above $5,157

Ex1: Average monthly income came out to be $3,000

- 90% of $856   = $770.40
- 32% of $2,144   = $686
  Total payout   = **$1,456.40**

Ex2: Average monthly income came out to be $5,000

- 90% of $856   = $770.40
- 32% of $4,144   = $1,326
  Total payout   = **$2,096**

Ex3: Average monthly income came out to be $6,000

- 90% of $856   = $770.40
- 32% of $4,301   = $1,376.32
- 15% of $843   = $126.45
- **Total payout**   **= $2,273**

Note: The benefit formula could change in future. The calculation gives a general idea how it works. In 2015, the maximum benefit with full retirement age was $2,663 per month. The graph below plots the social security benefits (x axis: avg. monthly income, and y axis: full monthly payout)

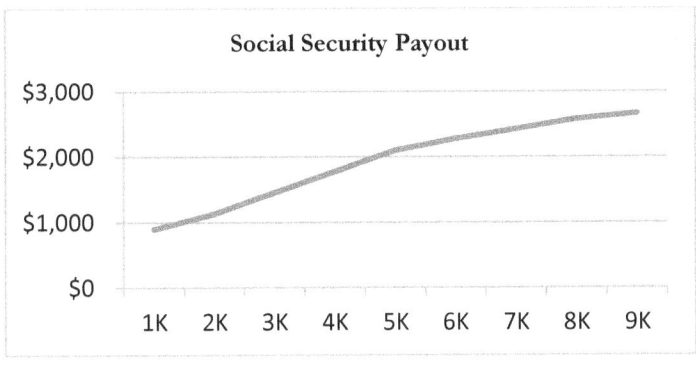

Fig. 27.3   **Social Security Payout**

27.3.4   Spousal Social Security Benefits

Both spouses are eligible to receive social security benefits starting at age 62. Each spouse can choose to receive the benefit based on his or her earned benefits or 50% of the benefit of the spouse if that is larger. The 50% benefit is based on full retirement age and will be reduced if a spouse starts collecting benefits before full retirement age.

Example1

One spouse has $2,000 monthly benefit, and the other spouse has $1,500 monthly benefit. In this case, it is better for each to receive the benefits based on their own numbers, as 50% of the spousal benefit is less than their own benefits.

Example2

> One spouse has $2,000 monthly benefit, and the other spouse has $500 monthly benefit. In this case, the spouse with $2,000 monthly benefit should claim based on his or her own $2,000 monthly benefit. However, the spouse with the benefit of $500 would be better off by taking 50% of his or her spouse's benefits, which comes out to be $1,000. Even if one spouse has no monthly benefit of his or her own, he or she can still claim 50% of the spousal monthly benefit.

27.4 Medicare

27.4.1   What is Medicare?

From https://www.medicare.gov: Medicare is the federal health insurance program for people who are 65 or older, certain younger people with disabilities, and people with End-Stage Renal Disease (permanent kidney failure requiring dialysis or a transplant, sometimes called ESRD). Medicare has four parts to it.

Medicare Part A (Hospital Insurance)

> Medicare Part A covers hospital stays, care in nursing facility, hospice care, and some home health care.

Medicare Part B (Medical Insurance)

> Medicare Part B covers certain doctors' services, outpatient care, medical supplies, and preventive services.

Medicare Part C (Medicare Advantage Plans)

> It is a type of Medicare health plan, offered by a private company, that contracts with Medicare to provide you with all your Part A and Part B benefits. Most Medicare Advantage Plans offer prescription drug coverage as well.

Medicare Part D (Prescription Drug Coverage)

Medicare Part D adds prescription drug coverage to Original Medicare, some Medicare Cost Plans, some Medicare Private-Fee-for-Service Plans, and Medicare Medical Savings Account Plans. These plans are offered by insurance companies and other private companies approved by Medicare.

27.4.2   How Much does it Cost?

Part A

It is free if you or your spouse paid Medicare taxes for 40 quarters (10 years). However, there is an annual deductible (it was $1,288 in 2016) that you have to pay and also have to pay portion of the expenses for hospital stays, longer than 60 days and nursing home stays beyond 100 days.

Part B

The premium is set by Medicare each year. It was $104.90 a month in 2016 for most people. However, it goes up for individuals with annual income over $85,000 and married people with income over $170,000. Part B premium can be higher if you did not enroll when you were first eligible.

Part C (Medicare Advantage Plans)

It is not free, and everyone pays the same premium.

Part D (Prescription Drug Coverage)

It is not free, and the premium and drug coverage vary from one insurer to another insurer.

Chapter

28

28 How They have Done it

28.1 Great Investors and Their Strategies

First of all, the list is not exhaustive, and there are many other great investors who have done it and proven to be very successful in investing. I have chosen sixteen great investors. Why do we want to talk about them? It is a tribute to their expertise and contributions to the investment world. What could be a better way of learning than studying about them and their styles? We will go over their investment philosophy, their attitude toward investing, and learn what made them so much successful.

28.2 Ben Graham (1894 - 1976)

Ben Graham, known as the "Father of Value Investing," was born in Britain in 1894 and later moved to America when he was one year old. He graduated from Columbia University and taught at Columbia University and UCLA Anderson School of Management. He was also a professional investor.

Graham introduced the concept of value investing where he analyzed how to do fundamental analysis about a company and figure out if the stock price is below its intrinsic (true) value or above the intrinsic value. He advocated that good companies selling below their intrinsic value not only provide high probability for appreciation but also offer a high factor of safety. He advocated to treat a stock not as a piece of paper but as part owner of the company. He calls the stock market as Mr. Market. Mr. Market knocks on your door every day and offers the stock each day at a different price. Sometime, Mr. Market, the salesman, behaves erratic and offers his products (stocks), at very high price or at deep discount. You do not have to buy the product; just politely say no to Mr. Market. However, when Mr. Market is offering a solid product at a deep discount, do not shy away from grabbing it.

Graham has contributed two very good books to the investment world. In his first book, **"Security Analysis,"** that he co-authored with David Dodd in 1934, he laid the foundation for value investing. His second book, **"Intelligent Investor"** was first published in 1949 and has been recently (2006) published with Jason Zweig with his comments relevant to today's investment world. This is one of the best books on investing in stocks. Graham had many famous and great investors as his students – Warrant Buffett, Charlie Munger, Philip Fisher, Peter Lynch, John Templeton, and Prem Watsa.

Some of Ben Graham's quotes....

- Have the courage of your knowledge and experience. If you have formed a conclusion from the facts and if you know your judgement is sound, act on it – even though others may hesitate or differ.

- To achieve satisfactory investment results is easier than most people realize; to achieve superior results is harder than it looks.

- The investor's chief problem – and even his worst enemy – is likely to be himself.

28.3 Warren Buffett (1930 -)

It will not be wrong to say that Warren Buffett is the greatest investor of all times. Moreover, it is a very difficult task to describe and capture Buffett's contributions in a few paragraphs where volumes have been written about him, and whose life is a living almanac of investing knowledge and wisdom.

Buffett was born in 1930 in Omaha, Nebraska. Buffett showed interest in business and investing from an early age. He got his first business experience by selling chewing gum, newspaper, and Coca-Cola bottles in the neighborhood. At the young age of 10, he visited New York stock exchange. At age 11, he bought his first stock, three shares of City Services. It was the start of a long and successful investing career that would change the face of investing and write the rules of investing. Buffett would do many small business ventures before he worked for Ben Graham, the father of value investing. He gained knowledge on fundamental analysis working with Ben Graham. Buffett met Charlie Munger in

1959 that would be the beginning of a very successful partnership that continues to today.

Buffett's investment philosophy is based on fundamental analysis and long-term investment. He talks about the famous "moat." He looks for companies that have inherent advantages over competitors, which can be maintained over the long run. He puts great emphasis on the management of a company, as good management is critical for long-term success of the company. Another key part of his investment tenet is the circle of competence. Before you buy a stock, you need to understand the company, its products, and its strength and weakness. There are hundreds of companies, and you do not have to buy all of them. To buy, you need to understand a few and buy what you understand. He buys good companies at fair value, but he is ready to increase the stakes when the price goes down. Knowing about the companies in details and understanding the fundamentals help him to make these gutsy decisions when others are bailing out.

Buffett has given many investing quotes that are like gems that we can use every day. We cannot go without mentioning a few here.

Warren Buffett quotes

- It takes 20 years to build a reputation and five minutes to ruin it. If you think about that, you'll do things differently.
- I don't look to jump over seven-foot bars; I look around for one-foot bars that I can step over.
- Opportunities come infrequently. When it rains gold, put out the bucket, not the thimble.
- Diversification is a protection against ignorance. It makes very little sense for those who know what they're doing.
- If you aren't willing to own a stock for ten years, don't even think about owning it for ten minutes. Put together a portfolio of companies whose aggregate earnings march upward over the years, and so will the portfolio's market value.
- It's far better to buy a wonderful company at a fair price than a fair company at a wonderful price.
- Price is what you pay; value is what you get. Whether we're talking about socks or stocks, I like buying quality merchandise when it is marked down.
- Rule No. 1: Never lose money. Rule No. 2: Never forget rule No.1
- And, the most famous one…
  Be fearful when others are greedy and greedy when others are fearful.

Warren Buffett, of course, is the greatest investor. His net worth was around $67B as of Aug 2015. He was the #1 richest person in 2008 and has been the within the top three on multiple occasions. But, more than his wealth, he is known as one of the greatest philanthropists and givers to charity. He has pledged most of his wealth to charity. Not only that, he and Bill Gates started the Buffett-Gates giving pledge, which is growing in numbers where many billionaires have pledged to give a significant part of their wealth to charity.

28.4 Carl Icahn (1936 -)

Carl Icahn has a stock phenomenon named after him, known as "Icahn Lift," and if you are lucky, you would also get the lift. When it becomes public knowledge that Icahn has taken interest or taken position in a stock, the stock price gets an immediate boost. In many cases, the stock has appreciated further after Icahn started buying stocks.

Carl Icahn's philosophy is that he looks for undervalued companies where management is not acting in the best interest of the shareholders and he can effect changes that will help share price to appreciate. He starts accumulating shares in these companies and architects change in management policies, such as stock buybacks, increasing dividends, spinning off companies, or change in management. Not everyone likes his style, but his end goal is to increase shareholders value.

Icahn was born in New York in 1936 and graduated from Princeton University in 1957. He joined New York school of medicine, but medicine was not his calling. He dropped out after two years. He started his investing career in Wall Street in 1961 and later formed Icahn & co, a securities farm in 1968. As we talked before, he has targeted many companies that fits his investment thesis and has been successful in unlocking shareholders values. Let us look at some of his quotes to get a glimpse of his thinking and investment style.

Carl Icahn Quotes.....

- I have to look out for the shareholder's interests, and I'm the largest shareholder.
- In takeovers, the metaphor is war. The secret is reserves. You must have reserves stretched way out ahead. You have to know that you could buy the company and not be stretched.
- In risk there is reward

- I look at companies as businesses, while Wall Street analysts look for quarterly earnings performance. I buy assets and potential productivity. Wall Street buys earnings, so they miss a lot of things that I see in certain situations.

Carl Icahn has been involved in many philanthropic works. Icahn made a large contribution to Princeton University to fund a genomics laboratory. He has made large contributions to Mount Sinai Hospital, New York. Among other philanthropic works, his foundation (Children's Rescue Fund) built a 65-unit complex for homeless single women.

28.5 George Soros (1930 -)

George Soros is known as the person who broke the bank of England. He made a profit of $1B by short selling British Pound during 1992 Black Wednesday UK currency crisis, where British government had to withdraw the Pound from the European Exchange Rate Mechanism (ERM). Soros was born in Budapest, Hungary. He emigrated to England in 1947 and became a student in London School of Economics. He moved to America in 1956 and worked as an arbitrage trader in New York. Soros is the chairman of Soros Fund Management.

George Soros' investing style can be best understood by his quote, "Markets are constantly in a state of uncertainty and flux, and money is made by discounting the obvious and betting on the unexpected." Soros turned initial investment of $12M in 1969 to a staggering $20B by end of 2000. Soros uses "Reflexivity" as the main plank for his investment thesis. **Reflexivity** refers to feeding each other relationships between cause and effect. An example would be confidence and success. If you are confident, you would be successful, and when you are successful, you garner more confidence.

Soros argues that reflexivity applies to investing that trumps the Efficient Market Hypothesis in the practical world. As per EMH, the price will increase where more people are buying a stock. When the price goes up, the demand will go down, bringing the stock price to equilibrium. However, as per reflexivity, the higher the price goes, more people pile on bringing the price even higher. Similarly, when the stock price falls, more people are prone to sell the stock bringing the price even lower.

Some of Soros' Quotes.

- The financial markets generally are unpredictable. So, that one has to have different scenarios. The idea that you can actually predict what's going to happen contradicts my way of looking at the market.
- I'm only rich because I know when I'm wrong...I basically have survived by recognizing my mistakes.
- The worse a situation becomes, the less it takes to turn it around and the bigger the upside.
- I contend that financial markets never reflect the underlying reality accurately; they always distort it in some way or another and the distortions find expression in market prices.

Apart from being a great investor, Soros has espoused political views and undertaken many philanthropic works. He is the founder and chairman of "Open Society," a network of foundations, partners, and projects in more than 100 countries.

28.6 Peter Lynch (1944 -)

Peter Lynch achieved average returns of 29.2% from 1977 to 1990 while managing Magellan funds at Fidelity Investments – a remarkable feat for being able to do it for 14 years. The assets under him increased from $18M to $14B. He is regarded as a legend in investment world for his performance record. He coined the word "ten bagger" which is a stock that increases by tenfold.

Lynch's investment philosophy is centered on investing what you know. He advises that if you know something well, you will be in a good position to know the trend and take advantage of it. He also argues that this is a plus for individual investors compared to fund managers. The individual investors are better positioned to spot the trend early (go to a mall or observe things in day-to-day life) and invest early.

Lynch has written several highly popular books on investments. He has co-authored three books on investing, One Up on Wall Street, Beating the Street, and Learn to Earn. He has been involved in philanthropic work and has donated millions. He views philanthropy as a form of investment. He donates money as an individual and through is foundations and trusts. Lynch has also given many wise quotes to the investment world. Some of these are...

- Behind every stock is a company. Find out what it's doing.

- In this business, if you're good, you're right six times out of ten. You're never going to be right nine times out of ten.
- During the Gold Rush, most would-be miners lost money, but people who sold them picks, shovels, tents and blue-jeans (Levi Strauss) made a nice profit.
- The simpler it is, the better I like it.
- Average investors can become experts in their own field and can pick winning stocks as effectively as Wall Street professionals do by doing a little research.

28.7 John Bogle (1929 -)

John Bogle founded Vanguard Group mutual funds in 1974, which is one of the most successful and respected investment companies. Bogle retired as CEO of Vanguard in 1999. In 1999, Fortune Magazine named Bogle as one of the four "investment giants" of the twentieth century. Bogle is known for creating the first index mutual fund, Vanguard 500 index fund, in 1975.

Bogle's investment philosophy has been to invest in low-cost index mutual funds. His has advocated that individual investors are best served by thinking long term, keeping investment cost low, and investing in index funds. There is a large audience and follower of Bogle's investing style. Bogleheads forum, in honor for Bogle, discusses financial news and theory. Some of Bogle's popular books are, *Common Sense on Mutual Funds: New Imperatives for the Intelligent Investor and The Little Book of Common Sense Investing.* Some of Bogle's quotes:

- If you have trouble imagining a 20% loss in the stock market, you shouldn't be in stocks.
- Time is your friend; impulse is your enemy.
- Investing is not nearly as difficult as it looks. Successful investing involves doing a few things right and avoiding serious mistakes.
- Index funds eliminate the risks of individual stocks, market sectors, and manager selection. Only stock market risk remains.
- The mistakes we make as investors is when the market's going up, we think it's going to go up forever. When the market goes down, we think it is going to go down forever. Neither of those things actually happens. Doesn't do anything forever. It's by the moment.
- Learn every day but especially from the experiences of others. It's cheaper!

28.8 John Templeton (1912 – 2008)

John Templeton was born in Tennessee in 1912 and graduated in Economics from Yale in 1936. He then went to Oxford and got a master degree in Law in 1936. He started his investment career in Wall Street in 1939 and went to become one of the most successful mutual fund investors of all time.

Templeton's investing philosophy was based on buying low and selling high, a form of value-contrarian investing. He picked up depressed shares at very low price during World War II and made large profit later when price recovered. He started Templeton mutual funds in 1954 and made it hugely successful. He sold family of Templeton funds to Franklin group in 1992, which is now known as the Franklin Templeton investments. Money magazine, in 1999, called him "arguably the greatest global stock picker of the century."

Templeton pioneered in investing globally. He would search for companies internationally that were severely undervalued and not noticed by others. He would meet many successful business people in his home in the Bahamas to exchange ideas with them and gather useful investment insights. Templeton was a great philanthropist, giving away over $1B to charities. Templeton founded the Templeton Foundation in 1987. Templeton relinquished American citizenship and adopted British Citizenship that saved him close to $100M, which he gave to charity. He is known as Sir John Templeton. Here are some of the famous quotes from Templeton...

- Bull markets are born on pessimism, grow on skepticism, mature on optimism, and die on euphoria.
- Invest at the point of maximum pessimism.
- If you want to have a better performance than the crowd, you must do things differently from the crowd.
- The four most dangerous words in investing are "This time it's different.
- It is nice to be important, but it's more important to be nice

28.9 Seth Klarman (1957-)

Seth Klarman is an American investor and was born in 1957. He graduated from Cornel University and later got his MBA from Harvard Business School. He founded Baupost Group, a private investment firm in 1982, and currently is the

President and CEO of Baupost Group. Klarman is regarded as an expert in value investing.

His investing style is based on value investing with high margin of safety. He would keep a significant cash reserve waiting for the right moment. This requires discipline and patience. Klarman is known for the popular book, "Margin of Safety: Risk-Averse Value Investing Strategies for the Thoughtful Investor." This book is regarded highly among the circles of value investors. The book is currently out of print but can be found in Amazon for $1,600 – like a closed-end fund that has done really well.

We are putting some apt quotes from Klarman, but here is a link of an interview of Klarman by Charlie Rose. The first part of the interview is about Klarman's philanthropic organization, "Facing History." However, the 2nd part of the interview where Klarman talks about value investing is a gem. https://vimeo.com/32333102. I encourage you to view it. One of the things that stood out for me was finding the real value-company and figuring that it is not a falling knife and not a perennially undervalued or under-performing company. Like Warren Buffett, Klarman puts a lot of emphasis on the management of the company. If the management is good, it will find a way to turn around the company.

Some of Klarman's quotes...

- The focus of most investors differs from that of value investors. Most investors are primarily oriented toward return, how much they can make and pay little attention to risk, how much they can lose.
- Investors buy securities that appear to offer attractive return for the risk incurred and sell when the return no longer justifies the risk.
- Being fully invested at all times will at best generate mediocre returns; at worst they entail both a high opportunity cost – foregoing the next good opportunity to invest – and the risk of appreciable loss.
- Value investing is the discipline of buying shares at a significant discount from their current underlying values and holding them until more of their value is realized. The element of a bargain is the key to the process.
- The trick of successful investors is to sell when they want to, not when they have to.

28.10   Jim Rogers (1942 -)

Jim Rogers is the co-founder of Quantum funds and the Chairman of Roger Holdings. Rogers was born in Baltimore, Maryland in 1942 and graduated from Yale in 1964 in History major. He later acquired second bachelor's degree in Philosophy, Politics, and Economics from Oxford in 1966. In 1964, he started his investing career by joining Dominick & Dominick LLC on Wall Street.

Rogers joined Arnhold and S. Bleichroder, an investment bank where he worked with George Soros. Soros and Rogers left Arnhold and S. Bleichroder in 1973 and founded Quantum fund. In the next 10 years, Quantum gained 4200% compared to S&P gain of 47%. In 2005, Rogers wrote, "Hot Commodities: How Anyone Can Invest Profitably in the World's Best Market." He currently lives in Singapore with his view that ASIA provides one of the best places for investment opportunities in the 21st century. He is regarded as an expert in international investing and a commodities guru. An interesting thing about Jim Rogers, he achieved a Guinness world record by travelling 116 countries, covering 245,000 kilometers with his wife, Paige Parker in a custom-made Mercedes. Following this, he wrote a best seller, Adventure Capitalist.

Some of his quotes....

- Bottoms in the investment world don't end with four-year lows; they end with 10- or 15-year lows.
- Commodities tend to zig when the equity markets zag.
- Right now I own shares of companies in 28 countries.
- Buy low and sell high. It's pretty simple. The problem is knowing what's low and what's high.

28.11   Bill Miller (1950 -)

Bill Miller was named by Money magazine as the "Greatest Money Manager of the 1990s." Miller was born in Laurinburg, North Carolina in 1950. He graduated with honors from Washington and Lee University in 1972 in Economics. Later, he pursued graduate studies in Philosophy from John Hopkins University. Miller joined Legg Mason investment firm in 1981 and co-managed Legg Mason Capital Management Value Trust from 1982, since the inception of the fund. His fund would later beat the S&P 500 for 15 consecutive years from 1991 through 2005. This was considered to be a feat, highly unlikely, according to efficient market hypothesis.

Miller and his team focused on detailed understanding of the business and their intrinsic value. He calls himself a value-investor, but he has his own style that differs from the traditional value investing in some regard. He attributes his long record of success to exhaustive security analysis and portfolio construction. According to him, the question is not growth or value but where the best value is. He asserts that value can be found in stocks with high PEs as well. Because of his outstanding returns, he was named by Money magazine as the "Greatest Money Manager of the 1990s." In 1999, he was selected as the "Fund Manager of the Decade" by Morningstar.

Some of Bill Miller's quotes....

- We try to buy companies that trade at large discounts to intrinsic value. What is different is we will look for that value anywhere we can. We don't rule out technology as an area to look for value.
- Our portfolio contains a mix of businesses, some of which we believe are cyclically mis-priced, and some of which we believe are secularly mis-priced.
- What you are trying to do as an investor is that you are trying to exploit the fact that fewer things will happen than can happen. So you are trying to figure out how that probability distribution works and stay in the middle of what will happen.
- When you get down toward the lower end of these valuations, value people find them attractive. The trap comes in when there is a secular change, where the fundamental economics of the business are changing or the industry is changing, and the market is slowly incorporating that into the stock price. So, that would be the case over the last several years with newspapers. They are a good example of where historical valuation metrics aren't working.
- Your profit is the difference between your average purchase price and your average selling price. Bernard Baruch said nobody buys at the bottom and sells at the top except liars. Your stock will go down after you buy it, and it will go up after you sell it. Being willing to lower your average cost is a great strategy. But, it's difficult.

28.12   David Tepper (1957 -)

David Tepper is a legendary hedge fund manager who has earned a name and lot of money by investing in distressed debts and companies. His hedge fund earned a staggering $7B by buying distressed financial stocks in 2009 (bought Bank of America for $3) and made huge profit later when stocks recovered. Tepper was born in Pittsburg, PA in 1957. Tepper earned his BA from University of Pittsburg in 1978 and MS in Industrial Administration from Carnegie Mellon University in 1982.

Early in his career, he understood the credit structure of financially distressed companies, and it became handy when he made a lot of money for Goldman Sachs during the junk bond market crash in 1989. Tepper co-founded Appaloosa Management in 1993 with $57M. Assets, as of 2014, were above $20B. Tepper's investment strategy has been buying debts of distressed companies (often in bankruptcy) very cheap and making huge returns later. Tepper made very successful bet during 2008 financial crisis by buying heavily beaten down financial stocks very cheap and made huge profit when market recovered.

Tepper has been very generous in donating money to philanthropic causes. He gave $55M to his alma mater, Carnegie Melon University in 2003 and donated $67M again in 2013. He has also donated to other institutions, such as, The Robin Hood Foundation, Teach for America, and Better Education for Kids.

Some of David Tepper quotes…..
- I think when it comes to decisions, I try not to be emotional. To drown out the noise and look at the important facts.
- I'm just a regular upper-middle-class guy who happens to be a billionaire.
- This company looks cheap, that company looks cheap, but the overall economy could completely screw it up. The key is to wait. Sometimes the hardest thing to do is to do nothing.
- There is a time to make money and a time to not lose money.
- I am the animal at the head of the pack. … I either get eaten, or I get the good grass

28.13   Ken Fisher (1950 -)

Ken Fisher is the founder, chairman, and CEO of Fisher Investments, an independent money management firm, managing over $68B in assets. Fisher is called the largest money manager in the United States. Ken was born in San Francisco, CA in 1950. His dad, Philip Fisher was an investor and the well-known author of a very popular book, "Common Stocks and Uncommon Profits." Ken graduated from Humboldt University in Economics in 1972.

Ken Fisher started Fisher Investments in 1979 with just $250 and has grown it to one of the premier and large money management firms. Fisher attributes his success to pursuit of passion and not the pursuit of money. He pioneered the use of P/S (Price to Sales) as a tool to pick stocks. He looks for stability in profit margin in picking stocks. He puts a lot of emphasis on the quality of management running the company. Ken is a prolific writer with 11 books with the latest (2015), "Beat The Crowd." The Only Three Questions That Count, The Ten Roads to Riches, How to Smell a Rat, and Debunkery were all New York Times bestsellers. Fisher is a lover of the redwood forest and an expert in logging. He has donated money to support Redwood ecology research.

Some of Ken Fisher quotes....

- The stock market is a discounter of all known information.
- A good way to think about successful investing is, it's two-thirds not making mistakes, one-third doing something right.
- I call the stock market The Great Humiliator. It wants to humiliate as many people as it can, for as long as it can, for as many dollars as it can.
- Indeed, bull markets are fueled by successive waves of prior skeptics finally capitulating as their fears fade. Eventually, fear turns to euphoria, and that's the stuff of bubbles.
- Both cheap value stocks and more glamorous growth stocks can work well in a portfolio - if done right.

28.14   Steven Cohen (1956 -)

Steven Cohen is a successful American hedge fund manager and the founder of Point72 Asset Management, a family owned asset management firm that he currently manages. He earned his fame and controversy in S.A.C Capital that he founded in 1992. He started S.A.C. with $20M of his own money and grew it to $14B. In 2012, he was charged by SEC for failing to prevent insider trading inside his company, but he himself was not directly charged. In November 2013, the case was resolved with a huge fine of $1.8B.

Steven grew up in New York and liked playing Poker during high school. He credits the game for teaching how to take risks. Steven received a degree in economics from the Wharton School in 1978. Steven started his professional investment career as a junior trader with Grunthal & Co. in 1978. He made his way up before starting S.A.C in 1992.

Steven is known for his rapid-fire trading style and never held positions for longer periods. He would trade stocks several times a year. Outside of investing, Cohen is an avid art collector. He is involved in philanthropic work. He and his wife have donated generously to projects involved in health, education, arts & culture, and New York community.

Some of Steven Cohen quotes...

- There's something to be said for giving and helping to change people's lives.
- I'm not an introvert. I'm media shy.

28.15   Bill Gross (1944 -)

Bill Gross, known as the Bond King, is an American investor and was born in Ohio in 1944. He graduated from Duke University in 1966 and got his MBA from UCLA Anderson School of Management in 1971. Bill co-founded PIMCO (Pacific Investment Management Company) and managed the world's largest bond funds, "Total Return Fund" at PIMCO until his departure in 2014. He joined Janus Capital Group after leaving PIMCO.

His investing philosophy is based on two major beliefs. It is important to formulate a long-term view of the market for the next several years and having the correct portfolio mix (asset allocation, diversification). If one is clear about the goal and expectation of the market ahead for next 3-5 years, the short-term fluctuations do not matter. He is also known to be flexible to change direction based on the market conditions.

Gross has authored two books, "Bill Gross On Investing" and "Everything You've Heard About Investing Is Wrong! How to Profit In The Coming Bull Markets." Gross donated $23.5 million to Duke University in 2005. Over the years, he has donated close to $25 million dollars to Doctors without Borders, a humanitarian non-government organization that serves across the globe.

Some of Bill Gross quotes...

- Whether a tops-down or bottoms-up investor in bonds, stocks, or private equity, the standard analysis tends to judge an investor or his firm on the basis of how the bullish or bearish aspects of the cycle were managed.
- Companies typically borrow money at less than their return on equity and therefore compound their return at the expense of lenders.
- The market can move for irrational reasons, and you have to be prepared for that, ... you need to make big bets when the odds are in

your favor -- not big enough to ruin you but big enough to make a difference.

28.16   Prem Watsa (1950 -)

Prem Watsa is a Canadian businessperson, the founder, chairman, and chief executive of Fairfax Financial Holdings, based in Toronto. He is referred as the Canadian Warren Buffett. He was born in India in 1950 and later moved to Canada to get his MBA from the Richard Ivey School of Business at the University of Western Ontario.

In 1985, Watsa founded Toronto-based financial services firm Fairfax Financial Holdings where he is the CEO. He modeled his business career after Warren Buffett by acquiring insurance companies that Buffett successfully executed by using the cash flow from his insurance companies to invest in stocks. Watsa doesn't come into the news and keep to himself. However, not long ago, he was in the news for taking stakes in BlackBerry, the beleaguered Canadian smart phone company. He is a member of the Board of Trustees for the Hospital for Sick Children. He is also in the Advisory Board for the Richard Ivey School of Business.

Some of Prem Watsa quotes....

- We put our heads down and worked hard and have gotten results. Once in a while we will talk if we have anything to say.
- Don't ever think that the [stock] market knows more than you do about the underlying business. That's the biggest mistake you can make.

28.17   Mohnish Pabrai (1964 -)

Mohnish Pabrai was an engineer by profession and an entrepreneur before he embarked on the path of investing in stocks. He was a successful engineer and businessman, but he had the natural talent and love for investing that pulled him to the world of investing. He was born in India and came to Clemson University in 1983. He is currently the managing partner of Pabrai Investment Funds that he founded in 1999. He is heavily influenced by the legendary investor Warren Buffett whom he considers his role model.

His modeled his investment style after Warren Buffett and built it around value investing. His philosophy is that one does not have to reinvent the wheel as great investment philosophies already exist that he or she can emulate to be successful. He is a very smart person, and I would consider it his humility. His extraordinary success in investing can be gauged by the 2013 headline in Forbes magazine, "How Mohnish Pabrai Crushed The Market By 1100% Since 2000."

He wrote a book on investing, The Dhandho Investor: The Low-Risk Value Method to High Returns. He has written another book, Mosaic: Perspectives on Investing. An interesting tidbit about him - in June 2007, he made headlines by bidding US$650,100 with Guy Spier for a charity lunch with Warren Buffett. In 2005, Mohnish, along with his wife, founded the philanthropic foundation, *Dakshana Foundation* with the goal of giving back most of their wealth to society.

Some of Mohnish Pabrai quotes....

- Wall Street sometimes gets confused between risk and uncertainty, and you can profit handsomely from that confusion. The low-risk, high-uncertainty [situation] gives us our most sought after coin-toss odds. Heads, I win; tails, I don't lose much.
- Mistakes are the best teachers. One does not learn from success. It is desirable to learn vicariously from other people's failures, but it gets much more firmly seared in when they are your own.
- You don't make money when you buy stocks. And you don't make money when you sell stocks. You make money by waiting.
- We Americans love original ideas. But truly, there are already plenty of good ones out there, ours for the taking. If I were too proud to copy the ideas of others, I likely wouldn't have even a fraction of my current success.

Chapter

29

29 Everything has a Purpose and Meaning

Money is a great servant but a bad master.

–Francis Bacon

Wealth is the ability to fully experience life.

–Henry David Thoreau

We make a living by what we get, but we make a life by what we give.

–Winston Churchill

Live as if you were to die tomorrow. Learn as if you were to live forever.

– Mahatma Gandhi

The real measure of your wealth is how much you'd be worth if you lost all your money.

–Anonymous

Before you speak, listen. Before you write, think. Before you spend, earn. Before you invest, investigate. Before you criticize, wait. Before you pray, forgive. Before you quit, try. Before you retire, save. Before you die, give.

–William A. Ward

Here, I have compiled a list of great quotes from some of the greatest people on earth. It summarizes the role of money and wealth in our lives. If we are successful in our careers, investing wisely, doing the right things, and have a bit of luck, the results will be most likely in our favor. Personal responsibility is the most important thing. Use money to live a good regular life, give the best education and opportunities to your kids, keep enough for retirement, and most importantly, donate and help out others so that they can be self-sufficient and avail opportunities for success.

30 Further Resources

Good Books

- The Intelligent Investor – Benjamin Graham
- Stocks for the Long Run – Jeremy J. Siegel
- A Random Walk Down Wall Street - Burton G. Malkiel
- Beating the Street – Peter Lynch
- Rich Dad, Poor Dad – Robert Kiyosaki
- Buy High Sell Higher – Joe Terranova
- Economics – David C. Colander

Websites

- http://www.investopedia.com
- https://www.wikipedia.org
- https://finance.yahoo.com/
- https://www.fidelity.com
- http://www.treasurydirect.gov
- http://www.treasury.gov
- http://www.cnbc.com
- http://www.bloomberg.com/markets/economic-calendar
- https://www.briefing.com/investor/calendars/economic
- http://bea.gov/national/index.htm : For GDP
- https://www.federalreserve.gov/monetarypolicy
- www.barchart.com
- https://www.irs.gov/Credits-&-Deductions

Index

31 Index

Index

Index

Index

Index

Index

32 About the Author

I am a resident of Silicon Valley working in computer chip design for the last 20+ years. I completed my undergraduate in EE from NIT Rourkela, one of the premier engineering colleges in India. Received MSEE from University of Toledo, Ohio. In early part of my professional career, I was fortunate to work with great chip design companies like Texas Instruments and Intel Corporation. For the last decade, I have been an entrepreneur and founded successful start-up companies in the Silicon Valley.

In 2004, I co-founded ASIC Architect, Inc., an IP (Intellectual Property) company. As CEO at ASIC Architect, Inc., I led the company with development and deployment of leading edge IPs. ASIC Architect, Inc. was acquired by Gennum Corporation in 2008 where I led productization of PCI Express Switch IP. The Switch IP has been used by some of the largest multinational companies.

My interest and work have been in the areas of chip development, PCI Express, SATA storage, memory controller, and power management/power savings. Recently, I worked on multi-core processor, cache coherency, and NoC (Network on Chip) design. I have presented papers in conferences on multiple occasions and hold several US patents. The industry had many good books on computer and logic design but lacked a book from the industry. With my deep love for chip design and first-hand experience in developing many of the IPs, I embarked on an ambitious project. After more than two years of effort, published 700+ page, "Advanced Chip Design" in 2013. It has been very well received throughout the world and has been Amazon's bestseller regularly in computer design and logic since its launch.

Besides my first love for computer design, I have a deep affinity and love for Economics and investing in stocks. What started as a casual curiosity is now a major involvement that I love and thoroughly enjoy. I focus on companies with strong fundamentals (solid balance sheet, increasing or steady income, positive and steady cash flow, good dividends, stock buyback, and good management). I start taking positions when they are out of favor where stock price is cheap compared to its true value. Generally, I average down when price falls further and rarely sell at a loss. I have gone through times where my portfolio was down 15%-20%. It was very tough initially. But, I stand the course and buy more when things are down. Things come back eventually, sooner or later. Going through these tough situations several times has helped me to be a better investor and less emotional about it.

I do not have a set time for holding. The holdings are from a few weeks to a few months but rarely over a year. My investment philosophy is based on increasing the probability of success and positioning for success. Once the goal (10%-20% gain) is achieved, I move the money to another investment that provides better probability of success. This has been working out well for the last several years where the stock market has been moving sideways. If I were to invest coming off a market crash like the 2009, I would consider holding long-term.

I generally keep some cash for good opportunities that come by from time to time. I sometimes take concentrated positions with solid companies that have been unduly punished in the market (based on my analysis) and where the downside risk is low. I use margin judiciously with a high degree of safety, and most of the times, the dividends offset the margin interest. **By nature, I am a safe investor and use the market inefficiency and the power of leverage to make many small (5%-20%) gains that eventually add up to respectable numbers.** Based on my analysis, I felt that Walmart was cheap at $56-60 in November 2015. I took some positions then. When the whole market dropped almost by 10%-12% in beginning of 2016, Walmart actually gained 10%-12%. When DOW and S&P were down 10%-12% in Jan-Feb of 2016, I bought financials, retails, semiconductors, and some other blue chip stocks using margin.

Was I certain that the market would come back in a month? Absolutely not! Was I nervous that it could fall further? Not much either. I felt that reward for upside is higher than the risk of further fall. I felt that it was worth taking the risk. I was prepared to hold them with dividends offsetting most of the margin cost. I had thought of the worst-case scenario and had an action plan for it. I still had margin money to use if the market were to fall further. No one looks for or yearns for a market crash, but to be a successful investor, one must have a plan to handle it if it were to happen. I learn every day. I keep an open mind and study the great investors of all times. I love writing, and this book is the product of my passion for investing and the desire to share my thoughts and experience with my fellow investors.

Other Books from the Author

Look inside ↓

Advanced Chip Design, Practical Examples in Verilog Paperback – April 16, 2013

by Mr Kishore K Mishra • (Author)

☆☆☆☆☆ • 22 customer reviews

#1 Best Seller in Computer Programming Logic

> See all formats and editions

Paperback
$37.80

15 used from $29.95
23 New from $34.31

Designing a complex ASIC/SoC is similar to learning a language well and then creating a masterpiece using experience, imagination, and creativity. Digital design starts with RTL such as Verilog or VHDL, but it is only the beginning. A complete designer needs to have a good understanding of the Verilog language, digital design techniques, system architecture, IO protocols, and hardware-software interaction that I call the **five rings of chip design**.

This book is the result of 20 years of experience and passion for chip design: love for the Verilog language, three years of focused research, and a genuine desire to share the practical design world with students and practicing engineers. I sincerely believe that you are not only going to get a jump...

Read more

---

www.ingramcontent.com/pod-product-compliance
Lightning Source LLC
Chambersburg PA
CBHW070312190526
45169CB00005B/1599